The Half-Life of Policy Rationales

The Half-Life
of Policy Rationales

How New Technology Affects
Old Policy Issues

EDITED BY

Fred E. Foldvary AND *Daniel B. Klein*

A CATO INSTITUTE BOOK

New York University Press

NEW YORK AND LONDON

NEW YORK UNIVERSITY PRESS
New York and London

Library of Congress Cataloging-in-Publication Data
The half-life of policy rationales :
how new technology affects old policy issues /
edited by Fred E. Foldvary and Daniel B. Klein
p. cm.
"A Cato Institute book."
Includes bibliographical references and index.
ISBN 0-8147-4776-0 (cloth : alk. paper) —
ISBN 0-8147-4777-9 (pbk. : alk. paper)
1. Technological innovations—Government policy—
United States.   2. Free enterprise—United States.
3. Technological innovations—Government policy.
4. Free enterprise.   I. Foldvary, Fred E., 1946-   II. Klein, Daniel B.
HC110.T4 H35 2003
330.973—dc21   2002015249

New York University Press books are printed on acid-free paper,
and their binding materials are chosen for strength and durability.

Manufactured in the United States of America
10 9 8 7 6 5 4 3 2 1

New methods may be found for making a service saleable which before could not be restricted to those willing to pay for it, and thus make the market method applicable to areas where before it could not be applied. Wireless broadcasting is an instance. [T]echnical advance might well open the possibility of confining reception to those using particular equipment, making the operation of the market possible.

—Friedrich A. Hayek, *Law, Legislation and Liberty*

Contents

Acknowledgments

Early in the process, Jim Koch, director of the Center for Science, Technology, and Society (CSTS) at Santa Clara University (SCU), warmed up to the idea of writing this volume. CSTS funded the conference at SCU in February 2000, "Technological Advance and the Changing Context of Public Policy Justification," at which the evolving set of contributors gathered. The conference was crucial in making connections and achieving a common focus on the intended themes. The editors are grateful to CSTS for that support, made at the most challenging part of the process: the beginning.

We also wish to thank Santa Clara University for the university grant used to hire Jock Doubleday for a preliminary round of fine copy editing. We thank Wayne Crews for shepherding the manuscript through the submission process and Bihn Chen at SCU for formatting the text.

Introduction

The Half-Life of Policy Rationales:
How New Technology Affects Old Policy Issues

Fred E. Foldvary and Daniel B. Klein

Writers have occasionally noted that a policy's appropriateness depends on the current state of alternative technologies and that technological changes make old policies obsolete and new policies worthwhile (Hayek 1979, 47; Rosen 1992, 68). This book addresses a related question: Does technological advancement generally enhance the case for one kind of policy over another?

The chapters offer a tentative conclusion: *Technological advancement tends to enhance the case for free-enterprise policy.* It reduces the strength of market-failure arguments and the case for intervention. Most market-failure arguments boil down to claims about invisible-hand mechanisms being obstructed by some kind of transaction costs. If technology trims transaction costs—by making it easy to charge users, define and enforce property rights, exit and utilize substitutes, gather information, gain assurance of quality and safety, enter and compete in markets—the invisible hand works better. An example is highways. Using electronic tolling, highway users can now pay highway tolls as easily as they pay a monthly phone bill, weakening the case for operating highways as freeways and strengthening the case for privatization. Technological advancement might not enhance the case for free enterprise in every area of policy, but it does in most.

Before explaining more fully the volume's central themes, it might help to state clearly . . .

What the Book Is Not About

In recent decades technological advancement has accelerated. Writers of diverse perspectives have pondered the effects and speculated on the future course of public policy. Some suggest that new technologies will enhance government power to survey, regulate, and enforce (Brin 1998). Others argue that technology will frustrate government efforts to control behavior and beliefs as technology enables people to circumvent controls (T. Friedman 1999; Gilder 1989, part V; Huber 1996; McKenzie and Lee 1991). It has been argued, for example, that counterdevices such as encryption and reverse surveillance will check government and enable individuals to remain a step ahead (Brin 1998; D. Friedman 1995; Henderson 2000). Thus, many have speculated on the governmental changes that technology *will* bring. But few have explored the changes that it *ought to* bring. This collection suggests that technological advancement ought to persuade policymakers to implement reform in the direction of free enterprise, but it does not predict that public policy will move in that direction. (One may hope that there is a direct connection between the *ought to* and the *will be*, but that hope is so often disappointed!)

The policy areas considered here are traditional ones like parking, postal services, and occupational licensing. The book is not about "technology policy" (taxation and regulation of the Internet commerce, copyright, privacy, encryption, and so on). We ask not how high-tech services should be regulated (a question asked by DeLong and Froomkin 2000) but how new technology ought to affect our thinking about traditional policy areas and whether technological advancement generally favors certain kinds of policy.

The Central Argument:
Technology Works to Resolve Market Imperfections

Theories of market failure and governmental remedies are not absolute doctrine but depend on the institutional and technological context.[1] The invisible hand—the nexus of voluntary social mechanisms—may fail, in a significant sense, if transaction costs obstruct gainful exchange. But better technology reduces such costs. Applications of market-failure theory may be found to have a technological "half-life," after which their validity dissolves. The contributors to this volume suggest that technological advancement tends to enhance the case for free enterprise, first, by resolving apparent market imperfections of various well-known categories—nonexcludability, information and assurance costs, natural monopoly—to which we shall return shortly.

Some would challenge the general claim, arguing that just as technology enhances the knowledge and capabilities of private entrepreneurs, so it enhances those of public-spirited regulators and officials. Government becomes more effective by virtue of technology. No doubt there is much to the challenge. Government agencies, too, can run highways as toll roads. Or consider a common argument against regulation, that it introduces non-compliance problems and requires costly enforcement. Insofar as technology facilitates government monitoring and enforcement, the case for government regulation gains strength.

However, if both free enterprise and the government are technically capable of, say, producing tomatoes, the sheer-incentive argument recommends free enterprise. Good government itself is a public-goods problem (Tullock 1971); government often fails to do the good that it is technically capable of. The free-enterprise system, however, generally creates for its participants incentives to pursue what is good for society. Hence, the incentive advantage recommends free enterprise, given technical and institutional workability.

The Complexity/Unknowability Argument
for the Volume's Claim

While admitting some symmetry in the effects of technology, we believe that there is an important asymmetry that goes against government. Any form of government intervention or enterprise depends for its justification on an understanding of what the private-enterprise economy would otherwise be lacking or failing to achieve. Justification for occupational licensing depends on consumers being unable, in a regime without licensing, to obtain quality and safety assurance. Utility regulation depends on theories of natural monopoly. Government activism is predicated on a belief that regulators or planners can *know the economy well enough* to restrict, manipulate, or supplement it beneficially.

After Adam Smith and Friedrich Hayek, the classic argument against government intervention is, aside from incentive problems, that the economy is too complex to know and therefore too complex to direct or manipulate in a beneficial manner. Like the spontaneous patterns of roller skating in a roller rink, the more complex the system is, the more mischievous the notion of centralized control will be. In a complex system such as that of two hundred skaters in a roller rink, we ought to rely on decentralized decision making. After all, even if the rink is without bound, the increased complexity does not pose a comparable problem for the individual skater. He does not interpret the whole; he utilizes pointed knowledge in pursuing opportunities of his particular time and place.

Technology enhances government's ability to gather, collate, and convey information and to monitor actions, identify transgressions, and enforce compliance. Technology expands the informational capability of government. But technology also accelerates economic change and multiplies the connections between activities. It integrates dimensions, connects multitudinous variables, and, moment by moment, alters constraints and opportunities. To know market arrangements—either those that are current or those that would exist under an alternative policy—the fundamentals of such arrangements would have to remain unchanged for the time being. Technology makes the whole economy—what is to be known—far more complex. It brings fundamental upsets, now and again, to even our best understandings of current arrangements and their shortcomings. After all, society includes the thoughts and potentialities of private individuals and organizations, each of whom has likewise enjoyed vastly expanded informational capabilities.

In his book *The Lexus and the Olive Tree*, Thomas Friedman relates comments from a friend that illustrates the contest between informational capability and complexity. He quotes Leon Cooperman, the former director of research for Goldman, Sachs:

> When I joined Goldman Sachs in 1967 . . . I was the head of research and I hired analysts. In those days, a typical analyst covered seventy-five companies. . . . I was recently talking to one of the analysts I had hired back then and he told me he was terribly overworked now because he had to cover twelve companies. I just laughed. Only twelve companies? But you have to look into those twelve companies so much more deeply now in order to get some edge that it takes up all of his time. (Cooperman quoted in Friedman 1999, 101–2)

One might imagine that because of today's high-speed data access, computation, and so on, the analyst would have better informational capabilities, enabling him to cover *more*, rather than fewer, companies. But his informational capabilities do not keep up with the complexity of the world to be analyzed.

In 1879, Cliffe Leslie, an Irish economist and keen expositor of Adam Smith, wrote: "The movement of the economic world has been one from simplicity to complexity, from uniformity to diversity, from unbroken custom to change, and, therefore, from the known to the unknown."[2] In later years Friedrich Hayek took the point further: the economic world has moved not merely to the unknown but to the *unknowable*. The effect of technology is asymmetric in the epistemic situations in which it leaves, respectively, private actors versus social planners (such as those at the FDA or the Anti-Trust Division). *Technology's heightening of society's complexity outstrips its heightening of the social planner's informational capabilities.*[3] Hayek, like Smith, drew a lesson for policy: Except in the most clear-cut cases of systemic harm, like air pollution, the supposition that government officials can figure out how to improve on the results of decentralized (i.e., voluntary) decision making becomes more and more outlandish. In his Nobel lecture, Hayek (1978) called that supposition the *pretense* of knowledge. As intellectuals who ponder the complex workings of the social world, we really know little aside from one hardy fact: If those who participate in an activity do so voluntarily, each is probably bettering his or her own condition. The more complex the system is, the more skeptical we ought to be about claims to knowledge that go beyond and against that hardy fact.

There are, then, two ways in which technological advancement enhances the case for free enterprise: (1) It reduces the transaction costs that had obstructed (actually or supposedly) invisible-hand mechanisms, and (2) it makes the economic system ever more complex and makes the notion that interventionists can meaningfully know and beneficially manipulate the system ever less credible.

Policy Areas in Which the Conclusion Is Doubtful?

Some cases seem to go against the general tendency. Technology might make it especially difficult to secure and appropriate the value of one's intellectual products, such as basic scientific research, patents, software, music, and writings, because technology vastly facilitates the replication of "knock-offs" and sharing without authorization. The situation might call for stepped-up government enforcement of patents and copyrights (is that government intervention or property rights enforcement?) or more interventionist measures like the subsidization of knowledge and cultural products—akin to European television subsidies financed by taxes on television ownership (a policy that DeLong and Froomkin 2000 sometimes seem to favor).

It may be argued that technology favors expanded government control of pollution because it enhances the effectiveness of detection, measurement, impact assessment, and enforcement. The case of auto emissions is considered in the chapter "Fencing the Airshed," in which it is argued that new sensing technologies offer powerful means of accosting gross-polluting motorists. It is not clear, however, that pollution abatement should be regarded as government intervention. Common law traditionally treated air pollution as a nuisance, and the scheme proposed in that chapter keeps to that spirit. Furthermore, the new technology offers an excellent alternative to many existing interventions. If government uses new technologies to define and enforce property rights in water, airspace, or animal resources, that might be seen as defensive nightwatchman functions compatible with the principles of free enterprise.

National security is another area in which technology might suggest a larger role for government. Capabilities to create advance quickly, but not as quickly as capabilities to destroy. New destructive capabilities in arms, biotechnology, and, eventually, nanotechnology might recommend vigorous national security measures. Again, depending on the measures, we might not deem them "government intervention" but, rather, nightwatchman functions.

Improved technology, as previously mentioned, might improve regulators' knowledge of particular sets of activities and cause some to recommend more interventions such as antitrust restrictions. Some might even suggest that new technologies will deliver the long-sought means of administering a centrally planned economy: "Indeed, with the development of mathematical programming and high-speed computers, the centralized alternative no longer appears preposterous. After all, it would appear that one could mimic the workings of a decentralized system by an appropriately chosen centralized algorithm" (Arrow 1974, 5). However, again, the growth of the complexity of the whole ought to humble even our latest technologies of knowing and intervening. Even at the level of piecemeal intervention such as antitrust policy, justification relies on a pretense of knowing that such interventions are likely to improve in the whole on what the un-intervened system would produce.

Finally, it might be argued that technology will make government more transparent and hence more accountable. We may put more trust in government because any abuse or outrage will be more readily exposed and investigated (Brin 1998). This optimistic factor surely has some validity. It may be extended: technology will facilitate public discourse, public understanding, and participation in direct democracy. Perhaps government can be made more accountable and reliable through "electronic town meetings," in which each citizen may delegate his or her voting rights to proxies (as in shareholders' meetings). If government were thereby improved, the case for activism would be strengthened.

Our conclusion, therefore, makes no claim to entirety or universality. We do not say that technology favors the case for free enterprise in all areas of policy. We thus submit a hypothesis that says "tends to," "mostly," "usually," "in general."

Arrangement of the Chapters

Each chapter in this book addresses an area of service provision and policy and tells how technological advancement affects the traditional debates in that area. The chapters show how technology weakens specific market-imperfection arguments against free enterprise. Thus, the chapters chiefly elaborate on technology's ability to reduce transaction costs and enhance competition. Only occasionally do they explicitly develop the complexity/unknowability point, even though it resides implicitly throughout.

Most of the chapters present a central market-imperfection argument to which the author brings new technology to bear. The chapters have been arranged around these central arguments.

Technology Enables Metering, Excluding, and Charging

A nonexcludable public good is one whose benefits cannot be withheld from nonpayers or noncontributors. Because users of the good cannot be made to pay and instead look to free ride, entrepreneurs who supply the good, goes the textbook story, cannot make profits. Hence the free market underprovides the good or service, and arguably, the government ought to levy taxes to finance its provision.

The lighthouse has long served as the classic example of a public good that cannot be supplied by purely voluntary means. Ronald Coase (1974)

explored the history of lighthouse provision in Britain and showed that private entrepreneurs built, owned, and operated lighthouses and made profits. Payments from ships for lighthouses were mandated at nearby ports,
however, so, as David Van Zandt (1993) explained, the arrangement depended in such cases, after all, on a form of taxation. Whatever the lessons
of the historical experience, the chapter on lighthouses by Fred Foldvary
shows that technology has dissolved any argument for government financing of lighthouse services. Because of radar, sonar, satellite-based electronic
guidance, and the feasibility of scrambled or encrypted signals, the lighthouse is largely antiquated as a navigational aid. Thus technology has
turned the canonical public good into a museum piece.

Governments are actively involved in transportation, but some of the rationales for that involvement, again, have been whittled down by technology. It has traditionally been argued that charging for highway use or parking space would entail significant transaction costs, such as delays and in-
convenience for motorists, the handling and securing of bulky cash, and
costly or unsightly toll booths or parking meters. Yet these difficulties have
been lessened considerably. Peter Samuels describes various systems for
electronic toll collection on highways. For parking, Donald Shoup describes
similar developments that dispense with on-street parking meters. Such
technologies help bring the relevant resource into the fold of market mechanisms and create strong arguments for privatization. Parking spaces along
the curb, for instance, could be turned over to adjoining property owners or
associations that use new methods of metering and collection. Such an approach would create profit opportunities that elicit supply, discovery, and
more efficient resource utilization. Debates over parking and highways involve market-imperfection arguments other than that of exclusion costs,
but technology clearly answers the central challenge to private enterprise in
these areas.

The foundation for the invisible hand is private property rights. Michael
De Alessi explores the ways in which new technologies are enhancing the
ability to define, secure, trade, and enforce private property in marine resources. He suggests that the promise of aquaculture and fisheries to feed
humankind is like the promise that was the American West. Just as ranchers and cattlemen secured and built up their property using innovations
like branding and barbed wire, today entrepreneurs can do likewise in
oceans using technologies of livestock herding, "fingerprinting," tagging,
sonar, satellite tracking, habitat creation, fencing, gating, and guarding.

Technology has strengthened the intellectual case for aquatic farming and ranching.

Can the virtues of property rights be realized in air resources? Air pollution remains one of the best examples of negative externalities (and pollution prevention one of the most compelling public-goods problems). In the chapter on auto emissions, Daniel Klein argues that the property-rights approach can be applied using sensors (paradoxically called "remote sensors") that directly measure a vehicle's on-road emissions. The new technology allows for very easy identification and apprehension of gross polluters. The airshed can be defined as the property of the relevant local governments, which guard against violations. This approach would punish only offenders by, say, imposing fines. The fines would, in a sense, be "charges" or "user fees," though they would also carry moral disapprobation. Governments could then dispense with many interventions in auto making, fuel usage, driving behavior, and scheduled inspection ("smog checks"). Policing against actual offenses alone would allow and align the invisible hand to keep down auto emissions.

That technology facilitates metering, excluding, and charging figures into several of the other chapters, though less prominently. That technological advancement thus favors free enterprise pertains also to many policy areas not covered here, such as other natural resource, wildlife, and pollution issues, security and firefighting, sanitation, and urban transit. (Highly relevant here is Anderson and Hill's 2001 valuable collection.)

Technology Facilitates Quality and Safety Assurance

Many "consumer protection" interventions suppose that quality and safety assurance cannot be adequately provided by voluntary practices and the tort system. Consumers suffer from "imperfect" or "asymmetric" information, which makes for transaction costs in marketplace decisions. The cost of overcoming ignorance is high or even insurmountable, and consequently, consumers are vulnerable in a free market to false representations of quality and safety. Services infrequently used or especially hard to understand need to be restricted according to government approvals and permissions. This line of thinking is used to rationalize many government policies and agencies, including the Consumer Product Safety Commission, the Food and Drug Administration, the Securities and Exchange Commission, the National Highway Traffic Safety Administration, the Occupational

Safety and Health Administration, and local and state occupational licensing, business licensing, and housing codes.

As consumers demand assurance, however, voluntary market processes find ways of supplying it. Service providers assure consumers of quality and safety by building and conveying a good reputation. They obtain certifications and seals of approval, seek affiliations with trusted sources, and develop a brand name. Consumers, for their part, also look to rating or recommending agents to ascertain reputations. All these methods and media depend on the generating, collecting, interpreting, formatting, storing, retrieving, and transmitting of information about service providers.

Information technologies are enhancing such methods. Shirley Svorny reexamines the rationales for medical licensing. Computer technology coupled with practice review and monitoring have given hospitals, clinics, health organizations, and insurers new means of evaluating practitioner performance. These institutions function as certifiers. Furthermore, through the Internet and other media, consumers themselves are more able to gain pointed expertise, by learning about available therapies, tapping the knowledge of fellow patients, and checking the credentials and affiliations of practitioners.

John Moorhouse explores the powers of the Internet to provide consumers with both technical knowledge and assurances. He surveys the information resources available from independent organizations, other consumers, and the vendors themselves. While such resources burgeon, entrepreneurs economize on the amount and complexity of information that consumers require. Rating organizations develop a good reputation for conveying accurate assessments of sellers and manufacturers. Using the Net, consumers may look merely for the "thumb's up" (or seal of approval), read detailed reviews, or click to another vendor who provides better assurance.

David Friedman and Kerry Macintosh consider the case against laissez-faire banking. Critics of free banking suggest that the system would be marred by bank runs and panics, hyperinflation, embezzling, and counterfeiting. These are lapses of quality. Can banks ensure quality? Will the free-banking system prevent such problems? The authors suggest that managing solvency and providing assurances of solvency are easier today because of technology; up-to-the-moment financial statements and assessments can be generated and made widely available. Contractual arrangements giving banks options to delay redemption can be more easily posted, managed, and conveyed to worried depositors. Hyperinflation and counterfeiting can be discouraged by rapid feedback mechanisms like adverse clearing. In an information age, reputation stays more current and counts for more. Friedman and Macintosh consider three models of free banking and explore how technology helps free-banking proponents respond to market-imperfection arguments.

Regulators claim that individuals suffer from an insurmountable ignorance of their own needs and the true quality of available options. Restrictions imposed in the name of quality and safety hamstring many important areas of business and everyday life. Yet in every instance new technology is making claims of consumer vulnerability less and less credible and proving that the demand for assurance elicits supply.

Technology Dissolves Natural-Monopoly Arguments

The so-called public utilities—water, sanitation, electricity, natural gas, telephone, and cable television—have long featured an interconnected network, or grid, by which water, gas, and electrons are distributed from central sources to users throughout the community. The construction and operation of the distribution system involve large up-front costs that are irreversible. Adding users to the system entails low marginal costs, and distributing product entails a low current cost. Thus, in this standard portrayal, a single distribution system continues to enjoy economies of scale as it adds volume over time. The cost structure therefore will, in a free market, give rise to a single provider: a natural monopoly. The single provider may then charge high prices, produce low quantity and quality, and make excessive profits. Would-be competitors do not enter and bid down prices because once they have invested in a competing system, the incumbent firm will lower its price and possibly bring losses to both firms. Hence no one would be foolhardy enough to challenge the monopolist. Using this reasoning, regulators and interventionists have argued that government ought to supervise such utilities and control their prices.

Whatever the historical validity of the natural-monopoly argument, it is clear that in many service areas, technology has brought alternatives to the traditional provider, alternatives that belie the traditional assumptions about costs and integration requirements. Furthermore, rapid change itself complicates the problem of regulators and planners. As Milton Friedman (1962, 28) put it: "In a rapidly changing society, however, the conditions making for technical monopoly frequently change and I suspect that both public regulation and public monopoly are likely to be less responsive to such changes in conditions . . . than private monopoly."

Alvin Lowi Jr. and Clyde Wayne Crews Jr. describe a significant trend in the delivery of electricity, toward what they call dispersed generation. Increasingly viable is small-scale generation by microturbines powered by diesel, natural gas, or other fuels. On-site generators offer users—office buildings, factories, housing developments, or even single homes—the option of creating their own self-contained loop. Lowi and Crews also explain that the costs of creating new and competing loops have fallen because of computer-controlled drilling and line laying, allowing workers to snake under streets and buildings without above-ground disturbance. These developments dissolve the assumptions of high fixed and sunk costs. Entry and competition in the market would, in a free market, be very viable. Furthermore, technology has greatly advanced the possibility of combining electricity generation with steam power, heat, and air conditioning and of combining electricity distribution with telecommunications, vastly complicating the job of any regulator who presumes to know how to improve on the invisible hand.

Alvin Lowi Jr., a mechanical engineer by profession and a social scientist by avocation, contributes his own chapter on water delivery. It nicely parallels the electricity chapter, as it too expounds on the viability of on-site utility management. Lowi argues that homes, developments, businesses, and so on would, if permitted, often choose not to hook up to the centralized utility grid. The substitute for transporting massive amounts of water via the grid, both to and from users (the latter to deal with wastewater), is developing on-site systems. Such systems would inventory a quantity of raw water, treat it according to a quality hierarchy for local uses, and then recover the raw water from the waste for inventory and reuse. On-site water and waste treatment requires refinement, disposal, and replenishment. Lowi explains the science of nine basic water treatment methods and describes the profusion of modern applications and apparatus now available on the market. So-called gray water could be treated and used for landscaping, cooling, firefighting, and sanitation. The small amount of water for sensitive human uses like bathing, cooking, and drinking would be distilled to a purity and a safety that the current one-quality-fits-all water systems could not hope to match. The "black water" from toilets and kitchen-disposal units would be treated and disposed of via sewage, vacuum truck, or other methods. Depending on recovery rates, the system would need replenishment from rainwater catchments, trucked water, or other sources. Lowi emphasizes that combining on-site utilities may yield economies of scope (the heat from an electricity generator could warm and distill water, for example). He concludes by highlighting the complexity of the institutional possibilities and rejecting the national-monopoly rationales for government control: "Technological advancements in water supply and delivery would allow the natural competition of many substitutes and alternatives, if permitted by law."

Rick Geddes looks at how technology affects the rationales for a government-created monopoly in postal services. One of those rationales is that free-market letter delivery would suffer from natural monopoly. After noting that the argument never really made much sense, Geddes explains how technology erodes whatever plausibility the argument enjoyed in matters of postal service. The main effect has been the development of powerful substitutes for letters, notably telephone, facsimile, and electronic mail, with broadband on the way. If we define "postal services" narrowly as letter delivery, these substitutes make the demand curve for postal services flatter or more elastic. Thus, the whole concern about a letter-delivery monopolist exploiting consumers loses plausibility. When people have easy alternatives, a provider cannot jack up prices without reducing revenues. Geddes identifies numerous other effects of technology, such as the facility it gives to contracting for pieces of the delivery system. Indeed, the whole notion of a postal service as a monolithic system is the artifact more of government intervention than of underlying economic conditions. Even today we have numerous delivery systems going to virtually every mailing address in the country, and where permitted by law, technology enhances the competition among them.

Other Areas in Which Technology Bolsters the Case for Free Enterprise

Several of the chapters do not fit so neatly into market-imperfection categories. A visionary and provocative chapter is that by Spencer MacCallum on what he calls entrepreneurial communities. He proposes that local governance of residential communities be proprietary and contractual. More specifically, he favors the model of the multiple-tenant income property (MTIP), a model familiar to us in the form of apartment complexes, office parks, hotels, and shopping malls. What has succeeded in the business world could also, if permitted, succeed in residential living. In MTIPs, the entrepreneurial firm retains the property title and leases space to tenants on a long-term basis. MacCallum argues that entrepreneurial ownership of the common resources and environs far surpasses the democratic governance that marks subdivided communities (whether homeowners' associations or municipal governments). MacCallum is advocating, in a sense, living in "company towns." He engages the arguments against such an arrangement, to wit, that tenants settle down and become attached to many of the features of that specific set of environs, enabling the firm to exploit the residents. Future desires cannot be known in advance, and future service and prices cannot be contracted for in detail. It is costly to negotiate, write, and enforce elaborate contingent contracts that would shield against opportunism. MacCallum contends that technology has greatly diminished these pitfalls. Modern transportation, particularly the private automobile, and telecommunications have made our lives less embedded in our residential locale. Facets of life (work, school, church, friends) are less rigidly tied to residence. Furthermore, technology facilitates our ability to switch locales. "Company towns," then, have to keep the customer satisfied. Also, technology enhances the reputational incentives for trustworthiness because any lapse would be more readily noted via the Internet and made known to other customers, both current and prospective. MacCallum envisions people living in residential communities that resemble hotels: common areas, amenities, and utilities would be managed by the property owner, with prudent regard for the tenants' desires for social interaction and communion. Meanwhile, local government could be largely dismissed.

The chapter on endangered species by Richard Stroup and Jane Shaw provides a striking variation on a theme. Whereas other chapters in this book explain how technology mitigates market imperfections, their chapter suggests that technology exacerbates the problems of the Endangered Species Act. In managing and sustaining wildlife, know-how comes in both low-tech and high-tech forms. Some of the most important breakthroughs are the discovery of breeding, nesting, migrating, or feeding patterns. Low-tech methods of enriching habitat, such as setting up proper nesting boxes for woodpeckers, are often as important as more sophisticated methods like tagging and monitoring. The tragedy of the Endangered Species Act is that it often drives landowners to put know-how to use *against* wildlife preservation. The act empowers federal officials to attenuate landowners' property rights, notably by restricting land use, if listed species are found on the land. The situation gives landowners the incentive to rid their land of listed (or potentially listed) species lest they attract the federal skunks. Landowners use know-how to eradicate fauna or make the land inhospitable in advance of their presence. Were landowners secure in their property rights, they would be more inclined to allow hobbyists, foundations, and other concerned parties to cooperate voluntarily, as guests, in wildlife management on the land, making the best use of both low-tech and high-tech methods. The chapter raises the question of whether technology intensifies government failure in other policy areas as well.

Concluding Remarks

The appropriateness of alternate policies depends on the state of technology. As technology advances, the intellectual case for specific policies changes. Thus, technology imposes on policies and their justifications what may be called an expected intellectual half-life. The faster that technology advances, the shorter the intellectual half-life of government policies will be.

This book suggests more specifically that technological advancement usually favors the effectiveness of free enterprise over government intervention. If that is the case, interventionists need to concern themselves especially with the intellectual half-life of their positions, lest they promote policies appropriate yesterday but no longer appropriate today or tomorrow.

Just as policy depends on the state of technology, so technology depends on policy. The technological advancements treated in this volume help solve social problems. In doing so, they bring affected parties some kind of profit. Technological advancement is itself a member of the invisible hand, the invisible hand's tending of its current shortcomings. "Just as technology can affect the formation of property rights, the institutional environment in which property rights evolve can also influence the development of technology" (Anderson and Hill 2001, xiii). Voluntary social mechanisms and technological advancement enjoy a complex dialectic of mutual improvement.

NOTES

1. Cowen 1988 is an excellent compilation of basic "market-failure" works and criticisms.

2. Cliffe Leslie 1879, 224. He writes also: "And just in proportion . . . as industry and commerce are developed, does the social economy become complex, diversified, changeful, uncertain, unpredictable, and hard to know, even in its existing phase" (223).

3. See Roger Koppl 2000, who writes, "The level of complexity is likely to outstrip our analytical engine" (105).

REFERENCES

Anderson, Terry L., and Peter J. Hill, eds. 2001. *The Technology of Property Rights.* Lanham, MD: Rowman & Littlefield.

Arrow, Kenneth. 1974. "Limited Knowledge and Economic Analysis." *American Economic Review* 64: 1–10.

Brin, David. 1998. *The Transparent Society: Will Technology Force Us to Choose between Privacy and Freedom?* Reading, MA: Addison-Wesley.

Coase, Ronald H. 1974. "The Lighthouse in Economics." *Journal of Law and Economics* 17 (October): 357–76. (Reprinted in Cowen 1988.)

Cowen, Tyler, ed. 1988. *The Theory of Market Failure: A Critical Examination.* Fairfax, VA: George Mason University Press.

DeLong, J. Bradford, and A. Michael Froomkin. 2000. "Speculative Microeconomics for Tomorrow's Economy." Available on DeLong's Web page: http://econ161.berkeley.edu/.

Friedman, David. 1995. "Why Encryption Matters." Available at www.best.com/~ddfr/Libertarian/Why_Crypto_Matters.html.

Friedman, Milton. 1962. *Capitalism and Freedom.* Chicago: University of Chicago Press.

Friedman, Thomas L. 1999. *The Lexus and the Olive Tree.* New York: Farrar, Straus & Giroux.

Gilder, George. 1989. *Microcosm: The Quantum Revolution in Economics and Technology.* New York: Simon & Schuster.

Hayek, Friedrich A. 1978. "The Pretence of Knowledge" (Nobel lecture, 1974). In Hayek's *New Studies in Philosophy, Politics, Economics and the History of Ideas.* Chicago: University of Chicago Press.

———. 1979. *Law, Legislation and Liberty.* Vol. 3, *The Political Order of a Free People.* Chicago: University of Chicago Press.

Henderson, David R. 2000. "Information Technology as a Universal Solvent for Removing State Stains." *Independent Review* 4, no. 4 (spring): 517–23.

Huber, Peter. 1996. "Cyber Power." *Forbes,* December 2, 142–47.

Koppl, Roger. 2000. "Policy Implications of Complexity: An Austrian Perspective." In *The Complexity Vision and the Teaching of Economics,* edited by D. Colander, 97–117. Northampton, MA: Edward Elgar.

Leslie, T. E. Cliffe. 1879. "The Known and the Unknown in the Economic World" (originally published in *Fortnightly Review,* June 1). Reprinted in his *Essays in Political Economy,* 221–42. London: Longmans, Green, 1888.

McKenzie, Richard D., and Dwight R. Lee. 1991. *Quicksilver Capital: How the Rapid Movement of Wealth Has Changed the World.* New York: Free Press.

Rosen, Harvey S. 1992. *Public Finance.* 3d ed. Homewood, IL: Irwin.

Shane, Scott. 1994. *Dismantling Utopia: How Information Ended the Soviet Union.* Chicago: Ivan R. Dee.

Tullock, Gordon. 1971. "Public Decisions as Public Goods." *Journal of Political Economy* 79, no. 4: 913–18.

Van Zandt, David E. 1993. "The Lessons of the Lighthouse: 'Government' or 'Private' Provision of Goods." *Journal of Legal Studies* 22 (January): 47–72.

Part I

Metering, Excluding, and Charging

Technology, Marine Conservation, and Fisheries Management

Michael De Alessi

It was once believed that the vast bounty of the oceans was inexhaustible. Not anymore. Around the world, the oceans' fisheries are more often than not suffering from decline and mismanagement. The World Wildlife Fund recently declared that "nearly everywhere fisheries have suffered catastrophic declines" and claimed that "without a doubt we have exceeded the limits of the seas" (Associated Press, June 7, 1996). A case in point is the cod stock off the Atlantic coast, once one of the world's richest fishing grounds. Though cod are an astoundingly fecund fish (an average female produces 1 million eggs), they now are close to commercial extinction.[1]

The basic problem is that no one owns the fish. There is no reason to exercise restraint—what is left behind may simply be caught by someone else—and so fishermen try to harvest all that they can. This reduces fish populations and harms the fishery, but because the harmful effects of each fisherman's actions are spread to all the participants, fishermen do not fully feel the harmful effects of their own actions. Depleting resources and destroying livelihoods may not make sense in the aggregate, but as Garret Hardin (1968) argued, when it is impossible to exert control over a fishery, tragedy may be inevitable.[2]

On land, the problem of the tragedy of the commons has typically been addressed by the creation of private property rights, either individual or communal. Owners' rights carry with them the inducement to behave responsibly by creating positive incentives for conservation and stewardship.[3] At sea, however, private ownership has been much more difficult to establish, and rules that fishermen have informally agreed on are often not recognized by the law. Over time, government intervention has become the norm in fishery-resource management.

Apart from the disastrous effects of subsidies for expanding various fishing fleets, government efforts to stem depletion have typically been confined to limiting catches through restrictions on gear, effort, and seasons. But because they have done nothing to address the incentives to overfish, these restrictions have resulted in overcapitalization, inefficient harvesting techniques, dangerous races to harvest fish, and little or no progress in stemming the depletion of fisheries.

Sometimes harvests are successfully restricted, but fishermen are adept at staying ahead of the restrictions. The Alaskan halibut fishery is one of the most telling examples of regulatory failure. Regulations attempted to limit overfishing by reducing the length of the fishing season. With each successive reduction in the season, however, fishermen improved their ability to catch fish by investing in better technology and bigger boats. Before long, a fishery that had once been open for most of the year had seen its season reduced to two days, but without a significant reduction in its actual harvest.

Still, many continue to favor the government regulation of fisheries. The reasons given are myriad and are normally couched in rhetoric about protecting "the common heritage of humankind." But many pleas for government involvement have something less than altruistic motivation. Dutchman Hugo Grotius, for example, was hardly feeling altruistic when he wrote of "the common heritage" in responding to attempts by the British navy, then stronger than the Dutch, to control access to the high seas (Christy and Scott 1965). Sadly, little has changed since the seventeenth century: opposition to private property rights is generally motivated by the improvement of some specific group or individual's welfare.

Not surprisingly, technology is often blamed for the rapid decline of many species, as improved methods for locating and harvesting marine resources have allowed more fish to be caught more quickly and effectively. Carl Safina, a noted marine environmentalist, tells us in a 1995 *Scientific American* article that the worldwide fisheries' "collapse" began with the explosion of fishing technologies during the 1950s and 1960s:

> During that time, fishers adapted various military technologies to hunting on the high seas. Radar allowed boats to navigate in total fog, and sonar made it possible to detect schools of fish deep under the oceans' opaque blanket. Electronic navigation aids such as LORAN (Long Range Navigation) and satellite positioning systems turned the trackless sea into a grid so

that vessels could return to within 50 feet of a chosen location, such as sites where fish gathered and bred. (Safina 1995, 48)

It is certainly true that improvements in fishing technology have enabled vast increases in harvesting capacity, but blaming technology for depletion fails to appreciate the importance of incentives. It is not technology but the institutional arrangements governing a fishery that determine whether or not a fishery will be depleted.

Technological Innovation and the Lesson of the American West

It is difficult to envision a system of private ownership in the marine environment, let alone the technologies that might make such a system feasible. However, the rapidly changing landscape of the American West at the turn of the century shows how a system of private ownership can foster the development of innovative technologies and approaches to resource management. When settlers arrived in the American West, land was plentiful. But as population rapidly grew, the West's water and land became progressively more scarce and therefore more valuable. Economists Terry Anderson and P. J. Hill (1975) showed that as the rights to land and freshwater resources became more valuable, more effort went into enforcing private property rights, which strengthened the incentives for resource conservation.

Initially, law in the West was simply transferred from the East, but it was not well suited to the frontier American West because it presumed that fencing material would be plentiful. It was not, however, and livestock frequently intermingled. Although defining private property by means of physical barriers was certainly desirable, the raw materials were not available. Government intervention was not an option, and so frontier entrepreneurs figured out new ways to define and enforce property rights.

The first such innovation was to devise a system of branding. Rapid improvements in branding technology, along with the development of cattlemen's associations which standardized and registered the brands, allowed cattlemen to identify, protect, and monitor a valuable roaming resource. Another important innovation came in the 1870s with the invention of barbed wire. Barbed wire radically changed the ability to define private property. It was inexpensive and effective at marking territory, excluding interlopers, and keeping in livestock.

The crucial element to spur change and improve the management of cattle and land was that private property could be fully enjoyed only if the rights to it could be defined and enforced. As the rewards to the private ownership were realized, owners stepped up their efforts to develop new technologies that would secure their property rights even further. Private ownership encouraged innovation.

Technological Innovation and the Oceans

The engineers who maintained the invisible fences of sound and electricity which now divided the mighty Pacific into manageable portions . . . [held] at bay the specter of famine which had confronted all earlier ages, but which would never threaten the world again while the great plankton farms harvested their millions of tons of protein, and the whale herds obeyed their new masters. Man had come back to the sea, his ancient home, after aeons of exile; until the oceans froze, he would never be hungry again.

—Arthur C. Clarke, *The Deep Range*, 1958

Sound will pen fish inside a sea ranch.

—headline in *Fish Farming International*, 1996

Arthur C. Clarke specialized in imagining the future. Nowadays, to understand technology's potential to revolutionize fishing and marine conservation, one need only examine the present. The territorial waters of the United States extend over a million square miles of ocean, and so monitoring animals or catching high-seas poachers is nearly impossible. If private property rights in the oceans were allowed to develop in ways similar to those in the frontier American West of old, a host of advanced technologies could be used to define and protect resources in the oceans.

Branding Technologies

Tags and Satellites

Scientists in Florida use transponders (small devices that beam information) and satellites to follow slow-moving manatees (O'Shea 1994). The manatees wear a belt with a platform-transmitter that emits an ultra-high-frequency signal. Using the Global Positioning System, or GPS, and radio telemetry, a satellite passing over a manatee detects the signal and records the identity of the manatee, the water temperature, and the angle at which the transmitter is tipped, allowing researchers to track the manatees and determine their migration paths. Similar electronic tags could be used to alert boaters to manatees in the water. Currently, boating accidents are the greatest threat to manatees, which have difficulty getting out of the way of speed boats. Although many waterways in Florida have speed limits, they are ineffectual. Advances in tagging could make monitoring and enforcement easier and could create a system of private property rights to protect the manatees.

Electronic Tags

Some fish populations can be monitored by less comprehensive—and less expensive—tagging technologies. Tagging of this kind involves inserting small computer chips into the fish, which are identified and recorded when the fish pass a monitor. Because live, tagged fish must pass through a small area, this method has limited applications. It is currently most effective in determining the success of hatchery programs for anadromous fish such as salmon that return to their native streams to spawn.

Salmon are already ranched in the same way that cattle are, except that their owners have no control over what happens to them once they are at sea, and so little work is being done to develop technologies to track them. Ranchers would devise branding technologies to control (i.e., protect) their salmon at sea *if their ownership of such fish were allowed and internationally recognized*. Ranchers might work out agreements with fishermen and/or fish packers so that owners would be compensated when their fish were caught by other ranchers or fishermen.

PIT Tags

Higher-tech tags have been developed that allow fish to be remotely identified. Such Passive Integrated Transponder tags, or PIT tags, are 9-mm-long electronic devices that send out signals when activated by a scanner (*Science* 1994). PIT tags can identify fish in rivers or ponds but not at sea (they have a short range of detection). In Maryland in 1995, four men illegally took protected largemouth bass from the Potomac to sell to wholesalers out of state (Mueller 1995). But many of the fish were tagged with these small electronic tags, which allowed police to identify the fish and catch the culprits.

Otolith (Inner-Ear) Markers

Biologists are learning that fish have their own natural tagging system, a bone in the fish's inner ear called an *otolith* (Kingsmill 1993). These small bones aid in balance and grow in concentric layers, producing daily rings much like those produced annually on a tree. These rings are influenced by environmental conditions. By altering water temperature, ranchers can induce distinct bone patterns that can be used to identify the fish. Fishery scientists at the Washington State Department of Fish and Wildlife have "branded" salmon otoliths by altering the water temperature and therefore the growth patterns in hatchery salmon (Volk et al. 1994). As yet, this technique has been applied only to hatchery fish. Nonetheless these internal growth patterns could allow different stocks of fish to be easily identified by being "branded" by their owners.

Genetic Markers

Genetic research provides much the same results as otolith research. Through a process known as *electrophoresis*, also known as genetic fingerprinting, scientists can determine the origins of anadromous fish and, in some cases, even the stream that the fish hatched in (*Pacific Fishing* 1989). As the sensitivity of this process improves, branding fish by their genetic makeup will become increasingly feasible. Genetic fingerprinting has a long way to go before it is fully reliable, but like otolith technology, it offers great hope for branding fish or mammals.

Fish-Scale Markers

Elemental Research, Inc., a firm in British Columbia, has developed a technology for identifying individual populations of salmon. This technology is known as *laser ablation ICP mass spectronomy* (Elemental Research 1995). The process works by using trace elements from the rivers, streams, or hatcheries to establish an elemental signature that can then be used to identify exactly where a salmon spawned. Fish scales are tested without harming the fish, and the process can accurately identify even the smallest populations of fish.

Sonar

Military technologies such as the Integrated Undersea Surveillance System (IUSS) are becoming available for environmental monitoring and research. IUSS is an integrated network of fixed and mobile acoustic devices for monitoring the oceans. These devices listen for acoustic waves such as those from submarines, underwater earthquakes, or cetaceans (the group of mammals that includes whales), some of which can be heard even thousands of miles away (Nishimura 1994).

In 1993 scientists at Cornell University used IUSS to track a single blue whale for nearly forty-three days without the use of tags or radio beacons. The songlike sounds of whales are as distinct as human voices, so that individual whales can be identified in almost the same way that voice prints identify people. Dr. Christopher Clark, a Cornell biologist, believes that the system will "rewrite the book on whale distribution and movement" (Broad 1993). IUSS will help scientists determine concentrations and numbers of whales worldwide, and it will be possible to monitor individual whales using technology that identifies their distinctive songs.

Fencing Technologies: Aquaculture

A decade ago, a fish Malthusian might have predicted the end of salmon as a food. Human ingenuity seems to have beaten nature once again.
    —Fleming Meeks writing in *Forbes*, 1990

Aquaculture—the practice of fencing in the oceans with nets, girders, and metal tanks—has experienced rapid growth and technological advancement. In 1994 it was reported that aquaculture generates $28.4 billion in revenues worldwide and is one of the world's fastest-growing industries (Herring 1994). In 1991, the world aquaculture production was approximately 13 million metric tons, double what it was seven years earlier (FAO 1992, 1993). By 1995 that number had jumped to more than 21 million metric tons (FAO 1997). It is one reason that the worldwide fish catch has remained relatively constant at 100 million tons, even though wild stocks are declining.

Just as they did in the American West, entrepreneurs have been motivated to tinker, experiment, and innovate. It is important to note in the frontier example that private ownership not only encouraged ranchers to think more carefully about cattle protection but also encouraged those with no stake in the cattle business to do the same. As the demand for cattle protection grew, so did the rewards of supplying that demand. Barbed wire was not developed by ranchers but by entrepreneurs looking to develop new markets for their wire products. This same dynamic has fueled much of the innovation and rapid growth of aquaculture.

One advantage of aquaculture is the stability of supply. Aquaculture facilities have fresh fish in holding tanks and can either slow or accelerate their growth as desired. Markets and restaurants can count on the availability of fresh fish of uniform quality and size year round. No wild fishery can ensure supply as aquaculture facilities can.

Salmon Aquaculture

Salmon are one of the most commonly farmed species, and fish farmers have developed remarkable ways to manage them. Through genetic manipulations as well as environmental and dietary control, aquaculturalists increase the fish's fat content for sushi chefs and reduce it for producers of smoked salmon. They can also increase a salmon's nutritional value, adjust its brilliant orange color, or set the flavor to bold or mild (Bittman 1996).

In 1980, the total worldwide catch of salmon (wild and farmed) was slightly more than 10,000 metric tons. Just ten years later, the volume of salmon farmed in Norway, Chile, Scotland, Canada, and Iceland amounted to more than 220,000 metric tons. The retail price of salmon in 1990 was about half of what it was in 1980 (Meeks 1990). In the United States, salmon are reared in Oregon, Washington, Alaska, and Maine. The success of salmon aquaculture operations demonstrates the vast potential for human ingenuity to protect and enhance species when private property rights channel that energy in a positive direction.

Genetics: "Fetch, Rover!"

One reason for the increase in aquaculture production is simply animal husbandry. The genetics of domesticated animals have been selected by thousands of years of breeding, whereas fish, in general, have simply been hunted in the wild (Smith et al. 1985). Not only have breeds of cattle and other livestock been improved over the centuries, but even common house pets like dogs and cats demonstrate how variability in size, temperament, and aptitude for certain tasks has been teased out to suit their masters.

Researchers are now manipulating the genetic traits of fish and shellfish, searching for hardier organisms that grow faster. Genetic research is especially promising for fish cultivation because fish have short life spans and are prolific breeders (a single fish normally produces thousands of potential offspring). Or in the case of oysters, researchers have found a way to produce triploid oysters that are sterile and therefore maintain their plumpness at those times of the year when oysters are normally dessicated from spawning.

Open-Ocean Fish Farms

Interest in offshore aquaculture is also growing, and a number of successful experiments have shown that fish can be grown offshore and successfully harvested despite the violent forces of the open sea (Champ and Willinsky 1994). Moving aquaculture operations offshore resolves conflicts in coastal areas but makes resources only partially exclusive. Although outsiders cannot take fish from cages, the fish cannot be kept out of the surrounding environment, and so pollution may be a problem. Allowing ownership of undersea areas would greatly encourage the investment in and the success of offshore aquaculture, just as private ownership has led to radical improvements in agriculture.

Indoor Aquaculture

Although they are more complicated and expensive, completely self-contained indoor aquaculture facilities allow for virtually complete control of the product. Aquafuture, a firm in Massachusetts, has had some success in raising striped bass in a closed tank system. The process uses very little water, produces wastes easily converted to fertilizer, and reportedly yields tastier fish than conventional fish farms do (Herring 1994). Regulating the temperature of the water affects the growth rate of the fish, enabling them to be grown to market size in half the time it takes in the wild or even in twice the time, depending on the current market.

An enclosed, sanitary environment also reduces disease. Aquafuture's mortality rate is half the aquaculture industry average. Traditional fish farms use about 1,000 gallons of water per pound of fish produced, whereas Aquafuture uses only about 150. Filtering out fish wastes and excess feed is a relatively simple task, and most of the waste is used by local farmers as fertilizer. Fish ponds use about 2.5 pounds of feed per pound of harvested fish, whereas the indoor system uses 1.4, in part because the count of the number of fish is always accurate (Herring 1994). Aquafuture already produces close to 1 million pounds of fish annually, and the owners plan to build plants that will yield ten times that amount.

Aquaculture and Pollution

Approximately two-thirds of all aquaculture facilities are located near the seacoast or in shallow estuaries. Environmental activists and others have recently targeted aquaculture as a threat to the environment because of the potentially detrimental effects of nutrient runoff and other wastes produced by aquaculture facilities. They have also raised concerns about the potential effects of escapees on the genetics of wild stocks. It is beyond the scope of this chapter to address the validity of these claims, but it is worth noting that if the problem is indeed serious, it would be yet another example of an unowned or government-managed resource that was not efficiently administered. If the resources in question were privately owned, any such injuries would be torts and presumably actionable in court.

Virtual Fences to Prevent Poaching

Sonar

Although the navy's underwater sound surveillance system (IUSS) is good at tracking whales, it was designed to monitor ship movements, which it does amazingly well. The IUSS is so sensitive that it can identify individual ships by the turbulence characteristics of their propellers (Grier 1994). The system locates the origin of a sound by comparing and triangulating information from hydrophones throughout an array, which effectively form a fence around a large coastal area, picking up and identifying any distinct noises within that area. Once ships are identified, logs of the ships that crossed an area can be kept, and if any unauthorized behavior takes place, the offenders can be tracked down.

Scientists at National Oceanic and Atmospheric Administration, or NOAA (part of the U.S. Commerce Department), picked up the early rumblings of an undersea volcanic eruption using IUSS. A ship rushed to the site and, for the first time, was able to monitor an undersea eruption from its inception. The kind of precise, real-time information that sonar delivers could drastically lower the costs of remote monitoring, making it easier to detect and apprehend poachers.

Satellites

Satellites can provide information about not only a ship's location but also its activity. Scientists at Natural Resources Consultants and the Pacific Remote Sensing Alliance in Spokane, Washington, have developed satellite hardware to monitor ships on the open ocean. These two private firms use Advanced Very High Resolution Radiometry (AVHRR) and Synthetic Aperture Radar (SAR) to discern whether ships are towing nets (Freeberg et al. 1992). When a ship tows a net, its engines must work harder, and this is reflected in the ship's heat profile, detected by satellite. These entrepreneurs have proposed that the government use this technology to prevent poaching, but fishermen who control offshore areas might be even better clients.

The *Financial Times* (Bowen 1999) reported that Peru's fisheries ministry is using satellite technology to monitor the eight hundred boats licensed to fish in Peruvian waters. Satellites monitor sea temperature and salinity, while instruments on the fishing boats transmit information about the types and quantities of fish being caught. The government requires boat owners to rent the technology for about $160 a month, hardly an overwhelming fee for a boat owner to pay to an industry association or other private monitoring group.

Global Positioning System (GPS)

Using the satellite-based GPS technology mentioned earlier, fishing vessels know exactly where they are at sea. Consequently, British fishermen are considering installing "black boxes" in their ships to link up with satellites that monitor their whereabouts (Deans 1995). Boats fishing legitimately would be identified by the signals from the box. Combined with the ability to tell whether ships are towing nets, monitors would have exact information about the position of ships in a given area and whether they were engaging in sanctioned activities. This strong antipoaching device could revolutionize the ability of owners to protect property and conserve marine resources.

Technologies to Herd or Fence Marine Life

We herd cows. Why not fish?
—David Barret, MIT researcher working on a "robo-tuna," 1994

Satellite Temperature Mapping

Satellite technology allows fishermen to receive maps detailing the heat profiles of the ocean's surface. Firms like Ocean Imaging in San Diego sell this information to commercial fishermen and charter boat captains because it provides accurate clues to the whereabouts of certain species of fish (Silvern 1992). Not knowing where fish are has been one of the greatest obstacles to controlling them, but the information provided by heat profiles of the ocean's surface could change that.

Submersibles

We know more about Venus, Mars, and the dark side of the moon than about the deepest ocean depths (Fricke 1994), but autonomous underwater vehicles (AUVs) are changing this. AUVs can explore and map the oceans without the drawbacks of ships, submarines, and remotely operated (but tethered) vehicles, whose range and mobility are limited. AUVs can be built cheaply and deployed continuously in large numbers. Communicating over networks similar to those for mobile telephones, AUVs will be able to share data with and receive instructions from surface buoys and via satellite. Scientists also will be able to talk back to the AUVs, sending information and instructions.

Using these features, AUVs could assist oil operations and aid in marine salvage, but more important, they could help manage fisheries and monitor pollution (Fricke 1994). Like a herd of sheep, a school of fish could be managed using AUVs, pushing them toward optimal feeding grounds and protecting them from unauthorized fishing. The technique would be perfect for valuable but elusive species like the giant bluefin tuna, one of which can fetch up to $30,000 at the Tokyo seafood market (Seabrook 1994). Such incredible prices leave little doubt that permitted the opportunity, owners would develop ways to monitor and protect such animals.

Creating Habitat

Artificial Reefs

Artificial reefs have been made from such disparate materials as buses, milk crates, and tires filled with concrete. Such reefs provide habitat that attracts some fish and propagates others and are especially popular with scuba divers and sports fishermen. To what extent artificial reefs either produce more species or simply lure them from elsewhere varies from site to site. There is no doubt, however, that artificial reefs do offer a recruitment site for larvae and juveniles that otherwise would not find a place to settle (Stone et al. 1979). We know that artificial reefs increase marine life, but not by how much.

The efforts of many private fishing and diving clubs, often working with local governments, demonstrate an interest and willingness to invest in artificial reefs. In Canada, the Artificial Reef Association of British Columbia was allowed to sink a warship in the barren, cold waters around Sechelt, British Columbia (Lamb 1995). This completely private venture has brought an influx of tourists, with divers flocking to the attraction. No one owns the wreck, but because locals control access to it, they can gain from enhancing the area and attracting diving business. Even partial ownership encourages protection and innovation.

Historically, Alabama has had the most lenient laws regarding the creation of artificial reefs. Reefs cannot be owned outright, but permit holders do not have to specify the exact location of their reef. The fishermen sink objects to form artificial reefs and attract fish and then hope to keep the location secret. Satellite systems, such as GPS, allow fishermen to return to their exact location at sea. A secret location allows for limited exclusion, so fishermen can capture some of the returns on their investment. As a result of artificial reef production, Alabama produced 33 percent of the recreational red snapper catch in the Gulf states in 1992, even though it has only 3 percent of the Gulf shoreline, a huge increase over catches before the start of the artificial reef program (Cisar 1993).

The Growth of Coral Reefs

Coral reefs are some of the most valuable and productive ecological sites in the oceans. They have suffered, however, from the same management failures as have many of the world's fisheries. Unlike most fisheries, they are very slow growing and take ages to recover from serious damage. A report in the *Sunday Times of London* (Hargrave 1999) documented the experiments in the Maldives in which an electrical charge was used to strengthen corals against environmental stress and, in another case, to accelerate the coral growth rate fourfold. The process creates high pH conditions directly at the growing mineral surface, which provides extra metabolic energy for the growth of corals (Goreau 1999).

Conclusions

Regulatory approaches to marine conservation, especially of fisheries, have all too often resulted in disaster, for both resources and the people that depend on them. Government intervention has precluded the evolution of private property rights. Resigned to government interference, entrepreneurs and fishermen have not taken steps to develop methods by which they could protect or even enhance marine resources. There is little incentive for private efforts to limit access when private property rights are not applicable to ocean territories.

Traditional governmental restrictions have failed in part because they maintain open access. Realizing this failure, fishery managers and policymakers are beginning to consider limited access schemes like the Individual Transferable Quota (ITQ) system. Under an ITQ system, government officials set annual catch limits, but rights to a percentage of the catch are privately owned and can be traded, allowing the market to allocate them. Political allocations like ITQs are always coveted and rarely secure, introducing uncertainty and harming the fishery. Thus, adapting government institutions to mimic private solutions is a step in the right direction but fails to eliminate the shortcomings of other regulatory programs. A purely private approach would be far superior.

Private conservation is becoming more and more feasible as emerging technologies increase the ability of owners to control marine resources. If private property rights are allowed in the oceans, stewardship and technological innovation will boom. Just as settlers in the frontier American West developed branding and fencing technologies to define and protect their property, sonar, satellites, tagging technologies, unmanned submersibles, artificial reefs, and aquaculture will permit owners of marine resources to do the same today. The challenge is to delineate control of the marine environment in a way that creates private property rights and induces owners to develop both technology and marine resources.

NOTES

1. Commercial extinction occurs when it is not economically viable to catch the remaining fish.

2. Hardin coined the phrase the "tragedy of the commons" but based many of his ideas on the work of economists H. Scott Gordon (1954) and Anthony Scott (1955).

3. Hardin's original essay caused some confusion over the word *commons*, which he used to mean an open-access regime (no limits on harvests). Other scholars, especially anthropologists, have used the word to connote a formal regime based on communal ownership of resources. See, for example, Ostrom 1990. The real problem seems not to be with commons per se but with resources that are not privately owned—that is, either "open access" and free to all or controlled by the state.

REFERENCES

Anderson, Terry L., and P. J. Hill. 1975. "The Evolution of Property Rights: A Study of the American West." *Journal of Law and Economics* 12: 163–79.

Bittman, Mark. 1996. "Today's Fish: Straight from the Farm." *New York Times*, September 18.

Bowen, Sally. 1999. "Peru Introduces the Science of Fishing—By Satellite." *Financial Times*, August 27.

Broad, William J. 1993. "Navy Listening System Opening World of Whales." *New York Times*, August 23.

Champ, Michael A., and Michael D. Willinsky. 1994. "Farming the Oceans." *The World and I*, April.

Christy, Francis, and Anthony Scott. 1965. *The Common Wealth in Ocean Fisheries.* Baltimore: Johns Hopkins University Press.

Cisar, Eric. 1993. "Artificial Reefs: Making Something from Nothing." *Tide*, November/December.

Clarke, Arthur C. 1958. *The Deep Range.* New York: Signet.

Crittenden, Jules. 1994. *Boston Herald*, October 30.

De Alessi, Michael. 1998. *Fishing for Solutions.* London: Institute of Economic Affairs.

Deans, John. 1995. "Tightening the Net: Spy-on-the-Bridge Could Curb Rogue EU Trawler Skippers." *Daily Mail*, March 20.

Elemental Research, Inc. 1995. "Application of the ERI Laser Ablation / ICPMS System to Salmon Migration Studies." Elemental Research, Inc. in-house study, November.

FAO. 1992. *Aquaculture Production 1984–1990.* Rome: Food and Agriculture Organization of the United Nations.

———. 1993. *Aquaculture Production 1985–1991.* Rome: Food and Agriculture Organization of the United Nations.

———. 1997. *The State of World Fisheries and Aquaculture.* Rome: Food and Agriculture Organization of the United Nations.

Fish Farming International. 1996. "Sound Will Pen Fish inside a Sea Ranch." April.

Freeberg, Mark H., E. A. Brown, and Robert Wrigley. 1992. "Vessel Localization Using AVHRR and SAR Technology." Paper presented at the annual meeting of the Marine Technology Society, Washington, DC, October 19.

Fricke, Robert J. 1994. "Down to the Sea in Robots." *Technology Review*, October.

Gordon, H. Scott. 1954. "The Economic Theory of a Common-Property Resource: The Fishery." *Journal of Political Economy* 62: 124–42.

Goreau, Tom. 1999. Untitled e-mail message to the Internet discussion group "Coralist" by the president of the Global Coral Reef Alliance in response to a *Sunday Times of London* article (Hargrave 1999), March 18.

Grier, Peter. 1994. "The Greening of Military Secrets." *Christian Science Monitor*, March 21.

Hardin, Garrett. 1968. "The Tragedy of the Commons." *Science* 162: 1243–48.

Hargrave, Sean. 1999. "Electrically Charged Frames Are Being Used to Create the Limestone on Which Coral Lives." *Sunday Times of London*, March 14.

Herring, Hubert B. 1994. "900,000 Striped Bass, and Not a Fishing Pole in Site." *New York Times*, November 6.

Kingsmill, Suzanne. 1993. "Ear Stones Speak Volumes to Fish Researchers." *Science* 260: 1233–34.

Lamb, Jamie. 1995. "Success of Private Enterprise Is Giving Our MLAs That Old Sinking Feeling." *Vancouver Sun*, January 30.

Meeks, Fleming. 1990. "Would You Like Some Salmon with Your Big Mac?" *Forbes*, December 24.

Mueller, Gene. 1995. "High-Tech Sleuthing Pays off for Md. DNR in Investigation." *Washington Times*, March 1.

Nishimura, Clyde E. 1994. "Monitoring Whales and Earthquakes by Using SOSUS." *1994 NRL Review.* Washington, DC: U.S. Naval Research Laboratory.

O'Shea, Thomas J. 1994. "Manatees." *Scientific American*, July.

Ostrom, Elinor. 1990. *Governing the Commons: The Evolution of Institutions for Collective Action.* Cambridge: Cambridge University Press.

Pacific Fishing. 1989. "Genetic Fingerprints." November.

Safina, Carl. 1995. "The World's Imperiled Fish." *Scientific American*, November, 46–53.

Science. 1994. "Bass Poachers Hooked by Bug." *Science* 267: 1765.

Scott, Anthony. 1955. "The Fishery: The Objectives of Sole Ownership." *Journal of Political Economy* 63: 116–24.

Seabrook, John. 1994. "Death of a Giant: Stalking the Disappearing Bluefin Tuna." *Harper's Magazine*, June.

Silvern, Drew. 1992. "For Company, Space Data Is Catch of the Day." *San Diego Union-Tribune*, October 10.

Smith, Emily T., Andrea Durham, Edith Terry, Neil Gilbride, Phil Adamsak, and Jo Ellen Davis. 1985. "How Genetics May Multiply the Bounty of the Sea." *Business Week*, December 16.

Stone, R. B., H. L. Pratt, R. O. Parker Jr., and G. E. Davis. 1979. "A Comparison of Fish Populations on Artificial and Natural Reefs in the Florida Keys." *Marine Fisheries Review* 41, no. 9: 1–11.

Volk, Eric C., Steven L. Schroeder, Jeffrey Grimm, and H. Sprague Ackley. 1994. "Use of Bar Code Symbology to Produce Multiple Thermally Induced Otolith Marks." *Transactions of the American Fisheries Society* 123: 811–16.

2

The Lighthouse as a Private-Sector Collective Good

Fred E. Foldvary

> Commerce has been bold and has searched out the dark corners of the world, but it stays longest where it is most welcomed and best entertained. Where there are light-houses there come ships; some may come where there are no lights, but with the welcome rays come the many and the richly laden.
>
> —Arnold Burges Johnson,
> *The Modern Light-House Service*, 1890

The lighthouse has become famous in economics as a landmark case of a good that, owing to its public nature, had been presumed to require provision by government, whereas as Ronald Coase (1974) pointed out in his famous article, some lighthouses were financed by user fees paid by the shippers. My chapter updates Coase's study by examining how advancing technology—the "welcome rays" having now progressed to electronic guidance signals—affects the feasibility of the private-sector provision of lighthouse services and hence the theoretical justification for the optimality or necessity of government provision. Coase cited John Stuart Mill, Henry Sidgwick, A. C. Pigou, and Paul Samuelson among those economists who suggested that lighthouses required governmental provision. But Coase showed how lighthouses in Great Britain have in fact been financed by user fees at harbors.

One example of private provision was the Casquets Lighthouse on Guernsey, one of the Channel Islands near France. In 1722 the owners of ships passing by dangerous rocks off the island of Alderney asked the owner of the rocks to build a lighthouse, offering to pay him according to the tonnage of the passing ships. It was erected by Thomas le Cocq, owner of the rocks. Lighthouses in Uruguay also originally belonged to private owners (IALA 1998, 103, 62).

If we define a "public good" in Samuelson's sense (1954) of any item impacting more than one person and the whole good impacting each person, whether or not it is excludable, lighthouses are public goods. As Coase showed, lighthouse service is to some extent excludable when it is tied to entry into harbors, where a fee can be charged.

Moreover, even a service that is nonexcludable does not by itself make private provision infeasible, because there can be benevolent sympathetic provision (Foldvary 1994) as well as or combined with provision based on social pressure, as occurred, for example, with the provision in the nineteenth century of toll roads in the United States (Klein 1990). The Royal National Lifeboat Institution is to a great extent run by volunteers and has been effective in rescue services in the British Isles (Meek 1999). Nonexcludable lighthouses could function similarly.

David E. Van Zandt (1993) countered that even though private lighthouses were built in Great Britain, including by some religious charitable providers, the government supplemented the services. (In fact, the collector had a warrant from the king.) Van Zandt also stated that the government was involved in all goods and services. Though true, this leaves open the question of whether even such broad involvement, along with the narrower aquatic lighting services, could be provided by more purely private enterprise if not preempted or even monopolized by government. A second issue is whether advancing technology provides even greater feasibility for private-sector provision.

Some Technical Elements of Lighthouse Services

A *lighthouse* is a fixed structure with an artificial light. In addition to lighthouses, moored lightships also offered similar services where the water was too deep to construct a lighthouse. The last of the Coast Guard lightships was removed from the Nantucket station in 1984 (*Lighthouse Facts* 1999).

Besides light, shipping protective services have included sound, such as from foghorns and sonar (high-frequency sound waves). Fog signals may be cannons, whistles, sirens, reed trumpets, bells, diaphones, or diaphragm horns. The source of light for a lighthouse is called a *lamp*, and its magnification is produced by a *lens* or *optic*. The most powerful optic has a range of 25 miles at sea. Its *characteristic* refers to the type of signal, such as fixed and revolving optics, colored lights, and the intervals for flashing (*Lighthouse Facts* 1999).

Ships and airplanes navigate using Zulu time, usually based on a 24-hour clock. "Zulu," the radio transmission articulation for the letter Z, refers to Universal Coordinated Time (UCT), formerly called Greenwich Mean Time.

According to Johnson (1890, 8),

> The theory of coast lighting is that each coast shall be so set with towers that the rays from their lights shall meet and pass each other, so that a vessel on the coast shall never be out of sight of a light, and that there shall be no dark space between the lights.

This concept implies that modern lighthouse services are not just isolated signals at dangerous protrusions or at harbors but an organized system of navigational aids.

The International Association of Lighthouse Authorities (IALA), a nongovernmental organization, was established in 1957 to provide global coordination and information for maritime navigation aids. During the 1970s it promoted a uniform international maritime buoy system (IALA 1988, 14). Currently the IALA is developing a global radio-navigation system. Even though the IALA works with national lighthouse administrations, it could also help coordinate private lighthouses.

A History of Lighthouse Technology and Provision

Light dues or fees have always been a primary source of revenue for lighthouses, providing evidence that it is feasible to collect charges for passage. In the first recorded instance of lighthouse fee collection, Edward, the Black Prince and administrator of the English province of Guyenne in France, erected the first seamark tower on Cordouan in 1370, and the keeper was authorized to collect dues of two groats (eight pence) from all passing ships (Blanchard 1978, 17–18). Before that, since 1092, monks had burned a light on Cordouan Island (IALA 1998, 136).

Before the U.S. Constitution was ratified, the colonies financed lighthouses by collecting light dues or shipping taxes. The first lighthouse in

North America was built at Boston harbor in 1715 and was supported by fees on both incoming and outgoing vessels (U.S. Dept. of Commerce 1915, 14). Customs collected the fees, and since the ships could be spotted as they arrived, there was little opportunity for evasion. Virginia and Maryland continued collecting such fees after they became states in 1776. In 1789, all lighthouses and beacons came under the control of the secretary of the treasury in accordance with the Act for the Establishment and Support of Lighthouses, Buoys, and Public Piers.

This act provided that all expenses of lighthouses and other navigational aids "shall be defrayed out of the Treasury of the United States" (Putnam 1933, 31). The Light-House Board was asked why it should not support itself by charging light dues:

> It has uniformly responded that light should be as free as air, that its work was done not only in the interests of commerce but for the sake of science and humanity, and that it should be supported from the national treasuries as is the Army, the Navy, or as is the Coast Survey or Life-Savings Service. (Johnson 1890, 112)

Alexander Hamilton was responsible for terminating the light dues, telling George Washington that light should be "as free as the air" (Wayne C. Wheeler, Lighthouse Society, interview, December 7, 1999). Clearly, the motive for financing American lighthouses out of general revenues was ideological; it was not that light dues were ineffective. After their revolution, the French also stopped collecting light dues (IALA 1998, 132).

Technological advancement during the 1800s provided for more effective lighting (e.g., revolving lights) and reflectors. Before this, whale oil was used with solid wicks until a parabolic reflector system was introduced around 1810. The Fresnel lens was invented in 1822 and began being used in the United States in the 1850s. Kerosene replaced oil during the 1870s, and electricity was used after 1900 (*Lighthouse Facts* 1999). David Porter Heap, called the "Great Improver" of the U.S. Lighthouse Service, invented improvements like the Five-Day Lens Lantern in 1889, better burners in 1888–92, the red-color characteristic (cylinders) in 1891, twinkling lights in 1890, occulting lights (obscuring at intervals) in 1890, and ball bearings in 1898 (Tag 1999).

In 1916, the automatic bulb changer was developed (Blanchard 1978, 774), and in 1921, the first successful radio beacon was erected in New York. Radio enabled signals to be sent to a specific station (Putnam 1933, 295). By the early 1930s, radio beacons were used in conjunction with fog signals as distance finders. Since World War I, automatic lights had eliminated the need for permanent lighthouse keepers (Blanchard 1978, 773, 774).

The U.S. Coast Guard obtained jurisdiction over lighthouses in 1939. Its LAMP (Lighthouse Automation and Modernization) project phased out tended lighthouses during the 1960s and 1970s (Blanchard 1978, 776). The last remaining Coast Guard–staffed lighthouse holdout is the Boston Light Station (*Keeper's Log* 1999). Microwaves or telephone lines can be used to monitor automated lighthouses. Other advances during the 1900s included sonar and radar, which was developed during World War II. In the early 1990s, solar-powered lighthouses became economical (Wheeler, interview, 1999).

The Role of Government

Van Zandt (1993, 56) distinguished among the government's various roles concerning lighthouses: (1) the provision of law by some agency; (2) government enforcement of property and contract rights; (3) government fixing of rates, establishment of monopolies, and enforcement of collections; (4) government provision from user fees; and (5) government provision from general revenues. Van Zandt claims that there is no historical example of purely private provision, his second category. Instead, the government granted monopolies to lighthouse owners, set the lighthouse fees ("light dues"), and assisted in enforcing the collection fees. As Johnson noted (1890, 113), "Payment of light dues is made to and enforced by the customs offices, and they are a lien on ship and cargo. They usually appear in the bill of port charges." In Gibraltar, many Latin American countries, and elsewhere, light dues were directly collected by governments (116). Light dues are still the source of revenue for lighthouses in Scotland and Ireland (IALA 1998).

These facts reduce the impact of Coase's conclusion. However, as Van Zandt pointed out, the feasibility of more purely private provision depends on the available technology: "When the available private technology of collection and exclusion is less effective than the government's enforcement powers, one should expect government support for the collection process" (1993, 57). By implication, the technology that makes the provision more excludable, plus the shift of property rights to enable lighthouse owners to charge for entering their territory, reduces the economic rationale for such government involvement.

The patents granted to British lighthouse keepers (or leases by Trinity House under a general monopoly patent for England and Wales) included exclusive territorial rights in exchange for paying rent (Van Zandt 1993, 65). The patent also fixed the charges to the ships, with the exception of Royal Navy ships, and permitted the holder to employ collectors provided by Trinity House, backed by the power of government, or to use customs officials. (In 1836, Parliament empowered Trinity to buy and direct most of the lighthouses in England, which it did by 1842.)

Nevertheless, it is not clear that monopoly privileges were necessary in order to make fee collection profitable, as competition could eliminate monopoly profits and economic rents or several harbor enterprises might form an association to operate the lighthouses. Moreover, because waterways are government property, payments for lighthouse services are required for their use.

But even if the waterways were not governmental property, using the government to enforce payments for lighthouse services is no different conceptually from using government courts and police powers to enforce any contract or property right.

Technology Today and Tomorrow

Current technological progress, such as global satellite-based electronic guidance signaling (Global Positioning System or GPS) combined with encryption, make electromagnetic signaling services more excludable and hence more amenable to private provision and financing. While such services have continued to be provided by government agencies—owing to inertia or political self-interest—the theoretical nonexcludable public-good argument has receded, if not vanished. An encrypted signal requiring a fee to unscramble creates exclusion aside from the harbor. Foghorn signals still seem to be nonexcludable once provided, but since electronic and sonar guidance signals are sufficient to warn of any dangers, in principle the service of protecting shipping from the danger of protrusions can be provided privately. According to Van Zandt (1993, 71), "All signs indicate that the days of lighthouses are numbered."

It is evident that the private operation of lighthouses, including modern signaling services, would be substantially less costly than governmental operation. For example, it costs $180,000 for the U.S. Coast Guard to paint a lighthouse according to government regulations, whereas it would cost only

$40,000 for it to be painted by a private contractor (Wheeler, interview, 1999).

Airline navigation is going through a transition similar to that of lighthouses. Air navigation first relied on pilots using aeronautical charts and comparing them with visual landmarks. Dead reckoning, used when landmarks are not visible, used a clock, compass, and later also a computer to track timing and direction. Current technology now uses VOR (Very high frequency Omnidirectional Radio) navigation and instrument landing systems as well as radar in conjunction with air route traffic control centers operated by the U.S. government. Aircraft navigation systems have been moving toward the use of the GPS (Global Positioning System) (Brewster 2000). Both air and sea craft have thus been moving toward electronic signals, although visual signals at the place of landing are still in use.

Conclusion

With modern satellite-based electronic guidance signaling, the possibility of encrypted signals, radar, sonar, and computerized tracking of ships, lighthouses have become obsolete. They are now quaint tourist attractions, often with bed and breakfast (a list of publicly accessible lighthouses is available from the National Maritime Initiative). Some lighthouses are now being transferred from the U.S. Coast Guard to preservation communities and organizations. Indeed, societies have been formed to preserve lighthouses "and their lore" for future generations (Wheeler 1999). For example, the United States Lighthouse Society, with 10,000 members, is a nonprofit organization "dedicated to the preservation of lighthouse and lightships" (Silva 1999). It sells artifacts and publishes the magazine *The Keeper's Log*. Such societies also obtain grants from foundations as well as federal and state governments for historic preservation, often as matching funds. The societies conduct tours of lighthouses and maintain libraries of lighthouse literature. Another publication is the *Lighthouse Digest*, a magazine for lighthouse enthusiasts.

From early times, lighthouses were financed from charges for ship passage. That governments were involved in setting and collecting fees does not alter the concept that, absent such preemption, private enterprise could provide lighting services and collect payments. Today, lighthouses are becoming obsolete. Government is using radio, sonar, and other signals that can be encrypted to require payment for reception, especially in conjunction with property rights to the passage of ships contingent on their paying the charges. As with other technological advances, the implementation of the technology that makes feasible more private provision depends on institutional changes. Even more so than when Coase made the lighthouse a famous example of a presumed governmental good that was not always historically so, it is politics, not economics, that now maintains the government's provision of signaling services to ships. Now the government is providing historic monuments and scenic amenities rather than navigational aids.

If the waters near a lighthouse are privately owned space or if the governing agency asserts similar property rights, then any entrants are trespassers unless explicitly welcomed. Radar, sonar, and other electronic signals can detect the presence of intruders and then alert them by radio that they are entering a private zone requiring payment. If the ship or boat does not stop, the private owner may be entitled to fine the intruder beyond the usual fees. Such property rights may conflict with traditional laws treating the oceans, even within countries' territorial waters, as commons with unrestricted and free passage.

Again, "commerce . . . stays longest where it is most welcomed and best entertained. . . . [W]ith the welcome rays come the many and the richly laden." In the twenty-first century, if set free to do so, private enterprise would have the incentive to invent and implement rays that would better welcome richly laden commerce.

REFERENCES

Blanchard, Leslie. 1978. "A Century of Lighthouse Engineering: Technology and Institutional Politics, 1800—1900." Manuscript available at the U.S. Lighthouse Society, San Francisco.

Brewster, Bill. 2000. "Aircraft Navigation Systems to Get GPS Upgrade." ABC-NEWS.com, June 14.

Coase, Ronald. 1974. "The Lighthouse in Economics." *Journal of Law and Economics* 17 (October): 357–76.

Foldvary, Fred E. 1994. *Public Goods and Private Communities.* Aldershot: Edward Elgar.

IALA. 1998. *Lighthouses of the World.* Old Saybrook, NY: Globe Pequot Press (compiled by the International Association of Marine Aids to Navigation and Lighthouse Authorities).

Johnson, Arnold Burges. 1890. *The Modern Light-House Service.* Washington, DC: U.S. Government Printing Office.

Keeper's Log. 1999. "Going to Boston Next Summer? Visit Little Brewster Island's Boston Light Station." *Keeper's Log* 16, no. 1 (fall): 31.

Klein, Daniel B. 1990. "The Voluntary Provision of Public Goods? The Turnpike Companies of Early America." *Economic Inquiry* 28, no. 4 (October): 788–812.

Lighthouse Facts. 1999. San Francisco: U.S. Lighthouse Society.

Meek, Nigel. 1999. "The Plausibility of Large-Scale, Hi-Tech, Voluntarily-Funded Emergency Organisations: The Example of the Royal National Lifeboat Institution." *Economic Notes*, no. 86.

National Maritime Initiative. 1999. http://www.cr.nps.gov/history/maritime/.

Putnam, George R. 1933. *Lighthouses and Lightships of the United States.* Boston: Houghton Mifflin.

Samuelson, Paul A. 1954. "The Pure Theory of Public Expenditure." *Review of Economics and Statistics* 36, no. 4 (November): 387–89.

Silva, Marian de. 1999. Letter to New Members. San Francisco: U.S. Lighthouse Society.

Tag, Thomas A. 1999. "The Great Improver." *The Keeper's Log* 16, no. 1 (fall): 24–29.

U.S. Department of Commerce, Lighthouse Service. 1915. *The United States Lighthouse Service.* Washington, DC: U.S. Government Printing Office.

Van Zandt, David E. 1993. "The Lessons of the Lighthouse: 'Government' or 'Private' Provision of Goods." *Journal of Legal Studies* 22 (January): 47–72.

Wheeler, Wayne C. 1999. Letter to New Members. San Francisco: U.S. Lighthouse Society.

3

Motorway Financing and Provision
Technology Favors a New Approach

Peter Samuel

The Standard "Market-Failure" Arguments

Classic expositions of "market failure" offered several ways in which the free-enterprise system could "fail"—fail, that is, to be perfect (Bator 1958; Musgrave and Musgrave 1976, chaps. 3 and 9). The relevance of a perfection standard is a matter of great importance, but let's take the standard critique for whatever it's worth. Two types of "market failure" have, in the past, pertained to highway provision. It once could have been said that users of highways cannot be made to pay for the service without incurring large costs of toll collection, including the erection of toll booths, the employment of toll collectors, the handling and securing of bulky cash, and the disruption and delay of traveling motorists—all of these being transaction costs. Highways were, to an extent, "public goods," and, the argument goes, their financing ought to rely on general taxation. Another way of phrasing the point is to say that the construction of tax-financed freeways will generate positive benefits not achievable by means of toll financing. (The public-goods problem can be expressed in terms of externalities, which can be expressed in terms of transaction costs.) This chapter deals primarily with this argument. New technology has made toll collection a trivial matter. The transaction costs have been reduced greatly, and highways are now perfectly "excludable." It can be as easy to pay a highway bill as it is to pay a telephone bill. And some highway companies now exclude nonpayers from usage just as easily as telephone companies do. Thus, toll-financed highways entail transaction costs no greater than (and arguably significantly less than) those of tax-financed highways.

The second textbook argument against the provision of free-enterprise highways is "natural monopoly" (see, for example, Stiglitz 1993, 411, 455). The argument runs as follows: Competition in provision is unlikely or un- workable because the up-front cost (or fixed cost) of providing a competing highway is very high and irreversible (or "sunk"), and the marginal cost of allowing another user is very low. These conditions make competition in the market an uninviting prospect: market battles driving price down to mar- ginal cost would probably yield mutual bankruptcy. An incumbent monop- olist, therefore, would not be checked, in its pricing and performance, by entry or potential entry. Clearly these arguments have weight with respect to local streets. For the owner of a single house or business, usually only one street provides access, so there is almost no opportunity for competition in the provision of local street access. At this level the issue is what level of gov- ernment—city, county, or state—is best equipped to manage the single road or whether it might best be handled by a cooperative or joint service con- tractor answerable to a homeowners' association or condominium. But as you go up the hierarchy of roads from the local street up through collector streets to arterial roads and motorways, the natural-monopoly objection to market provision of roads becomes somewhat less compelling. True, one route is never a perfect substitute for another, but for most trips there are usually alternative routes and sometimes competing modes.

Even if the free marketer were to concede the natural-monopoly argu- ment, that argument could cut against free enterprise only so far as to sug- gest regulation or antitrust scrutiny of the respective private monopolists. Even the conventional wisdom of the textbooks does not recommend gov- ernment ownership of public utilities. Yet in the matter of highways, public ownership is what we see all around us, mostly financed by taxes. Thus, new technology—transforming, as it does, highways into perfectly excludable goods—clearly argues for both tolling and private enterprise, if not *free* en- terprise.

"Market-failure" reasoning is used to point to government provision and tax financing, but it contains a terrible paradox. On modern "freeways," a severe and common problem is congestion. The absence of pricing results in a "tragedy of the commons," which again is a kind of externality problem. Also, the pavement damage inflicted by heavy trucks has been turned into an external burden on the taxpayer. Both of these problems may better be dealt with by flexible tolls than by taxes (U.S. Federal Highway Administra- tion 1997; Winston and Shirley 1998). As Gabriel Roth has long argued (see Roth 1996), "free" government provision has created some of the most serious externality problems of motorway service. Politicizing society's resources often creates, rather than resolves, externality problems (Tullock 1971).

A Retrospective on Toll Collection and the Gas Tax

In the last century, transactions costs were the main argument for having governments build and manage roads. A toll or fee for use of the road was often seen as too expensive and cumbersome. A toll collector in a booth can collect anywhere between 300 and 600 tolls per hour, depending on the complexity of the toll, the familiarity and speed of the motorists, and how often change needs to be made. At an all-up labor cost of $30 per hour, toll collection by collectors costs an absolute minimum of 5 cents per transaction and often 20 cents or more, given that there will be periods of slack traffic. At these costs a toll facility must package its roadway into discrete segments of a size that warrants a toll greater than those numbers in order to make a toll worth collecting. That translates into interchanges at least 5 and more often 10 miles apart—which lose a lot of local traffic.

Typically manned toll facilities in the automobile era have been found on highways of *motorway* class (*motorways* is the international term for so-called freeways in the western United States, and *expressways*, in the east and south). Their feature of controlled access prevents motorists from avoiding tolling points. Also, such roads have been favored for tolling because they most often generate the volumes of traffic needed to exploit tolling economies of scale. And the speeds that they allow offer motorists time savings that make them attractive despite the tolls.

But generally such motorways carry only about one-quarter to one-third of the total road traffic as measured by vehicle miles traveled. Two-thirds or more of traffic is on local streets and signalized arterial roads, the kinds of mixed-use roads on which human toll collection is, as yet, infeasible. In Japan, France, Italy, Greece, and South Korea, the motorway system is almost exclusively tolled; in Australia, about half is tolled; whereas in the United States and Canada, less than 10 percent is tolled. In Germany, Belgium, Holland, and the United Kingdom, motorways are completely untolled. In most countries, however, tolls are used to fund very expensive bridges and tunnels.

With the advent of petroleum-fueled internal combustion engines, the technology of oil refining to manufacture motor fuels was the tax collector's dream. Here was a standardized product produced by a relatively small number of corporations with large centralized facilities, careful measurement of production, and sophisticated accounting procedures. A tax per gallon was irresistible. Politicians were easily able to "sell" it to the public as a "user fee" for financing roads, which in the early days rarely supported the numbers of vehicles that would justify toll collection and, if tolled, were prone to toll evasion. That the gas tax is highly regressive, in the sense that it takes a larger proportion of income from a poor person than from a rich person, was not significant. Today, a newly imposed tax of such regressivity would cause an uproar, but because we've had the gas tax all along, it causes little stir.

The technology of centralized fuel refining and ease of tax collection facilitated the government's domination of road provision in the first century of the automobile. It has to be said this was also a period in which the government was growing with a progressivist optimism about the beneficent impact of central planning. Interest groups followed the trend. Farmers were one group, truckers another. Because the first government road-building programs were to pave farm-to-market roads and the markets tended also to be railheads, a coalition of organized interests could be assembled to lobby. "Getting the farmers out of the mud" of unpaved roads was the early slogan for government road building. But it was the triumph of the gasoline internal combustion engine over electric batteries and steam as propulsion between 1900 and 1920 that made it a soft option for state governments to institute gasoline taxes in the early 1920s as the standard revenue raiser for roads. That helped entrench the government as the dominant road service provider.

Mechanization eventually started to undercut the popular logic of tax financing. Indeed, electromechanical devices such as automatic coin machines, introduced in 1953 on New Jersey's Garden State Parkway, allowed toll roads to begin their break away from labor-intensive toll collection (*Toll Roads Newsletter*, no. 34, December 1998, 12). Able to handle coins or tokens thrown by the patron into a receiving basket, they allowed a doubling of throughput per toll lane to 600 to 1,000 vehicles per hour. And since one worker could service dozens of coin machines, they represented a leap forward in toll collection productivity. They made it possible to introduce more interchanges into toll roads, and hence serve traffic better by picking it up closer to its points of origin and letting it off close to its points of destination. Coin machines are especially helpful at rather low volume ramp plazas. And at mainline "barrier" plazas they also enable managers to sharply reduce costs by removing human collectors from booths at times of low traffic, as at night, while still having the toll lane profitably open for business. A major limit on automatic coin machine collection has been the decline of coinage in America and inflation's erosion of the value of the quarter. Increasingly, tolls require a bunch of quarters, and patrons simply don't want to carry that many quarters in their purses or pockets.

Another new form of mechanization was the combination of punched-hole cards and mainframe computers. Later, magnetic stripe cards or "tickets" were substituted for the punched-hole cards. At the entry ramp the motorist picks up the card, which carries a record of the time and place of entry so that on exiting the road, the toll collector's terminal quickly computes the trip length and toll due. In this period there was a tension in the design of toll roads with the objective of minimizing the number of congestion-causing stops. The "ticket" technology made economic sense for long trips, so that the motorist was limited, however long the trip on the toll road, to a maximum of two stops, one to obtain the "ticket" at the beginning and the other to pay the toll at the end. Of course, point tolling is more economical for short trips within a urban setting where a combination of barrier toll plazas and ramp plazas can limit the stops to one for each of many trips being made. As suburban development has changed the nature of stretches of toll roads from being principally long-distance interurban facilities to intraurban commuter facilities, a number of facilities have abandoned trip tolling for point tolling, but at considerable expense in refitting their toll plazas.

Electronic Tolling

A far greater advance in toll technology came in the late 1980s with the successful application of new radio-signal technologies to introduce electronic tolling. As radio has gone to higher and higher frequencies, the antennas have become smaller; the signal has become more directional; and power demands have dropped. Thus, ever smaller batteries have become viable as a power source. Deployed first in June 1989 on the Dallas North Toll Road, such electronic tolling (ET) enables the use of a cigarette pack–size transponder mounted on the windshield to respond with an account number to queries transmitted by an antenna on an overhead gantry. In North America, such transmissions use the 915-MHz frequency band which is already in widespread use by cellular and cordless telephones, so the transponder parts can be bought cheaply in a mass-production market. With a 7- or 8-year life battery, they cost only about $20 each. Because the radio transmissions of electronic tolling occur within a narrowly tuned beam forming a defined "footprint" on the roadway, at low power, and at short range (100 to 200 feet maximum), interference is not a significant problem. The major application so far has been to retrofit ET to existing toll lanes in physically unaltered toll plazas. In this setting, the cars with ET transponders have to be restrained to slow to somewhere between 10 mph to 30 mph, not because of any speed limitations of the ET technology itself, but for the safety of toll collectors walking between booths and to reduce the hazards of cash-paying customers merging with ET vehicles at the exit throat as the toll plaza narrows to the regular roadway. ET retrofitted in this way allows throughput of 1,000 to 1,200 vehicles per hour per lane.

Developments in Electronic Tolling

A number of toll roads have rebuilt the central portion of their toll plazas to take full advantage of ET, isolating the traditional toll collection with long lengths of Jersey barrier and mandating that toll collectors use an over-bridge or tunnel. This allows full highway speed or express ET. Almost all new toll roads under construction are providing for electronic toll express lanes in the configuration of their toll plazas. Full highway speed ET will be achieved on new toll roads including Delaware's state route 1 between I-95 and Dover, the Suncoast Parkway north of Tampa, three new toll roads in southern California, the President George Bush Turnpike in Dallas, the second span of the Tacoma Narrows Bridge in Washington state, E-470 in Denver, Highway 407-ETR in Toronto, the Western Expressway in Orlando, and the last stage of the Mon-Fayette in Pittsburgh. Where ET is conducted at full highway speed in free-flow conditions, 1,800 to 2,400 vehicles per lane per hour can be accommodated, and the technology requires no departure from normal driving.

In these cases, toll collection by means of any cash booths or coin machines is set off to the side of the toll road, much like a service plaza or interchange ramps. For ET-equipped cars the only sign of a toll collection point is a gantry over the roadway, rather similar to sign gantries. The gantries deploy radio antennas for communications with the transponders, vehicle presence detectors to trigger other systems, laser profiling devices that classify vehicles to apply the correct toll rate, and license plate cameras to catch an image of the violators who buzz through without the windshield-mounted toll transponder.

The ET technology is being enthusiastically embraced by toll agencies and their customers. It is a major boost to the productivity of toll collection. Customers get their toll bills, itemized like a telephone bill, and pay monthly. Some facilities allow tollsters to directly debit their bank or credit card account. As of the end of 1998 Canada and the United States had about 5 million ET transponders in use on about 2,000 miles of toll lanes with 550 dedicated exclusively to electronic tolling. These represent about one-tenth of the toll miles in operation north of the Rio Grande. About 2.5 million tolls were taken electronically, approximately one-sixth of the total of all tolls taken. A number of major agencies have not yet implemented ET but are near to doing so, while a number of others are in the very early stages of deployment. Many of those with ET are taking new measures to boost its usage. ET is destined to become the major mode of toll collection within five years (*Toll Roads Newsletter*, no. 35, January 1999, 5).

ET is especially popular with commuters and others who travel on toll roads as part of their everyday business. It does away with the complexities of the toll plaza—of maneuvering for the shortest line offering the right payment mode, assembling the requisite coins and bills, winding down the window, and stopping and starting as the line advances. Removing payment from the road reduces the driver's workload and speeds vehicles by the tolling point. There is an overhead expense in establishing and maintaining a transponder account, and usually a minimum monthly charge, so transponders are not likely to be obtained by occasional users. But three large regions of the country, in California, Florida, and the Northeast/Mid-Atlantic/Midwest states, will have a single transponder that will work for virtually all toll facilities. The E-ZPass system centered mainly in New York and New Jersey but extending to Toronto, New Brunswick, Massachusetts, Illinois, and Maryland is the largest in which "interoperability" is being actively pursued. As the use of E-ZPasses becomes more widespread in one area, out-of-towners will come equipped with transponders. Those who don't get them—a small number of people are highly concerned about them as privacy busters—can be accommodated by cash payment lanes. Alternatively, the facility may simply declare that only transponder-equipped vehicles may use the road. Someday transponders may be a standard feature in new vehicles. That day is probably quite close with heavy trucks, but there are no signs of it with automobiles, especially because there are three separate regional standards in the United States.

Electronic tolling has boosted economic viability by making the toll facility more attractive to patrons and cutting labor costs substantially. Integrating ET with other systems in a toll plaza has been extremely demanding on engineers' ingenuity and on software writers' time, but once the problems have been worked out, the systems have been deemed a great success by toll operators and patrons alike. Toll industry leaders such as Michael Ascher, head of the New York Triborough Bridge and Tunnel Authority, say that it has been the most dramatic advance in transportation technology in their lifetime and that it has greatly improved the morale of their staff (Michael Ascher, interview, January 1999).

New Possibilities

As one would expect, tolling technology is advancing apace, and the possibilities of integrated features and applications are enormous.[1] Transponders mean that tolling no longer need be confined to a conventional toll plaza. They are being used in San Diego; in Orange County, California; and on the Katy Freeway in Houston to impose a toll on express lanes while other vehicles go free on adjacent lanes. Tolling need no longer be confined to access-controlled motorway type facilities but could be used on arterial or collector roads, because the transceivers are quite cheap. To be successful, tolling must offer patrons an improved travel benefit that is at least commensurate with the toll, or motorists won't use it.

The technology opens up many new opportunities:

- Signalized arterials could be concessioned to companies with the right to toll traffic in return for converting them into "superarterials" in which vehicle sensors would work with optimizing algorithms to manage traffic signals to maximize the use of green-light time. At selected places the concessionaire might install and electronically toll an overpass to allow free flow on the superarterial.
- Special truck toll lanes could be designed and managed to isolate commercial patrons from commuters' traffic jams.
- A network of toll express lanes on urban motorways could be developed to offer road users a premium service for a toll, for those trips for which a fast trip and punctuality are especially important—such as trips to the airport to catch a plane or to an important meeting.

- Transponders could be used for the collection of parking charges, for access control to gated communities and other controlled parking lots (see the parking chapter by Donald Shoup in this volume).

Need for Traffic Management Entrepreneurship

Most metropolitan areas have at least one "traffic management center" where operators have TV monitors to view roadway conditions and to zoom in on problems. They also have access to the data from traffic-sensing devices deployed either in the pavement (inductive loops mostly) or vehicle-counting and classifying equipment using radar, digital video, and other sensors deployed overhead on gantries or poles. They are able to quickly identify problems and dispatch patrol vehicles to deal with stranded motorists or debris that has fallen off vehicles. And in case of serious incidents, they can help deploy emergency fire, ambulance, and tow services. These centers do little in the way of regular traffic management; rather, they are, at best, an incident-surveillance and emergency-coordination system.

Traffic in congested urban conditions badly needs to be systematically and routinely managed. Beyond about 2,000 vehicles per hour per lane, the entry of extra vehicles into a traffic lane imposes heavy costs on the motorists behind them as each struggles to maintain a comfortable distance from the vehicle ahead. This produces the familiar caterpillar-type waves of stop-and-go traffic and low average speeds. As more traffic enters, the problem dramatically worsens. Quite suddenly, driving goes from being tight but brisk to being clogged, and average speeds plunge. A graph of vehicle throughput (on the horizontal axis) versus traffic speed (on the vertical axis) is shaped like a rightward-pointing, snub-nosed bullet. The maximum throughput (the tip of the snub nose) is achieved at about 50 mph. On congested motorways with speeds below 50 mph, therefore, throughput would be increased by reducing the number of cars entering the road.

Given this characteristic of unmanaged traffic flows, great gains can be made by limiting the number of entering vehicles to slightly lower than breakdown volumes. For 30 years, traffic engineers have attempted to do this roughly with "ramp meters" or simple red/green signals positioned near the top of freeway ramps and timed to allow one or two vehicles at a time to enter the main lanes. This is effective within certain limited ranges of congestion. But beyond that range, the ramps cannot accommodate the traffic being stored, and congestion backs up onto the approach streets. At that point, clearing the intersection traffic becomes a higher priority than flow on the main lanes, and most ramp meter systems are set so that when the backup extends to fill the ramp (the backup is measured by a pavement loop detector), the meters change to a setting that will speed entry into the main lanes from the front of the queue.

By contrast, using a variable toll or price to manage traffic flow offers an opportunity to reduce real demand for rush-hour travel by giving that proportion of motorists who attach the least value to the trip the incentive to rearrange their affairs so that they do not have to make the trip or shift their time of travel to pay a lower toll. (Notice that the gas tax and sales taxes do not enable price-sensitive—perhaps low-income—motorists to reduce their outlays by shifting their route or time of travel.) Those who *do* value the rush-hour trip more greatly than the toll and take the priced lane will gain a free-flow trip, which will increase speed, enhance productivity, reduce tailpipe emissions, and make the travel safer. Their cost of entry is a monetary transfer to the motorway agency, whereas the cost of entry in the ramp meter case is dead time that cannot be recovered by society.

The world's first toll express operation, in Orange County, California, runs in the median space of an unpriced freeway (State Route 91). The private venture charges between 50 cents and $3.50 for the 10-mile ride, depending on its time advantage over the adjacent unpriced lanes. The "right-now" price is shown on large electronic boards along the approach to the separation of lanes, and the motorist must choose between the two sets of lanes in real time, moments before the separation. The road became profitable for its investors in its third year of operation.

Implementing Tolling One Lane at a Time

A widespread view is that the existing road is "paid for" by past taxes. Actually, no road is ever "paid for" because it has ongoing operational costs and deteriorates from traffic and weather from the moment it is built. But the toll management of traffic is likely to be introduced first as an option for motorists as part of a widening of the road (as in the case of the Route 91 express lanes in California). The 1998 federal highway funding legislation (known as TEA21) includes specific provisions allowing states to impose tolls on interstate highways, but so far there have been no takers. More feasible from a political standpoint is developing a new tolled facility—a new section of roadway or a new express lane—so that people can see that they are getting tangible new pavement for their tolls.

A toll lane on an otherwise crowded freeway can now be presented in classic business fashion as an option or higher-class service: something customers can buy if they wish, or decline. Tax-financed highway lanes will remain "free" to use, but because they are unmanaged, they will not guarantee a free flow for extended periods of the workday. The "toll-express lane," however, will be able to offer a premium service: free-flow speeds, a higher level of maintenance and patrol assistance, a better riding pavement, and so on. As with a package delivery service in which most people probably won't specify overnight delivery, it will offer a very worthwhile option to customers for those occasions on which a speedy unimpeded trip is especially valuable. As in many other walks of life, one size doesn't fit all customers or all occasions.

"Underutilized high occupancy vehicle lanes" ("diamond lanes") are an obvious place where toll-express services could be offered (Poole and Orski 1999). Indeed, toll-express lanes are being planned as expansions of existing major highways in Dallas (I-635), San Diego (I-15), Sonoma and Marin Counties in the northwestern Bay area (US-101), for special truck lanes in the greater Los Angeles area (CA-60, I-5, I-710, I-15, I-215), and in Houston (I-10). Clearly, when they are operated right alongside unpriced lanes, the tolls will have to be extremely flexible because the advantage offered by the express lane over the free lanes will vary very greatly according to the time of day. When the free lanes are flowing freely, the toll express lanes will be able to earn only a small toll, if any, but at times of heavy congestion they may be able to collect quite large tolls.

The automated toll technology makes it possible for the roadway system to be concessioned to investors to operate, or even simply sold off. The most challenging issues remaining are political ones of how to handle the widespread public perception that roads are already paid for in gasoline taxes, registration fees, and other charges.

The Natural-Monopoly Argument, Briefly Revisited

As mentioned at the outset of this chapter, motorways demonstrate the increasing-returns conditions of the natural-monopoly model. Also, there are plainly monopoly-access issues, and it is perhaps inevitable that the state will turn to easements and even eminent-domain powers. But these problems would not cut against the principle of user fees and private ownership. Investor operations can be subjected to competitive "concession" bidding and re-bids after a contract period (Fielding and Klein 1993). Some have identified peak conditions as having the potential for excessive tolls and suggested that governments could alleviate this problem by requiring private operators to offer "toll cutter" or unlimited use passes. In the case of the privatization of the Highway 407-ETR (electronic toll route) in Toronto, the contract of sale to the Spanish-led investment group sets penalties to prevent the operators from setting toll rates so high that they push much of the traffic onto local streets, and incentives to widen the roadway to accommodate increasing traffic in the future rather than to price it off the facility.

Conclusion

In the modern economy, the private sector has the financial and technological capability of financing, building, maintaining, and operating motorways. Electronic tolling dispels any doubts about the viability of pricing and exclusion, and pricing enables us to seek entrepreneurial private ownership. Almost all the advantages of private ownership can be realized by privatizing motorways. Besides looking forward to innovation and economical management of existing routes, the pursuit of the honest dollar enables supply to respond to demand. Rather than leaving infrastructure decisions in the hands of government officials, market mechanisms unleash creative entrepreneurship to figure out where society most urgently needs new infrastructure and to respond to those needs. Transportation planners too often pretend they already have—or can gather—the knowledge relevant to making sound infrastructure decisions. Market mechanisms, however, are the surest means of digging up, representing, and responding appropriately to the dispersed knowledge relevant to such decisions.

NOTE

1. Major sources of news on new transportation technologies are C. Kenneth Orski's "Innovation Briefs," Urban Mobility Corporation, Washington, DC (www.innobriefs.com); ITS International magazine published by Route One Publishing, Swanley, Kent, United Kingdom (www.itsinternational.com); and *Traffic*

Technology International magazine, Dorking Surrey, United Kingdom (www.ukint-press.com).

REFERENCES

Bator, Francis M. 1958. "The Anatomy of Market Failure." Quarterly Journal of Economics, August, 351–79.
DeSalvo, Joseph S. 1973. "The Economic Rationale for Transportation Planning." In Perspectives on Regional Transportation Planning, edited by J. S. DeSalvo. Lexington, MA: Lexington Books.
Fielding, Gordon J., and Daniel B. Klein. 1993. "How to Franchise Highways." Journal of Transport Economics and Policy 27, no. 2 (May): 113–30.
Kain, John F. 1999. "The Urban Transportation Problem." In Essays in Transportation Economics and Policy, edited by J. Gomez-Ibanez, W. B. Tye, and C. Winston. Washington, DC: Brookings Institution Press.
Lay, Maxwell G. 1992. Ways of the World: A History of the World's Roads and of the Vehicles That Used Them. New Brunswick, NJ: Rutgers University Press.
Musgrave, Richard A., and Peggy B. Musgrave. 1976. Public Finance in Theory and Practice. New York: McGraw-Hill.
Poole, Robert W. Jr., and C. Kenneth Orski. 1999. "Building a Case for HOT Lanes: A New Approach to Reducing Urban Highway Congestion." Policy Study 257, Reason Public Policy Institute, Los Angeles, April.
Roth, Gabriel. 1996. Roads in a Market Economy. Aldershot: Avebury Technical.
Stiglitz, Joseph E. 1993. Economics. New York: Norton.
Tullock, Gordon. 1971. "Public Decisions as Public Goods." Journal of Political Economy 79, no. 4: 913–18.
U.S. Federal Highway Administration. 1997. "Federal Highway Cost Allocation Study." Report HPP-10/9-97(3M)E. Washington, DC: U.S. Department of Transportation, August.
Winston, Clifford, and Chad Shirley. 1998. Alternate Route: Toward Efficient Urban Transportation. Washington, DC: Brookings Institution Press.

4

Buying Time at the Curb

Donald C. Shoup

I'll tell you how to solve Los Angeles' traffic problem.
Just take all the cars off the road that aren't paid for.
—Will Rogers

American children first learn about free parking when they play *Monopoly.* Players buy houses, build hotels, or go to jail after a toss of the dice, and sometimes they land on "Free Parking." When children grow up and get their own cars, their odds of landing on free parking increase dramatically because drivers park free for 99 percent of all automobile trips in the United States.[1]

You probably feel that you pay for parking on more than 1 percent of *your* automobile trips, and perhaps you do. Many of us undoubtedly pay for parking more frequently than others do. Americans make 230 billion vehicle trips a year, so motorists pay for parking 2.3 billion times a year (1 percent of 230 billion), but they also park free 228 billion times a year.[2]

If motorists don't pay for parking, who does? Initially, developers pay for it when they provide all the parking spaces required by zoning ordinances. The cost of land and capital devoted to required parking raises the cost of all development, and this cost translates into higher prices for everything else, so everyone pays for parking indirectly. Residents pay for parking through higher prices for housing. Consumers pay for parking through higher prices for goods and services. Employers pay for parking through higher office rents. Only in our role as motorists do we *not* pay for parking because motorists park free for most trips. *Everyone but the motorist pays for parking.*

Minimum parking requirements collectivize the cost of parking. When the cost of parking a car is included in higher prices for other goods and services, people cannot pay less for parking by using less of it. Bundling the cost of parking into higher prices *for* everything else skews consumer choices toward cars and away *from* everything else.[3]

This chapter argues that free parking is the unstudied link between transportation and land use, that urban planners make serious mistakes in dealing with parking, and that these mistakes gravely distort the markets for both transportation and land. It then describes several new technologies for charging for curb parking spaces. Finally, a modest change in planning practice is proposed that has high benefits and low costs, that is fair, and that the new technology makes feasible.

Another Planning Disaster

Urban planners typically set off-street parking requirements high enough to satisfy the peak demand for free parking. These requirements increase the supply and reduce the price—but not the cost—of parking. Parking requirements bundle the cost of parking spaces into the cost of development and thereby increase the prices of all the goods and services sold at the sites that offer free parking. Minimum parking requirements subsidize cars, raise housing costs, reduce urban density, and seriously distort transportation and land use.

Off-street parking requirements in zoning ordinances have severed the link between the cost of providing parking and the price that motorists pay for it. The cost of providing parking has ceased to influence most decisions about whether to own or use a car. Motorists own and use cars as if parking costs nothing because they pay nothing, and the added driving intensifies traffic congestion. When citizens object to congestion, planners restrict new development in order to reduce traffic. Minimum parking requirements then force development to subsidize cars, and planners must limit the density of development (and of people) to limit the density of cars. Free parking has become the arbiter of urban form, and cars have replaced people and buildings as zoning's real density concern. Form no longer follows function, fashion, or even finance. Instead, form follows parking requirements.

Curb Parking as a Commons Problem

Cities adopted minimum parking requirements because citizens and politicians understand that they solve a real problem: the commons problem. If curb parking is free and if buildings do not provide enough off-street parking to serve their own uses, curb parking will quickly become congested. In his famous essay "The Tragedy of the Commons," Garrett Hardin used curb parking to illustrate the commons problem in Leominster, Massachusetts, but many other cities offer this seasonal gift to motorists:

> During the Christmas shopping season the parking meters downtown were covered with plastic bags that bore tags reading: "Do not open until after Christmas. Free parking courtesy of the mayor and city council." In other words, facing the prospect of an increased demand for already scarce space, the city fathers reinstituted the system of the commons. (Hardin 1968, 1245)

Voters who see the gift-wrapped parking meters may thank their mayor and city council, but free parking at the time of peak demand makes curb spaces even harder to find. Drivers who circle the block searching for a free space add to traffic congestion and air pollution, and when they do find a free space they park longer than if the meters had not been gift wrapped. The mayor and city council are giving motorists a commons problem for Christmas.

Planners solve the parking commons problem by requiring developers to increase the parking supply by as much as they increase the parking demand. A new building may raise the demand for parking, but if the building provides enough parking spaces to meet this greater demand, competition for the existing parking supply will not get worse.

A big problem with this solution is the way planners estimate demand. They do not calculate it as a function of price. Instead, they make the unstated (perhaps even unconscious) simplifying assumption that all parking is free. That is, planners estimate the demand for *free* parking and then require enough parking spaces to meet this demand. In effect, *urban planners treat free parking as an entitlement, and they consider the resulting demand for free parking to be a "need" that must be met.*

The Immaculate Conception of Parking Demand

The planning "vision" behind minimum parking requirements is a world with ample free parking. Cities legislate this vision into reality for every new building, no matter how much the required parking spaces cost. The immense supply of parking creates a surplus of parking spaces most of the time. This excess supply drives the market price of parking to zero, and motorists park free for 99 percent of all trips. Free parking inflates parking demand, and this inflated demand is then used to set the minimum parking requirements. Because of this circular relation, free parking dictates the design of urban development. Minimum parking requirements that meet the peak demand for free parking are, in reality, free-parking requirements.

Urban planners may believe that they are simply requiring enough parking spaces to satisfy demand, but this demand was not immaculately conceived. Others may believe that the demand for cars is simply the result of consumer preferences being expressed in a free market. Instead, planners and the market coupled long ago and created today's swollen demand for cars and parking.

Planning without Prices

Urban planners diagnose the parking problem in a way that makes it extremely expensive to solve. Thinking that there is a parking shortage, planners require developers to supply at least enough parking spaces to satisfy the peak demand for free parking. Robert Weant and Herbert Levinson offer one of the few attempts to explain how planners set parking requirements:

> Most local governments, through their zoning ordinances, have a parking supply policy that requires land uses to provide sufficient off-street parking space to allow easy, convenient access to activities while maintaining free traffic flow. The objective is to provide enough parking space to accommodate recurrent peak-parking demands . . . parking demand is defined as the accumulation of vehicles parked at a given time as the result of activity at a given site. (Weant and Levinson 1990, 35–37)[4]

In effect, Weant and Levinson are saying that planners define the number of cars counted at peak periods as the parking demand (with no reference to the price of parking) and then require developers to supply at least this many parking spaces (with no reference to their cost).

Because parking is free for most automobile trips in the United States, parking must be free at most of the land uses where planners measure the peak-parking demands.[5] When they set parking requirements, planners thus do not define demand and supply in the same way that economists define them. For example, economists do not define the demand for food as the recurring peak quantity of food consumed at all-you-can-eat-for-free buffets where diners eat until the last bite has zero utility. And economists do not say that this recurring peak quantity of food eaten must be supplied, whatever the cost. Yet planners *do* define the demand for parking as the recurring peak number of parking spaces occupied when parking is free. Planners *do* require this number of parking spaces to be supplied, no matter what the cost is. Planning for parking is planning without prices.

Parking is an essential part of the transportation system, and the parking supply produces enormous benefits. Nevertheless, these enormous benefits do not imply that we need more parking or that parking should be free. Similarly, the food supply produces enormous benefits, but these enormous benefits do not imply that we need more food or that food should be free. Many of us already eat too much, and free food would encourage us to eat even more. Nevertheless, some cities' zoning ordinances explicitly require *free* parking. For example, the zoning ordinance for Wilshire Boulevard in Los Angeles, which has the best public transit access in the city, requires that "for office and other commercial uses there shall be at least three parking spaces provided for each 1,000 square feet of gross floor area available at no charge to all patrons and employees of those uses" (Los Angeles City 1989, 616). The only unusual aspect of this ordinance is that it mentions the price of parking. Free parking is the only reference to the price of parking that I have seen in any city's parking requirements.

Let Prices Do the Planning

Most markets benefit so much from using prices to allocate resources that it's hard to imagine they could operate in any other way. Nevertheless, cities have tried to manage the parking market almost entirely without prices, and the result is a disaster. Planning without prices has worked poorly almost everywhere it has been tried, and parking is no exception.

As an alternative to setting time limits on curb parking, cities could charge the market price for curb parking. The market price for curb parking is the price that balances (1) a parking demand that varies and (2) a parking supply that is fixed. If cities charged flexible market prices to balance the varying demand with the fixed supply—prices high enough to keep a few curb parking spaces vacant on every block—motorists would always find a place to park near their destination.

With prices to restrain the demand for curb parking, developers and businesses would be able to decide on their own how much off-street parking they wanted to provide. This arrangement—*charging market prices for curb parking and deregulating off-street parking*—would increase public revenue and reduce private costs. Instead of planning without prices, we could let prices do the planning.

Two major obstacles have prevented cities from charging market prices for curb parking. First, the technology of charging for curb parking was primitive until quite recently. Second, motorists don't want to pay for parking on the street or anywhere else. I first describe how new technology has removed the first obstacle to charging for curb parking: the practical difficulty. I then argue that a new distribution of curb parking revenue can remove the second obstacle: the political difficulty that motorists don't want to pay for parking.

The First Parking Meter

Carl Magee of Oklahoma City filed his patent application for a "coin-controlled parking meter" on May 13, 1935, and the world's first parking meter was installed in Oklahoma City on July 16, 1935 (Neraci 1985, 77). From the user's point of view, most parking meters are still identical to the 1935 model: you put coins in the meter to buy a specific amount of time, and you risk getting a ticket if you don't return before your time runs out.

Parking meters ensure a turnover of curb parking spaces, and their original purpose was simply to enforce the time limits for curb parking. The time limits on metered parking and the prohibition against feeding a meter to gain extra time show that the primary purpose of most parking meters is still to ensure a turnover rather than to charge the market price for parking.[6]

Figure 4.1 shows Magee's drawing of his invention. The proposed parking meter looks more streamlined than today's models, but one could

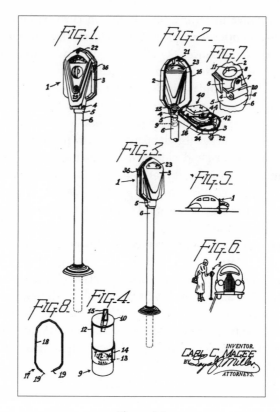

Figure 4.1

easily think that the sketch represents a present-day parking meter on any city street. Few technologies have advanced so little since 1935.

In his 1964 article on transaction costs, Harold Demsetz mentions the transactions costs of charging for parking as a reason to offer it free:

> Our first example is zero-priced parking. . . . It is true that the setting and col-lecting of appropriate shares of construction and exchange costs from each parker will reduce the number of parking spaces needed to allow ease of entry and exit. But while we have reduced the resources committed to constructing parking spaces, we have increased resources devoted to market exchange. We may end up by allocating more resources to the provision and control of parking than had we allowed free parking because of the resources needed to conduct transactions. (1964, 14)[7]

Demsetz later comments, "The preceding discussion has taken as given the state of technical arts." The technology of charging for parking has changed greatly in recent years, however, and this change has undermined the case for free parking.

The Technology of Charging for Curb Parking

Minimum parking requirements in zoning ordinances explain *why* the technology of charging for curb parking has stagnated. Because urban planners require enough off-street parking spaces to satisfy the peak demand for free parking at all new land uses, there is no need to charge for curb parking. By eliminating the need to charge for an important public service, urban planners have succeeded where nuclear physicists have failed. Advocates once predicted that nuclear power plants were so efficient that they would soon make electricity "too cheap to meter." That prediction failed spectacularly, but parking *is* free for 99 percent of automobile trips. Most parking in America is, literally, too cheap to meter.

Even though the parking meter was invented in the United States, the minimum parking requirements in this country have inhibited subsequent technological change. Cities rapidly added parking requirements to their zoning ordinances in the 1940s and 1950s, and parking meters are now used mainly in areas developed before cities required off-street parking. Most new ways to charge for curb parking were invented in Europe because the scarcity of parking in many older European cities created a demand for more sophisticated metering.

One severe defect of the traditional parking meter is that motorists must decide in advance how long they want to park. Furthermore, motorists' subsequent concern about returning before the meter expires can create "meter anxiety." Until recently, this handicap was assumed to be an inherent feature of paying for curb parking, but new technology allows motorists to pay for curb parking without deciding in advance how long they want to park. Buying time at the curb can now be as convenient as buying other goods and services.

Describing how one city—Aspen, Colorado—uses the new parking meter technology shows how any city can use it. Aspen is hardly a typical American city, but it has suffered from all the usual parking problems. With 5,000 residents and 25,000 visitors a day during the winter and summer seasons, curb parking is scarce. Until 1995, curb parking was free and restricted only by a 90-minute time limit. Time-limited free parking created predictable problems. As described by Aspen's assistant city manager, Randy Ready,

> Most of the downtown parking spaces in Aspen were being occupied by locals and commuters working in downtown and moving their cars every ninety minutes to avoid parking tickets in what we affectionately called the "90 Minute Shuffle." Few if any spaces were available for shoppers, restaurant patrons, and guests. The result was a commercial core full of employees' parked cars and streets congested with angry guests' and shoppers' cars endlessly trolling for a parking space. (Ready 1998, 7)

Aspen attempted to reduce its parking problem by building a 340-space underground municipal parking garage in 1991, but "despite its convenient location and $1.50 a day rate, only during special occasions did it ever fill. On most days the garage remained over half empty, while tremendous congestion and competition raged for free on-street parking a block away" (Ready 1998, 10).

After several years of preparation, in 1995 Aspen began to charge for curb parking in order to reduce traffic and parking congestion. Parking is now priced highest in the city center: $1 an hour in the commercial core and declining with distance from the core. Aspen also established residential parking permit (RPP) districts in neighborhoods surrounding the commercial area, and it allows nonresidents to park in RPP districts for $5 a day.

Aspen's success with paid parking stems in part from two new technologies it uses to charge for curb parking: (1) multispace meters placed on the street and (2) personal in-vehicle meters issued to individual motorists.

Multispace Meters

In the commercial area, Aspen places one "pay and display" multispace parking meter midblock on each side of the street. After parking, motorists walk to the meter and pay for the length of time they wish to park. The meter delivers a receipt imprinted with the time of issue, fee paid, and date for which parking has been purchased; the motorist then displays the ticket inside the car's windshield. One inexpensive and unobtrusive multispace pay-and-display meter usually controls twenty to thirty parking spaces. Aspen is one of only a few cities in the United States to use multispace parking meters, but many European cities use them for both curb and off-street parking.

Aspen has found several important advantages in using multispace pay-and-display meters:

- Ease of payment. Multispace meters accept coins, bills, tokens, charge cards, or smart cards. Motorists do not need to carry exact change to feed the meters.
- Flexible prices. Multispace meters can charge different prices at different times of the day or different days of the week.
- Better revenue control. Multispace meters provide excellent revenue control, and they reduce the manual labor of collecting, transferring, and counting coins.
- Better urban design. One multispace meter replaces twenty to thirty individual post-mounted meters, and the pay-and-display procedure does not require striping the street to mark individual curb spaces. Multispace meters thus reduce street clutter, hardware, and signs.
- More parking spaces. Because individual spaces are not marked on the street, more cars can typically park at the curb than when the permanent placement of individual meters requires every space to be long enough to accommodate full-sized cars.
- Economy. One multispace meter costs less to purchase and maintain than the twenty to thirty individual meters that it replaces.
- Better data collection. Electronic technology provides excellent records of parking occupancy rates on each block.

Aspen carried out an extensive education and public relations program when it introduced the new technology. It gave one free $20 smart card to every Aspen resident to familiarize them with the new multispace meters, and it voided one parking ticket per license plate for violations of the new paid parking program. Parking control officers also carried smart cards offering an hour of free parking to motorists who were confused by the new meters (Ready 1998, 11). These public education and consumer relation efforts are often overlooked but can pay big dividends in the acceptance of new technology.

Another form of multispace parking meter—pay-by-space—also works well for curb parking. The city paints a number on the sidewalk beside each curb space and installs signs directing parkers to the pay-by-space meters. Berkeley, California, installs one of these meters for every eight curb spaces, and they are simple to use. John Van Horn described their operation:

> The driver parks his car, notes the space number and goes to the machine. He selects the space number and inserts the appropriate coins. The machine displays the amount of time purchased. Enforcement officers can easily see which spaces are in violation by observing small windows in the back of the machine. When a space is in violation, a red fluorescent dot appears. . . . On the face of the machine, in addition to the space numbers, is an "information" button that when pressed gives the parker additional information about the unit and whatever else the city wishes to place on the display. The city has also placed its toll-free number on the machines, but so far has received no complaint calls. (1999, 42–44)[8]

Berkeley's assistant city manager noted, "The feedback has been positive—as positive as you can get for a parking meter" (Levi Holtz 1999, A17). Beyond the previously mentioned advantages of the pay-and-display meters, these pay-by-space meters offer four additional advantages:

- Convenience. Parkers who have entered the number of their space in the meter do not need to return to their vehicles, and they do not need to display a receipt on the dash.
- Grace period. The meters can offer a "grace" period before displaying a violation.
- Networks. All multispace meters in an area can be networked so that parkers can extend the time on their space by paying at the nearest meter without returning to their vehicles.
- Less "meter anxiety." Parkers who pay by credit card or debit card can pay for more time than they expect to use, and to obtain a refund for the unused time, they can reinsert their cards when they return.

Personal In-Vehicle Meters

In addition to using multispace meters, Aspen issues personal in-vehicle parking meters. Describing these electronic meters in some detail shows the recent rapid advances in technology. Personal in-vehicle parking meters are similar in size and appearance to a small pocket calculator, and they operate like prepaid debit cards. Motorists prepay the city an amount (typically up to $100) that is programmed into the motorist's personal meter. Motorists can then use the in-vehicle meters to pay for curb parking on any block where there is a charge.

The city demarcates the zones where curb parking is priced, assigns a number to each zone, and posts the price charged for parking in the zone. After parking, the motorist keys in the parking zone's number, switches on the meter, and hangs it inside the car's windshield with its liquid crystal display (LCD) visible. The timer debits the prepaid account for the parking time elapsed until the motorist returns and switches it off.[9] Enforcement personnel can easily see whether a parked car's meter is running because they can see the zone code flashing in the LCD window. Motorists can see the remaining prepaid value at both the beginning and the end of each use and are thus constantly made aware of the cost of parking.

Europeans call the in-vehicle meter an "electronic purse" because of its convenience. Paying for parking with an in-vehicle meter is like paying for telephone calls with a debit card. Callers pay for telephone calls according to where they call, when they call, and how long they talk. Similarly, motorists pay for parking according to where they park, when they park, and how long they park.

Arlington, Virginia, was the first local government in the United States to introduce the in-vehicle parking meters in 1989. Surveys have shown an overwhelming positive response from motorists who use the new meters (*Public Technology* 1990, 4). Cities that have adopted the in-vehicle meter system report the following advantages:

1. No need for cash. Motorists do not need coins, tokens, or exact change because the in-vehicle meters operate like debit cards.

2. Accurate payments for parking. Motorists pay for the exact parking time they use—no more, no less. Motorists do not pay for "leftover" meter time that they don't use.

3. No "meter anxiety." Motorists do not need to decide in advance how long they want to park, and they do not need to return to their cars by a specific time. Motorists therefore do not suffer from meter anxiety.

4. Higher turnover. In-vehicle meters encourage parking turnover because motorists pay for parking by the minute. Drivers will not use up time at the curb simply because they have paid for it.

5. Lower cost. The city does not need to buy and install conventional post-mounted meters or to pay for the manual collection, transfer, and counting of coins. The city collects the parking revenue in advance, and in-vehicle meters provide excellent revenue control at low cost.

6. Flexible prices. In-vehicle meters can charge different rates in different areas, at different times of the day, and for different parking durations.

7. Compatibility with conventional meters. Motorists can use their in-vehicle meters to pay for parking at conventional post-mounted parking meters or multispace meters. Rather than pay for parking by putting coins in the conventional meter, motorists display their in-vehicle meters. Visitors who do not have in-vehicle meters can pay at the conventional meters.

8. No theft or vandalism. To deter theft each in-vehicle meter has a personal identification number (PIN) entered by the user, and the meter is useless without the PIN. In-vehicle meters also eliminate the risk of vandalism commonly directed against post-mounted meters.

9. Better urban design. In-vehicle meters reduce the need for conventional parking meters on the sidewalk and do not require painting stripes on the street to mark the curb spaces.

10. Fewer parking violations. If legal parking spaces are available, motorists with in-vehicle meters usually pay for parking rather than risk getting a ticket.

These substantial advantages come at a very low cost. Aspen requires a one-time deposit of $40 per in-vehicle meter. Users can prepay for as much parking time as they want, and they can add value to their meters' remaining balance whenever they like. In-vehicle parking meters are extremely popular with Aspen residents; the city sold three hundred meters in the first three days and has sold more than five thousand since 1995 (in a city with five thousand residents) (Ready 1998, 9).[10]

"Honk If You Hate Paid Parking"

Prices for parking in Aspen did not come without protest. Opponents organized a "Honk If You Hate Paid Parking" campaign at the end of 1994, just before Aspen's pricing program began.

> Precisely at noon on the Friday before the New Year, employees of the downtown shops and restaurants (and more than a few from City Hall) poured out of their workplaces, walked to their cars parked right in front a few steps away, and proceeded to honk their horns for half an hour in protest of the parking regulations that would soon go into effect. . . . The local chapter of the Sierra Club added flavor with several of their members parading in gas masks, including one dressed as a clown riding a unicycle and carrying a sign that read, "Honk if You Love Dirty Air." (Ready 1998, 7)

Despite the loud protests, paid parking has worked extremely well. When parking was free, downtown parking space occupancy during peak periods ranged from 95 to 100 percent, and finding a space was usually difficult. Average parking space occupancy declined to about 70 percent after paid parking began, and finding a parking space is usually easy. Most residents now support the paid-parking program.

> Much to the horn-honkers' chagrin, the paid-parking program was supported by a 3 to 1 margin by voters in the municipal election in May 1995. . . . Most downtown business people now agree that the attractiveness of available convenient parking for their shoppers and patrons has far offset any disadvantages of paid parking. Likewise, the Residential Permit program has helped residents of neighborhoods around the commercial core to find a place to park in the block on which they live instead of several blocks away. The municipal parking structure now fills routinely during the winter and summer months and has begun to generate surplus revenues that can be reinvested in transportation improvements. The paid parking programs are generating about $600,000 a year in new revenues (out of a $1.4 million

total budget) over and above all parking-related expenses. (Ready 1998, 8, 12)

Aspen's solution to the parking problem has several assets. It makes conveniently located parking spaces available to all who are willing to pay for them. It reduces traffic congestion and pollution emissions from cars searching for curb parking. It improves urban design. And it generates substantial revenue for the city. Aspen's success therefore raises an important question. If charging the market price for parking is so easy and works so well in Aspen, why don't most cities do it? The answer to this question lies, I believe, with the distribution of parking meter revenue. I conclude by arguing that a fair distribution of the revenue will lead citizens to insist on charging market prices for curb parking.

Parking Benefit Districts

Money that you feed into a parking meter seems literally to disappear into thin air. Who *does* receive the money that parking meters swallow, and how is it spent? According to the only survey on the question, 60 percent of all cities deposited their parking meter revenues into their general funds, and 40 percent deposited them into special funds that typically were used to provide public off-street parking (Robertson 1972). Few motorists want to feed either the general fund or special parking funds, and cities have found it politically easier to require off-street parking rather than to charge for curb parking.

If the yearning to park free is such a powerful political argument for cities *not* to charge for curb parking, why did 75 percent of the voters in Aspen support market prices for their curb parking? One explanation is that 5,000 residents benefit from the 25,000 nonresidents' payments for parking. Aspen has followed Monty Python's advice to tax foreigners living abroad, and I contend that other cities can do the same. How can a city allocate its parking meter revenues so that residents will want the city to charge market prices for curb parking?

My proposal is for cities to dedicate each neighborhood's curb parking revenue to pay for public services in the neighborhood where the revenue is earned. If each neighborhood charges *nonresidents* for parking and spends all the revenue to improve the neighborhood, market prices for curb parking can become a popular source of neighborhood revenue. The resi-

dents' desire to improve their neighborhood with money paid by nonresidents will create the necessary political support for market-priced curb
parking.

To explain the proposal for neighborhood-based curb parking charges, I
describe two settings in which market prices for curb parking can be politically popular: (1) commercial districts and (2) residential neighborhoods.

Business Parking Benefit Districts

First, consider the case of an older commercial district where off-street
parking is scarce and most customers rely on curb parking. Parking is hard
to find because the meter price of curb parking is below the level that leaves
a few spaces vacant. The streets are congested with cars hunting for a parking space about to be vacated, and everyone complains about the shortage
of parking. Raising the price of curb parking will create a few vacancies,
eliminate the need to hunt for parking, reduce traffic congestion, and produce revenue, but merchants typically fear that higher meter rates will chase
customers away.

Suppose in this situation the city creates a "business parking benefit district" where the city dedicates all parking meter revenue to pay for public
services in the district, such as cleaning the sidewalks, planting street trees,
providing bus shelters, and removing graffiti. That is, curb parking revenue
will pay for public amenities that attract customers to the local businesses.
Dedicating the revenue to improving the area where it is collected can create a strong local self-interest in using market prices to solve the parking
problem.

The goal of pricing curb parking is to yield about an 85 percent occupancy rate so that motorists can quickly find a place to park near their destination (Shoup 1999). The price should be lowered if there are too many
vacancies and raised if there are so few vacancies that motorists must drive
around to find a place to park. The total number of curb spaces will not
shrink, and market prices will ensure that motorists can always find a few
vacant parking spaces wherever they want to park. Parking may not be free,
but it will be easy to find.

The market price for curb parking will not "chase away" potential customers who would park at the curb if the price were lower. *The market price
of parking is the price that keeps only a few spaces vacant to allow convenient
access.* A below-market price will create a parking shortage that *does* chase
potential customers away. The purpose of charging market prices for curb

parking is to allocate curb parking spaces efficiently, not to maximize meter revenues.

Market prices allocate curb parking to drivers who are willing to pay for it without having to hunt for a vacant space. If parking prices are high enough to ensure vacancies, those who arrive in higher-occupancy vehicles will pay less per person because they can split the parking charge. Those who park for only a short time also pay less because they use less parking time per trip. Therefore, market prices (1) ensure that everyone can park quickly, (2) favor shoppers who arrive in higher-occupancy vehicles, and (3) encourage parking turnover by favoring shoppers who stay a short time. Market prices for curb parking will thus attract more customers who will spend more in the adjacent shops because more drivers and passengers per hour will use each curb parking space. In contrast, free parking allocates curb spaces to drivers who will spend a long time hunting for a rare vacant space and park longer once they find it.

A Precedent: Business Improvement Districts

Business improvement districts (BIDs) are a precedent for the proposed business parking benefit districts. BIDs are special taxing jurisdictions formed by merchants and landowners to finance improvements that benefit their area. They are self-governing public/private partnerships, and they have spread rapidly since the first one was formed in Toronto in 1965.[11] Many cities encourage the establishment of these BIDs to finance public improvements in older commercial areas. BIDs are thus ready-made recipients for curb parking revenue, and their governing boards are legitimate bodies that can decide how to spend parking meter revenues earned in their districts.

Suppose that a city offers to dedicate to a BID the parking meter revenue earned within that BID. The parking revenue may be used either to reduce the taxes that businesses must pay to the BID or to raise the amount that the BID can spend. This arrangement encourages local businesses to form BIDs. If the total revenue from market-priced curb parking in a business district is high enough to finance a BID's total expenditures, the merchants and landowners will receive a free BID. The purpose of BIDs is to finance public improvements in older commercial areas, so using parking meter revenue to encourage the formation of BIDS stimulates commercial revitalization.

Dedicating curb parking revenue to fund BIDs encourages the businesslike management of curb parking. There can be no quicker way to educate businesses about the best policy for curb parking in their neighborhood than to give them control over parking revenue and pricing decisions. Each BID can examine how other BIDs deal with curb parking, and they can weigh the benefits and costs of alternative policies, such as free parking versus market-priced parking. BIDs have every incentive to choose the best policy for curb parking for their area because they will be the first to suffer from their own bad decisions. For example, BIDs can see that they will increase their revenues by installing more parking meters, extending meter hours, or increasing meter rates. They can also see that market-level prices will encourage parking turnover, so that more curb spaces will be available to short-term parkers.

If curb parking revenue finances a BID, merchants will also see that motorists who park at meters without paying are reducing the revenue available to fund public improvements in the immediate area. Parking without paying may therefore come to be seen like shoplifting from the BID, and merchants should therefore be eager to support meter enforcement. The city will receive the citation revenue, which often exceeds the revenue from parking meters themselves, so even the city's general fund can gain from dedicating parking meter revenue to BIDs.

If cities use market prices to manage curb parking efficiently in business districts, they will no longer need to require off-street parking in these districts. Businesses can voluntarily provide or validate off-street parking for their own customers and employees, but urban planners will not need to *require* off-street parking to prevent on-street parking congestion.

Creating a Market for Parking in Residential Neighborhoods

Dedicating curb parking revenue to BIDs encourages merchants and property owners to form BIDs and to support charging market prices for scarce curb spaces. These market prices for curb parking also allow cities to reduce or eliminate off-street parking requirements. But charging for curb parking and eliminating minimum parking requirements in commercial districts can cause parking spillover into nearby residential neighborhoods. Many neighborhoods already suffer spillover from adjacent commercial areas, and eliminating parking requirements might make this situation even worse. How can cities avoid this problem?

Many cities solve the problem of parking spillover into residential neighborhoods by creating residential parking permit (RPP) districts that reserve on-street parking spaces for residents and their guests. For example, high-rise office buildings and hotels are often near single-family residential neighborhoods, but RPP districts have eliminated parking spillover into these neighborhoods by reserving curb parking for residents. RPP districts have spread rapidly throughout the United States since 1977 when the U.S. Supreme Court upheld the constitutionality of the statute in Arlington, Virginia, that set up the first RPP district in the United States (*County Board of Arlington County, Virginia, et al. v. Rudolph A. Richards, et al.*, October 11, 1977).

Despite their advantages, RPP districts create a high vacancy rate for curb parking in residential neighborhoods while nearby commercial developers must build expensive parking structures for commuters and customers. The many underused curb parking spaces in RPP districts are an overreaction to the problem of overused free curb parking.

As an alternative to both overused and underused curb parking, creating a market in curb parking offers important benefits to both residents and nonresidents. The goal of creating this market is not merely to minimize the political opposition to pricing curb parking but also to generate strong political support for it.

To set the scene for this market, suppose you own a home near a busy commercial district that generates spillover parking into your neighborhood. Strangers park in front of your house all day, every day. You can't find a place to park your own car on the street, and neither can your guests. Suppose also that the city installs a parking meter at the curb in front of your house and that *you* get to keep all the revenue. As a resident you can park free at your own meter, but you can also make your curb parking space available to the public rather than occupy it yourself. Finally, suppose that a meter rate of $1 an hour on your block produces a 15-percent vacancy rate, so that anyone willing to pay that price can always find parking. At this price and vacancy rate, your parking meter will yield $7,446 a year if you make your curb space available to the public.[12] Or you can park free in front of your house.

Curb parking can also yield substantial revenue even where the demand is modest. At a price of 50 cents an hour for eight hours each weekday—and no charge at night or on weekends—each curb space will yield $884 a year.[13] In comparison, the median property tax for owner-occupied housing in the United States was $1,116 in 1999 (U.S. Census Bureau 2000, 9). Because many neighborhoods allot two curb parking spaces to each house, curb parking revenue can *easily* exceed the current property tax revenue in neighborhoods subject to spillover parking.

Although these private parking meters would lead many residents to demand market prices for curb parking, cities cannot give private property owners the revenue from parking on public streets. Is there another solution that can create political support for market prices without simply giving the revenue to property owners? I believe that there is, and it requires only a minor modification to existing residential parking permit districts.

Residential Parking Benefit Districts

My proposal is to create residential parking benefit districts. The new parking *benefit* districts resemble the existing parking *permit* districts in that residents can park free on the streets in front of their homes, but they differ from existing districts in two ways:

1. Nonresidents can park on the streets in the benefit district if they pay the fair market price. The price of curb parking is set high enough to ensure that vacancies are always available for residents (who can park free) and nonresidents (who must pay to park).
2. The city dedicates the resulting curb parking revenue to finance public services in the benefit district where the revenue is collected. For example, the benefit district revenue can be used to clean and light the streets, repair the sidewalks, plant trees, remove graffiti, preserve historic buildings, or put utility wires underground. These new public services in the neighborhood are provided above and beyond the conventional public services provided everywhere in the city.[14]
3. Parking benefit districts are a compromise between one extreme of free curb parking—overcrowding—and the opposite extreme of existing permit districts—prohibiting nonresident parking. Unlike conventional permit districts that prohibit nonresident parking, benefit districts supply public services financed by nonresidents. Nonresidents also benefit from benefit districts that allow parking at a fair market price rather than simply prohibiting parking at any price.

A few cities already allow nonresidents to pay to park in permit districts. As mentioned earlier, Aspen charges nonresidents $5 a day to park in its permit districts. West Hollywood, California, sells a limited number of permits allowing daytime parking by employees of nearby commercial areas, and the permit fees paid by these commuters are used to lower the permit fees charged to residents. Because many residential permit holders drive to work during the daytime and park on their own streets only in the evening, commuters who work in the area and residents who live in the area time-share their curb parking spaces.

The simplest way to convert an existing *permit* district into a new *benefit* district is to sell "daytime" permits that allow nonresidents to park in the district when many of the residents have taken their cars to work. The residents of an existing permit district might be happy to have a few employees of nearby business pay the market price to park in the neighborhood if the revenue is dedicated to improving the neighborhood. Residents who benefit from parking charges paid by strangers begin to see curb parking through the eyes of a parking lot owner. Seen from the residents' side of the transaction, a parking benefit district collects and spends curb parking revenue to make the neighborhood a place worth living in and visiting, rather than merely a place where anyone can park free.

The *economic* argument to charge market prices for curb parking is *efficiency*: the benefits far outweigh the costs. Motorists don't need to hunt for curb parking, and cities don't need to require off-street parking. The *political* argument to create parking benefit districts is *distribution*: the benefits for the neighborhood can persuade residents to support market prices for curb parking. Curb parking revenue needs the appropriate claimant—its own neighborhood—before residents will advocate market prices for parking.

Parking benefit districts offer neighborhoods a valuable, income-earning property: curb parking spaces. Charging for curb parking can be politically acceptable because residents want to improve neighborhoods at the expense of nonresidents. The reciprocal nature of the payments—you pay to park in my neighborhood, and I pay to park in yours—is fair. In addition, motorists compensate neighborhoods that suffer from spillover parking, and this also is fair.

Do It in My Front Yard

If curb parking is free, most nearby residents will say "Not in My Back Yard" to developers who want to provide fewer parking spaces than required by the zoning code. For example, if the minimum parking requirement for an office building is four spaces per 1,000 square feet, residents will obviously oppose the nearby development of a new office building with only one parking space per 1,000 square feet. Spillover parking from the new building will congest their streets and leave them no curb spaces to park their own cars.

A parking benefit district creates a symbiotic relationship between commercial development and its nearby residential neighborhood because any commuters who park in the neighborhood must pay for the privilege. Charging market prices for curb parking can solve the spillover problem because prices can be set to yield any curb vacancy rate the neighborhood wants. Commercial development that has few off-street parking spaces increases the demand for what the nearby neighborhoods sell to nonresidents: curb parking. Residents who collectively profit from curb parking might welcome a new office building with few off-street parking spaces because it will raise their parking revenue without increasing the number of cars parked at the curb.

The higher price for parking at an office building with fewer parking spaces will divert some commuters to carpools, mass transit, cycling, or walking to work. An office building with fewer off-street parking spaces will thus attract fewer vehicle trips, another benefit for the nearby neighborhoods. This combination of benefits—fewer vehicle trips but more revenue for neighborhood public services—may lead residents to say "Do It in My Front Yard" when a proposed development will raise the demand for curb parking.

Emancipated from minimum parking requirements, land and capital shift from parking to uses that employ more workers and generate more tax revenue. The option of making improvements without providing off-street parking encourages the adaptive reuse of older buildings, and in-fill development on sites where providing parking is difficult. It also promotes land uses that rely on pedestrian and transit access and that offer shopping opportunities for nearby neighborhoods.

In general, older and denser central cities built before the automobile gain much more from RPB districts than do newer suburbs built to accommodate the automobile. Neighborhoods that now suffer the most from spillover parking immediately earn the most RPB revenue. Spillover parkers who now congest these neighborhoods become paying guests, their numbers kept manageable by charging prices high enough to keep demand below capacity (just as commercial parking operators charge prices high enough to maintain vacancies). These neighborhoods might prosper like silent screen star Gloria Swanson in *Sunset Boulevard*, who explained to young William Holden the source of her income: "I've got oil in Bakersfield, pumping, pumping, pumping. What's it for but to buy us anything we want?" Each outsider's car will become a new resource "pumping, pumping, pumping" revenue to buy anything the neighborhood wants. If the price of curb parking is set high enough so that everyone can easily find a vacant space, curb parking revenue in neighborhoods subject to significant parking spillover can easily exceed the current property tax revenue (Shoup 1995, 23). After a few neighborhoods profit from charging outsiders for parking, many other neighborhoods will surely follow.

Conclusion: We Shall Overcome

Parking requirements in zoning ordinances bundle the cost of parking into the prices for all goods and services. Parking requirements thus "collectivize" the cost of parking, and we cannot reduce what we pay for parking by using less of it. In contrast, market prices for parking "individualize" the cost of parking, and they give us an incentive to economize in our decisions about whether to own or drive a car.

Off-street parking requirements emerge from a political, not an analytical, process, and better analysis alone does not affect this process. But the technology of charging for curb parking has radically improved in recent years. The political calculus that produces free curb parking and off-street parking requirements can change to keep pace. Voters will want to charge market prices for curb parking if the city dedicates the resulting revenue to the right recipient: the neighborhood where the revenue is collected.

The constraints on charging for curb parking are now political rather than technological. Aaron Wildavsky described this situation perfectly: "Constraints are not mere obstacles, but are opportunities asking (daring, pleading) to be shown how they can be overcome" (1979, 59). Technology no longer constrains curb parking to be free, and public concern has shifted to problems that off-street parking requirements make worse, such as traffic congestion, energy consumption, and air pollution.[15] Free curb parking is a constraint asking, daring, pleading to be overcome.

NOTES

1. The 1990 Nationwide Personal Transportation Survey (NPTS) asked respondents, "Did you pay for parking during any part of this trip?" for all automobile trips made on the previous day. Ninety-nine percent of the responses to this question were "no." Free parking at home does not help explain the high percentage of trips with free parking because the NPTS asked the "pay for parking" question for all vehicle trips *except* the trips that ended at home. *Monopoly*® is the trademark of Hasbro, Inc., for its real estate–trading game. See Stewart (1996) for the probability of landing on "Free Parking" in the game of *Monopoly.*

2. The total of 230 billion vehicle trips per year was calculated from the "travel day" file in the 1995 Nationwide Personal Transportation Survey. The 177 million licensed drivers in 1995 made about 1,300 one-way vehicle trips per person per year (230 billion, 177 million), or about 1.8 round-trips per day.

3. As soon as motorists park their cars and assume another role—shopping, eating in a restaurant, going to a movie—they begin paying for parking, but this payment is bundled into the prices for merchandise, food, or movies and does not affect the decision about how to travel to the store, restaurant, or movie theater.

4. Similarly, the PAS (1971, 3) reports that in surveys to determine parking demand, "Most of the developments studied provided adequate parking spaces to meet the observed peak demand without overflow conditions. This was important because in order to develop standards for parking space requirements, the peak demand had to be identified."

5. The 1990 Nationwide Personal Transportation Survey (NPTS) asked 48,000 respondents, "Did you pay for parking during any part of this trip?" for all automobile trips made on the previous day. Ninety-nine percent of the 56,733 responses to this question were "no." The responses outnumbered the respondents because some respondents made more than one automobile trip per day.

6. The Reverend C. H. North was the first motorist cited for overstaying a parking meter's time limit. The reverend's then-novel excuse that he "had gone to get change" persuaded the judge to dismiss the citation (*Allright Parking News,* summer 1985, 5).

7. Demsetz was referring to parking in shopping centers rather than at the curb. De Alessi (1983, 66) also used parking as an example to explain why transactions costs imply that the rights to some resources will not be priced. One reason that parking in shopping centers was too cheap to meter, however, is that minimum parking requirements increase the supply and reduce the market price of off-street parking.

8. Van Horn also reports an additional advantage of multispace meters: "Berkeley has some areas where the parking rules change space by space. For example, in three of the spaces controlled by a unit, there is no parking from 7 A.M. to noon. In other spaces controlled by the unit, parking is available from 9 A.M. to 6 P.M. The

machine displays which spaces are available during which times, and if a parker selects a space that is illegal during that time, the unit will so note and not allow the parker to insert a coin" (1999, 43).

9. If the motorist overstays the time limit, the time display will turn negative and show the excess time; traffic enforcement officers can then issue a ticket just as they do when a conventional parking meter shows a violation. Alternatively, the city can set in-vehicle meters to charge for parking at an accelerated rate for those who overstay the time limit.

10. In 1996 Aspen received the International Parking Institute's Award of Excellence for its transportation and parking plan.

11. Houstoun (1997) explains the details of planning, organizing, and managing business improvement districts.

12. $7,446 = $1 x 24 x 365 x 0.85. If the demand for parking in front of your house is inelastic, a higher price will produce both a higher vacancy rate and even more revenue. For example, if a price of $2 an hour produced a 50-percent vacancy rate, your personal parking meter would yield $8,760 a year ($2 x 24 x 365 x 0.50). After some experimentation, you could find the price of parking that yielded the combination of vacancy rate and total revenue that suited you best, just as the owners of off-street parking lots do.

13. This includes the effect of a 15-percent vacancy rate: $884 = 8 x $.50 x 5 x 52 x 0.85.

14. That is, the city agrees to a "maintenance of effort" for general public services provided in the new RPB district. The RPB revenues pay for *additional* public services in the RPB district.

15. Columbus, Ohio, introduced the country's first minimum parking requirement in 1923, and Oklahoma City introduced the country's first parking meters twelve years later, in 1935 (Witheford and Kanaan 1972).

REFERENCES

De Alessi, Louis. 1983. "Property Rights, Transaction Costs, and X-Efficiency: An Essay in Economic Theory." *American Economic Review* 73, no. 1 (March 1983): 64–81.

Demsetz, Harold. 1964. "The Exchange and Enforcement of Property Rights." *Journal of Law and Economics* 7 (October 1964): 11–26.

Hardin, Garrett. 1968. "The Tragedy of the Commons." *Science* 162: 1243–48.

Houstoun, Lawrence. 1997. *BIDs: Business Improvement Districts.* Washington, DC: Urban Land Institute in cooperation with the International Downtown Association.

Levi Holtz, Debra. 1999. "Parking Meters Going High-Tech in Berkeley." *San Francisco Chronicle,* August 30, A17.

Los Angeles City. 1989. *Planning and Zoning Code*, 1989 ed. Los Angeles: Bni Books.

Neraci, Jack. 1985. "The First Parking Meter." *Motor Trend,* November, 77.

Pickrell, Don, and Paul Schimek. 1999. "Growth in Motor Vehicle Ownership and Use: Evidence from the Nationwide Personal Transportation Survey." *Journal of Transportation and Statistics* 2, no. 1 (May 1999): 1–17.

Planning Advisory Service (PAS). 1971. *An Approach to Determining Parking Demand.* Planning Advisory Service Report no. 270. Chicago: American Planning Association.

Public Technology. 1990. November/December, 4.

Ready, Randy. 1998. "Public Involvement, Understanding, and Support: Lessons Learned from the City of Aspen Transportation and Parking Plan." *Journal of Parking* 1, no. 2: 7–12.

Robertson, William. 1972. *National Parking Facility Study.* Washington, DC: National League of Cities.

Shoup, Donald. 1995. "An Opportunity to Reduce Minimum Parking Requirements." *Journal of the American Planning Association* 61, no. 1: 14–28.

———. 1999. "The Trouble with Minimum Parking Requirements." *Transportation Research A* 33: 549–74.

Stewart, Ian. 1996. "How Fair Is Monopoly." *Scientific American*, April, 104–5.

U.S. Bureau of the Census. 2000. *American Housing Survey for the United States, 1999,* H150/99. Washington, DC: U.S. Bureau of the Census, October. Available online at http://www.census.gov/prod/2000pubs/h15099.pdf.

Van Horn, John. 1999. "Berkeley Makes the Move to Multi-Space Parking Meters." *Parking Today* 4, no. 8 (September 1999): 42–44.

Weant, Robert, and Herbert Levinson. 1990. *Parking.* Westport, CT: Eno Foundation for Transportation.

Wildavsky, Aaron. 1979. *Speaking Truth to Power.* Boston: Little, Brown.

Witheford, David K., and George E. Kanaan. 1972. *Zoning, Parking, and Traffic.* Westport, CT: Eno Foundation for Transportation.

5

Fencing the Airshed
Using Remote Sensing to Police Auto Emissions

Daniel B. Klein

In a famous article, Garrett Hardin explains the problem:

> The tragedy of the commons reappears in problems of pollution. . . . The
> rational man finds that his share of the cost of the wastes he discharges into
> the commons is less than the cost of purifying his wastes before releasing
> them. Since this is true of everyone, we are locked into a system of "fouling
> our own nest." . . . [The air] surrounding us cannot readily be fenced, and so
> the tragedy of the commons as a cesspool must be prevented by different
> means, by coercive laws or taxing devices. (Hardin 1968, 116–17)

Where Hardin says that the air "cannot readily be fenced," he is pointing
out that transaction costs stand in the way of otherwise mutually advanta-
geous agreements.

In very local matters of air quality, traditional tort doctrines such as Nuisance can cope with unneighborliness. Whether a laissez-faire society working within a reasonable tort system could cope with large-scale and not very
local matters of air quality involving tens of thousands, even millions, of
people, such as smog in the Los Angeles basin, is a matter of speculation. In
such a society there would be private ownership of roads, which, like stationary sources, would be subject to class-action suits for emissions-related
damages (Rothbard 1982, 90). Libertarians might argue that tort action, as
well as social esteem and moral suasion, would discourage fouling of the
common nest.

Putting such speculation aside, let's agree that government ought to pursue proactive policies against air pollution where the problem is serious. In
pursuing proactive policies the government might be able to choose be-

tween either *property-rights approaches* or *command-and-control approaches*. Economic principles strongly support the conclusion that property-rights approaches, provided that they are available, impose a smaller burden on society and produce better results. New technologies are making available a sound property-rights approach to the problem of auto emissions. Rather than maintaining and enlarging the current array of expensive and burdensome controls, government can "fence the commons" using new technologies.

Auto Emissions, Remote Sensing, and Smog Checks

Most auto emissions come from the dirtiest 10 percent of the fleet, the gross polluters. More than 50 percent of on-road carbon monoxide (CO) comes from just 5 percent of the cars. The same is true of hydrocarbon (HC) emissions. In each case the cleanest 90 percent of cars—the low and marginal emitters—taken together generate less than 15 percent of the pollution (Lawson 1998; see also the data at www.feat.biochem.du.edu). Because of the extreme skewedness of emissions and because most of the reductions of emissions come from the gross polluters, the chief task is targeting the gross polluters (Glazer, Klein, and Lave 1995; Lawson 1995).

A new device called a *remote sensor* is capable of doing just that. An infrared beam is shone across the road. As a car passes along the road, the exhaust plume absorbs some of the beam's light waves, and the sensor receiving the beam can measure the concentrations of pollutants in the exhaust. The remote sensor can be set up on many streets and highway ramps and can be attached to video and computer equipment that automatically reads the license plate of the passing vehicle. The device is mobile and extremely inexpensive per test. If government can use this device to identify the minority of gross polluters, it can clean the air at a low cost to the public.

Smog check programs around the nation usually require cars and light trucks to pass an inspection every two years (in some cases, every year). Motorists, of course, can prepare for the inspections, but on the other 729 days of the biennium they can drive a dirty car. Some motorists get their gross-polluting cars through the smog check by tampering with the car or bribing the private inspectors. Some keep their defective vehicle unregistered, thereby avoiding smog checks altogether (Glazer, Klein, and Lave 1995; Lawson 1993). Some register defective vehicles just outside the smog check region but drive inside the region (Stedman et al. 1998). Some station mechanics often tinker with cars so they can pass the test without fixing serious problems. Some cars simply deteriorate long before the next scheduled inspection. The program requires all motorists, even the vast majority with clean cars, to incur the cost and hassle of obtaining a smog certificate.

Smog checks are an example of the command-and-control approach to the problem. In command and control, the government regulates *your use of your property*, whether or not you have damaged the property of others. At present, governments rely mainly on command and control for auto emissions. The major examples of command-and-control policies are

- Smog check programs.
- Restrictions on the content of gasoline.
- Quotas and mandates for the use and development of alternative fuels and alternatively fueled vehicles.
- Quotas and mandates for the use and development of electric vehicles.
- Design and emission requirements imposed on automobile manufacturers.
- Promotion of carpool lanes and (in the past) mandatory carpooling.

By contrast, in a property-rights approach the government regulates *your use of others' property*; that is, the government monitors for infractions but otherwise leaves people free to use their own property. The government is the sentinel guarding and securing the fair use of property. It is the quiet nightwatchman, called in only when a tort or wrong has been committed.

The common airshed may be regarded as the property of the local or regional government. In 1968, when Garrett Hardin wrote his famous article on the tragedy of the commons, the air around us could not readily be "fenced." But technology has since enabled government (or others) to monitor fouling of the common nest and otherwise leave citizens free in the use of their automobiles.

In this paper I juxtapose remote sensing and smog check, but smog check is only one of a number of command-and-control approaches whose effectiveness often also pales relative to remote sensing.

The Economist's Framework: Thinking about How Inputs Are Best Combined to Yield the Desired Output

When we go into a restaurant and order a bowl of French onion soup, we specify only the desired output. We do not tell the chef how to slice the onions, grind the pepper, or grate the cheese. We do not tell the restaurant manager where to get the ingredients, how to store them, or how to train the employees. Customers merely specify the outputs, and entrepreneurs in the market attend to the inputs. Successful entrepreneurs are expert in finding local opportunities for effectively combining inputs, and they compete for customers by producing outputs that customers desire.

As steward of the commons, the government must attend to the problem of air quality. The logic of incentives still applies: if technology permits, government ought to address the problem by treating outputs directly, not by treating inputs. In other words, it should police abuses of the common property, not indiscriminately restrict individuals in the use of their own property.

The alternative is command and control, which tries to achieve output goals by specifying inputs. Those who favor command and control do not put much faith in the invisible hand. They do not believe that once property rights are established and outputs are specified, people will respond to those incentives and arrange the inputs appropriately.

Figure 5.1 is a conceptual diagram for the smog check program. Fleet-emissions reduction is the state's output goal. An *input* it has pursued to serve this goal is the smog check program. But from the motorist's point of view, the program creates the *output* goal of passing the test. One way that motorists or their mechanics serve this goal is to keep their cars running clean. But other ways are tampering with the car, obtaining temporary emission reductions, and obtaining a smog certificate illegitimately. Because such tactics are common and inspection is infrequent, the connection between the state's goal and the motorist's goal is *weak and distant*. In regulating your use of your property, the state has mandated an input process that doesn't deliver. Rather, it has implemented an *input-oriented program*, which is expensive and burdensome for all motorists.

A remote-sensing program would better connect state and motorist goals, as illustrated in figure 5.2. The state pursues its output goal by deploying remote sensors, automatically reading license plates, and sending warnings and citations to gross polluters. For motorists, the program

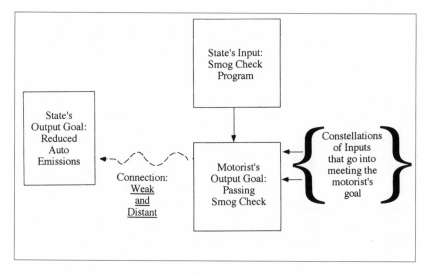

Figure 5.1

generates the output goal of avoiding smog citations. We say that this program is *output oriented* because the connection between the state's goal and the motorist's goal is *strong and close*. This program is very similar to the consumer's asking for a bowl of soup and leaving the rest to the entrepreneurs.

Five Reasons That Property-Rights Approaches Are Superior

There are five reasons that property-rights / output-oriented programs (assuming they are available) are superior to command-and-control / input-oriented programs. Each reason poses a criticism of input-oriented programs, illustrated by actual experience with smog check programs.

1. Programs that specify inputs are not tailored to individuated conditions but tend toward a policy of one size fits all. Yet the technique for transforming inputs into outputs is not singular but *plural*. Every motorist has his own distinct sets of opportunities for getting his car to run clean. In the absence of governmental regimentation, the entrepreneurship of the market would discover better ways to keep cars clean. Nonetheless, the required inspection by a certified station lays down a blanket procedure for getting

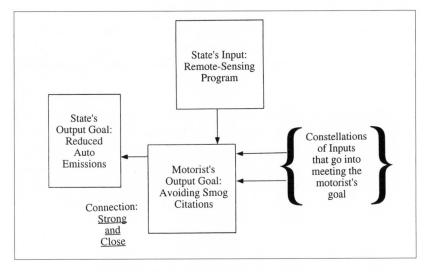

Figure 5.2

cars clean, a procedure that forsakes special opportunities and diverse conditions and chokes off entrepreneurial creativity.

Smog check experience: The smog check program forces most motorists to participate in a biennial practice that they may not need. As many as 90 percent of all vehicles are clean for all relevant pollutants, but most of them must participate in an input ritual (smog check) that may be appropriate only for the other 10 percent of cars. Indeed, only 3 percent of 1982-and-newer model cars failed the test for tailpipe emissions in Colorado's smog check program in 1998 (Colorado AQCC 1998, 1999). And owners of the dirtiest 10 percent might be able to make their cars clean by obtaining proper and legitimate service from *unlicensed* stations or *unlicensed* inspectors. Without input mandates, entrepreneurs would come up with good ways of serving motorists' desire to avoid smog penalties.

2. A government program that specifies inputs runs the risk of specifying the *wrong* inputs. Government proceeds by the blunt forces of bureaucratic, interest-group politics. Rather than relying on competitive market selection of inputs, the government adopts input strategies that may well be *ineffective* in producing the desired outputs.

Smog check experience: California's smog check program has not lived up to its original promises. Most research indicates that smog check programs have hardly any smog-reduction benefits (Hubbard 1997; Lawson 1993; Lawson and Walsh 1995; Scherrer and Kittelson 1994; Stedman et al. 1997; Zhang et al. 1996). Indeed, Lawson (1995) found, remarkably, that 40 percent of the vehicles repaired at smog check stations were found to have an *increase* in emissions.

3. The government's input strategies display very little ability to adapt to changing conditions. Unlike the free-enterprise market, which is driven to discover new combinations of inputs to produce the outputs that consumers desire, command-and-control programs become locked into yesterday's ostensible solutions and are very difficult to restructure or dismantle.

Smog check experience: Smog check programs have become part of "the Establishment." Because smog checks belong to the status quo, they have become a focal point for discussion and planning. And as the status quo, they have created concentrated and well-organized interest groups standing behind it, including both private smog check mechanics and inspection facility contractors.

4. A program that specifies inputs inevitably entails large administrative and bureaucratic costs for managing the program and policing compliance. If these efforts are inadequate, corruption, fraud, and malfeasance may become widespread.

Smog check experience: It is well known that corruption, fraud, and malfeasance have significantly undermined the effectiveness of smog check programs (Glazer, Klein, and Lave 1995; Hubbard 1997; Stedman et al. 1997, 1998). Smog check programs must attend to the training of licensed inspectors, the integrity of inspection equipment, the enforcement of honest inspection service, and the evaluation of the program procedures. Corruption, fraud, and policing costs inevitably grow larger as government requirements reach deeper into the input stages of the production process.

5. The less directly that programs are connected to public-interest goals, the more likely it is that they will be hijacked and led astray. Influential special interests, including regulators, are tempted to favor their own interests in deciding which inputs should be adopted. When policies treat outputs directly, it is much more difficult for interest-group tendencies to cloud the issue and usurp power.

Smog check experience: Debates rage over the input specifications of smog check programs. Should the inspection use treadmill-style dynamometers or less expensive equipment? If it chooses dynamometers, should they simulate loads over a continuous range or only discrete loads? Should they report an emissions trace over the entire test or only peaks and averages? And so on. Every interest group takes its place in the political process and, in doing so, often obscures the fundamental issue, which is clean air at the lowest cost. These politicized debates could be largely avoided if we had a strategy that dealt directly with outputs and was *silent about inputs.* The public interest would then be better recognized and have a greater chance of being well served.

Remote Sensing: A Feasible Technology for Treating Outputs

The success of an output-oriented policy for auto emissions depends on a "fencing" technology that is accurate and withstands circumvention. Does remote sensing measure up to the task?

Accuracy of Remote Sensing

All kinds of test systems can make two types of errors. A *false failure* occurs when the system identifies a clean car as dirty; false failures cause motorists to incur unnecessary costs. A *false pass* occurs when the system identifies a dirty car as clean; false passes are undesirable because high-emission cars are not cleaned up.

It is well established that remote sensing takes a reasonably accurate snapshot of the CO, HC, NO, and CO_2 emissions from a car's tailpipe and does so relative to levels in the ambient air (Ashbaugh et al. 1992; Lawson et al. 1990; Popp, Bishop, and Stedman 1999). In determining whether CO emissions, say, are excessive, CO emissions are measured in relation to CO_2 emissions. It is the ratio of CO to CO_2 that really matters. A low ratio is good; a high ratio is bad. That's why accelerating or idling does not matter as much as one might have thought: if CO and CO_2 increase proportionately, the ratio stays the same.

The "snapshot" taken by remote sensing is perhaps a little "blurry," but it tells us whether we are looking at an antelope or a vulture. The potential problem with emission snapshots is that they might capture the car's emissions performance at an uncharacteristic moment. A simple case is the cold start: during the first one to two minutes it takes to warm up, many cars produce high emission ratios. Vehicle emission ratios also vary with speed, grade, load, and acceleration. Rain and fog may prevent remote sensors from working properly. If there were no way to control for these factors, the usefulness of remote sensing would indeed be doubtful.

But these factors can be controlled. Officials can select sites removed from residences and parking areas to eliminate the cold-start problem and find road features or use orange cones to put narrow bounds on the grade, speed, and acceleration variables. They might be confined to work in dry weather or, during precipitation, in covered areas such as underpasses or tunnels. Remote sensing is most accurate when it reads cars under light acceleration, so a slight incline would be a benefit. Highway exit ramps are ideal. If site selection cannot eliminate variation in driving modes, program officials can easily measure speed and acceleration using light beams that cars break as they pass by.

In one remote-sensing study, cars that had been read by a remote sensor were pulled over and given a regular smog check on the spot. Of those cars that had exceptionally high CO readings (above 4 percent), 91 percent failed the on-the-spot smog test (Lawson et al. 1990). Other studies have replicated this high correlation, and further developments would surely make the match even closer (Ashbaugh et al. 1992; Lawson et al. 1996). (For a thorough overview on accuracy, see Schwartz 1998, 4–19; for on-line scientific data on remote sensing, see the University of Denver site www.feat.biochem.du.edu.)

Errors Must Be Construed on a Systemwide Basis

A report on California's smog check program (Calif. I/M Review Committee 1993, 129) discusses how likely it is that a remote sensor will wrongly identify a car as "clean" or "dirty." Let's say the sensor identifies a car as dirty if it reads the CO emissions as exceeding 4 percent of adjusted emissions. A car in the set of clean vehicles, with "clean" defined in the study, has, on average, less than a 1 percent chance—0.64 percent—that it will exceed this 4 percent "cut point" at a single reading. A car in the set of dirty vehicles has, on average, a 66 percent chance that it will *not* exceed the cut point at a single reading. If we must use only a single snapshot, we apparently must accept a lot of false passes. Alternatively, we could reduce the false passes by lowering the cut point, but doing so would then increase the number of false failures.

But officials do not face such a harsh trade-off. Instead of thinking of the errors in a remote-sensing program on the basis of a single snapshot, we should construe errors on a systemwide basis of *multiple snapshots*. Remote sensing is a remarkably inexpensive test—a conservative estimate is 75 cents per test—so we can multiply the remote sensors on the roads and use a pass/fail criterion based on a *pattern* of readings. In a significant sense, it really is the biennial scheduled test (regardless of its technical sophistication) that is limited to a once-every-two-years snapshot, while pervasive remote sensing could get a bona fide "nickelodeon" show capturing the emissions during the biennium.

Consider a remote-sensing program whose average number of readings for the entire fleet over a biennium is eight. Cars that travel more than average are read more than eight times, and cars that travel less are read fewer than eight times. Consider a standard that fails a car if it exceeds the 4 percent CO cut point at least once over the entire biennium.

- A clean car, tested eight times, stands (on average)[1] a 95 percent chance of never exceeding the cut point. That's a 95 percent chance of remaining undisturbed, which (unless it is a new car) is 95 percent better than its prospects under the current program!
- A dirty car, read eight times, stands (on average)[2] a mere 3.5 percent chance of not exceeding the cut point and getting away with a false pass over the course of the biennium.

On a *systemwide* basis, the program registers few false failures *and* few false passes.

Remote sensing is a little less accurate at reading NO emissions than it is at reading CO and HC emissions, but again the issue in not one of pinpoint accuracy. When gross polluters emit three times or ten times as much as normal cars do, catching them with multiple sensors is a turkey shoot. By increasing the cut point, officials can reduce the number of false failures, and by increasing the number of tests per year, they can reduce the number of false passes.

Moreover, the margin of error can be further reduced. The straight cut-point criterion just presented is unnecessarily simple. Deploying many remote sensors would generate a wealth of information, leading to the development of more sophisticated criteria. A salesman who travels a lot in his clean car would have a chance of exceeding the 4 percent CO mark during the biennium greater than the 5 percent just implied. But the system will have registered *numerous clean readings* for this motorist and, on that basis, can pardon a single dirty reading. A criterion might say, for example, that three clean readings cancel a single dirty reading. Or it can forgive first offenses or evaluate on the basis of running *averages rather than cut points.* It can blend the readings for the different pollutants into a composite variable. It can scan for engine behavior that alternates between running clean and running dirty (sometimes called "flipper" behavior). It can adjust for the measured speed and acceleration of the vehicle at the moment of emissions readings. And so on.

Outputs That Remote Sensing Does Not Measure

Policymakers can police the CO, HC, and NO exiting the tailpipe. But are tailpipe CO, HC, and NO the only outputs that matter? Are there other emissions that in fact cannot be found by remote sensing at the output stage and hence need to be controlled by other means?

Evaporative Emissions
Another source of noxious outputs is evaporative HC emissions. These are produced when gasoline mixes with air in a carburetor, when the fuel line has a leak, when the charcoal canister system malfunctions, or, most simply, when the gas cap is missing. There is considerable debate about the magnitude of these types of emissions (Calif. I/M Review Committee 1993, 97; Gertler et al. 1993; Douglas R. Lawson letter to Richard J. Sommerville, November 6, 1992; U.S. EPA 1992). Evaporative emissions of the fleet are declining steadily as new engine technology has replaced older technology, particularly the replacement of carburetors by fuel-injection systems. Evaporative emissions are continuing to decline as fuel tank vapor recovery systems come into use. These positive developments are, however, the direct result of federal command-and-control regulations imposed on automakers.

Although remote sensing does not read evaporative emissions, it might help reduce evaporative emissions because they are correlated with tampering and inadequate maintenance, and these in turn are correlated with high tailpipe emissions (Lawson et al. 1996; Pierson et al. 1999). Motorists who are induced to cut their tailpipe emissions make repairs that sometimes also reduce nontailpipe emissions.

Evaporative emissions elude not only remote sensing but also any inspection system. No existing inspection system can test the vehicle's evaporative filter/purge system. Although the EPA has proposed doing pressure/purge testing, it has been abandoned because those tests were too intrusive and actually damaged hoses, for example.

Particulate Matter

Another form of noxious emissions is particulate matter, like the smoke from diesel engines. Remote sensors (based on reflectometry or absorption) have been created to measure the concentration of particulates in auto exhaust (Lowi 1996; Stedman, Bishop, and Aldrete 1997). Researchers believe that better roadside units could be developed. Hence, particulate matter does not elude the output-oriented approach of remote sensing.

CO_2

Some people might argue that excessive carbon dioxide (CO_2) emissions exacerbate global warming. Views on global warming vary greatly. To some people also, it is unclear that global warming is (or will be) a reality, whether the supposed warming should be deemed detrimental, and whether, in the case of warming, it could be mitigated by simple, low-cost cooling strategies rather than emission-control strategies (Benford 1997).

CO_2 emissions are closely and inversely correlated with the car's gas mileage (the distribution of CO_2 emissions does not look like that of CO or HC), so controlling CO_2 emissions amounts to regulating gas mileage. One might argue that regional governments would not have an incentive to mitigate global warming, so command-and-control programs at the national level are necessary. In response, it could be said that the potential benefits of such a policy are too hypothetical and too insignificant to warrant intrusive measures at the national level. Command-and-control damages general prosperity, and general prosperity is the surest aid to environmental improvement (Wildavsky 1988).

Lead

A car running on leaded fuel emits lead. Federal command-and-control laws between 1976 and 1986 virtually eliminated the availability of leaded gasoline. The current remote-sensing technology cannot measure lead emissions, however, and Donald Stedman reports that remote-sensing technology *cannot* be adapted to do so. Lead emissions, therefore, cannot be controlled at the output level, so some form of input control is presumably necessary. It bears consideration whether federal law is the appropriate way to do so. Regional governments could rule on the permissibility of selling leaded gasoline in their own territory and leave manufacturers and distributors free to work around such regional restrictions. In areas where lead emissions are not deemed a serious problem, consumers would be free to enjoy the benefits of leaded gasoline.

Remote sensing, then, is not able to measure the full range of emission outputs that concern us, but its ability to measure CO, HC, and NO covers most of the problem. In an otherwise laissez-faire society, the problems of evaporative and lead emissions might remain and might call for measures farther down the command-and-control end of the policy spectrum.

Will Scofflaws Learn to Foil Remote Sensing?

Output-oriented policy remains silent on inputs. It unleashes entrepreneurial creativity to discover and combine inputs to produce customers' desired outputs. However, the output that a remote-sensing program sets for motorists is avoiding smog citations. It is possible that the process of entrepreneurial discovery will respond not by cleaning up cars, but by foiling or circumventing the system. A pure remote-sensing program will yield emission reductions only if human cunning cannot find convenient ways of foiling its efforts. (Smog check itself is an object lesson of this hazard.)

To thwart circumvention, a remote-sensing program should deploy a small number of on-road pullover teams. If a car exhibits a suspicious feature, the computer will signal the attendant, and the car can be stopped on the spot. On-road teams would not stop mere gross polluters, but those suspected of subterfuge or rank noncompliance.

The five methods of foiling remote sensing are as follows:

1. Obstructing the license plate with mud or putting a trailer hitch in front of it. This problem can be easily policed by pullovers. When the computer receives information that a car has an illegible plate *and* high emissions, it will signal authorities to pull the car over. Even without on-road forces, the problem could be resolved with elementary detective work using multiple video images of cars with illegible plates.
2. Keeping the car unregistered so the program is not able to identify the car and notify the motorist. Again, the computer could be programmed to signal on-road forces to nab unregistered vehicles.
3. Evading remote-sensing sites. This will be difficult for motorists because the sites could be numerous, unannounced, and disguised and be changed daily.

4. Conniving to eliminate the exhaust plume as observed by the remote sensor, such as altering the tailpipe or turning off the car as it passes by a remote sensor. The computer could flag these cars for pullover.
5. Tampering with the contents of the exhaust plume. This requires an additional gas source, to be mixed with the true exhaust, or perhaps an additive to the gasoline. More specifically, motorists might be able to foil remote sensing if they can make their car emit excessive carbon dioxide emissions (CO_2), because remote-sensing measures CO, HC, and NO_x each as a ratio to CO_2 emissions. Increasing the CO_2 content would therefore disguise gross emissions of the regulated pollutants. That motorists would go to such lengths is highly unlikely.

It appears that scofflaw tactics pose no real threat to a program vested with on-road pullover power. That power, even if exercised only rarely, would place a significant check on evaders. The accumulated record of license-plate snapshots that are taken concurrently with remote-sensing measurements would supply incontrovertible evidence of subterfuge.

Recommended Features of a Remote-Sensing Program

The desirable features of a remote-sensing program are carefully explored elsewhere (Klein and Koskenoja 1996; for similar and more current analyses, see Schwartz 1998). Here I summarize the basic components of a property-rights policy based on remote sensing:

- *On-road remote-sensing units coupled with automatic license plate readers*: The program should deploy numerous unannounced remote-sensing teams. In addition, many units could be permanently bunkered and operate unmanned.
- *No periodic inspection*: The program would deploy enough mobile remote-sensing units to read cars an average of four to eight times over two years. The cost of traditional ("decentralized") smog check inspection is about sixty times higher than the cost of a single remote-sensing inspection (Klein and Koskenoja 1996, 19). Periodic inspections add little to the surveillance achieved by remote sensing and should be discontinued.

- *Smart signs*: At the Speer Boulevard exit ramp off southbound I-25 in Denver, a consortium of public and private sponsors erected, with public-sector approval, a permanent "Smart Sign." It operated around the clock for sixteen months and has lately been relocated. Motorists driving by see an electronic billboard that automatically and instantaneously reports (at a cost of 3 cents per reading) the car's emissions as "good," "fair," or "poor." Governments should install these inexpensive "smart" signs to allow motorists to check their emissions and to advance public awareness and understanding. (On smart sign costs and performance, see Bishop et al. 2000; Schwartz 1998, 29.)
- *Early driver notification*: The program should notify motorists whose cars are within smog limits but are approaching the limits or showing deterioration. The state would invest in a postcard to notify the motorist that he may wish to service his car. The notification card would cite three good reasons for doing so: helping clean the air, improving gas mileage, and reducing the likelihood of being subject to future penalties. Early driver notification would be a positive service to the motorist as well as a sort of warning. It would prompt some people to reduce their emissions preemptively before being compelled to do so. Demonstration projects have proved the power of voluntary notification to clean the air (Bishop et al. 1993). The program should also extend a "notice of appreciation" to motorists with clean cars, perhaps after a series of readings has been compiled. This would reassure the motorist of his clean status and would build goodwill with the public.
- *Citation by mail and clean screening*: The program would issue citations by mail to motorists with high-emission vehicles. The citation would call for some kind of redeeming action to be made within a certain time period. Perhaps the motorist would be allowed to escape penalty by visiting a fixed remote-sensing site and demonstrating low emissions—an arrangement that remote-sensing advocates call "clean screening."
- *Monetary Fines Imposed on Gross Polluters*: When a motorist receives a citation for exceeding the speed limit, driving recklessly, or parking illegally, he is to pay a fine. A similar system of penalties could also be used for smog violations and would have those who damage the common property *compensate* those who have been harmed. Revenues from fines would go toward financing the program, which would benefit the community as a whole. Like speeding tickets, fines for smog violations could be graduated with the extent and frequency of the vio-

lation. A program of monetary penalties would induce motorists to value and, if necessary, to seek in the marketplace their own prevention of citations. Under such a program, this good would be a normal private good like hamburgers or handkerchiefs; the free, private market would be best at producing and supplying it. Consumers might demand and mechanics would offer a warranty on smog repairs. Perhaps entrepreneurs would open drive-through testing facilities using remote sensing and charging just a few dollars (like the "smart sign" proposal). Getting one's car tested might be quicker and cheaper than getting a car wash.

- *Enforcement: DMV records and on-road pullovers*: The California Department of Motor Vehicles is empowered to impose fines, deny vehicle registration, and impound vehicles that do not comply with citations (California Health and Safety Code, sec. 44081, 1994). In a remote-sensing program, driver's licenses, vehicle titles, and registration could be frozen until fines were paid. Using automatic license plate readers, on-road units could easily identify and pull over rank noncompliers and impound their vehicles. *Remote sensing is a means of both identifying gross polluters and apprehending them.* But the pullover forces would act only as the last resort. They should not be authorized to accost the mere gross polluter, the mere unregistered vehicle, the mere license plate obscurer, and so forth. Rather, they would pull over only gross polluters who are unregistered, who have illegible license plates, and who have not complied with previous citations. Thus, only the hard-core problem cases would be subjected to an on-road pullover. The program might create its own "smog squad," separate from existing police forces, that enforces only emissions violations, just as parking patrols enforce only parking violations.

- *Repair subsidies and waivers*: For reasons of equity, enhanced compliance, and political acceptability, it makes sense for the program to offer repair subsidies to the poor. Using deductibles and copayments, a subsidy program could mitigate opportunism and moral hazard. For cars in need of extremely expensive repairs, the government might issue waivers, as do smog check programs today.

A detailed examination indicates that a program consisting of all these features would cost society much less, and benefit it much more, than do current smog check programs. The cost of valid remote-sensing readings would range from \$0.35 to \$1.35 per reading (see Klein and Koskenoja 1996, 18–33; Schwartz 1998, 26–27).

Enforcing Property Rights Means Cleaning the Air

Besides offering lower costs, the remote-sensing approach delivers more air quality benefits than do smog check and other command-and-control policies. As mentioned, most of the fleet emissions comes today from about 10 percent of the cars. The majority of high emitters would receive a warning or a citation. And the majority of those receiving citations would consequently make their cars clean because leaving their car dirty would put them in constant jeopardy of penalty. We do not know how long a repaired car remains low emitting, but we do know that repairs vastly reduce the emissions of high emitters (Lawson 1995) and that if the car resumed high emissions, the system would probably detect it promptly.

Remote sensing has been used on a pilot or supplemental basis in Arizona, California, Colorado, and Ontario. Schwartz (1998, 22) summarized the results: "[Remote sensing] seems capable of identifying significant portions of the on-road fleet that are low-emitting, while allowing relatively few high emitters to slip through the cracks."

The EPA and most allied agencies have been slow to embrace remote sensing; indeed, the EPA's guidelines deflect state governments from remote sensing. The bad politics of remote sensing appear to stem from several unfortunate factors: (1) a not-invented-here attitude toward remote sensing; (2) an apprehension that remote sensing will find fault with long-favored auto-emission control programs; (3) an apprehension that remote sensing will work so well, so easily, that bureaucracies will lose budget and staff; (4) the possible influence of the smog check industries and other command-and-control related industries; (5) the ownership of important remote-sensing patents by a company that sells expensive alternative smog check equipment and therefore has an incentive to suppress remote sensing; (6) the lack of support by environmental groups, who seem more interested in imposing command-and-control and combating automobility than in cleaning the air (Klein and Saraceni 1994; Stedman 1995).

The Challenge to Auto Emissions Command and Control

Smog check is just one program aimed at reducing fleet emissions. Other programs are carpooling programs, emissions requirements on new cars, electric vehicle quotas, and alternative fuel mandates.

The case against command and control applies to these other programs as well. They are extreme examples of input-oriented strategies that fail to go to the heart of the problem and impose enormous costs. Recent literature shows convincingly that these programs rate low in cost effectiveness (for example, Orski 1994).

Although smog is a problem in only certain regions, the EPA's new-car emission requirements mean that many car buyers have to pay more for a new car even when they do not live in an area with a smog problem. The smog problem is thus best addressed by regional, decentralized programs. With a functioning remote-sensing program, regions can police excessive emissions. To pass muster with remote sensors, motorists will have to keep their cars clean. That demand will induce automakers, the energy industry, and the repair and inspection industry to produce cleaner cars. In the property-rights approach, made possible by new technology, inputs are selected by competitive, spontaneous market forces, not by government agencies. The likely result is less bureaucracy and cleaner air.

NOTES

I thank Gary Bishop, Douglas Lawson, and Donald Stedman for important feedback.

1. We should further recognize that of the cars in the set defined as "clean," the relatively dirty ones are most likely to fail. They may not be officially guilty, but they won't be entirely innocent.
2. The relatively less guilty cars are most likely to sneak by.

REFERENCES

Ashbaugh, Lowell L., et al. 1992. "On-Road Remote Sensing of Carbon Monoxide and Hydrocarbon Emissions during Several Vehicle Operating Conditions." In *PM10 Standards and Nontraditional Particulate Source Controls*, vol. 2, 885–98, edited by J. C. Chow and D. M. Ono. Pittsburgh: Air & Waste Management Association.

Benford, Gregory. 1997. "Climate Controls." *Reason*, November. Available online at reason.com/9711/fe.benford.html.

Bishop, Gary A., et al. 1993. "A Cost-Effectiveness Study of Carbon Monoxide Emissions Reduction Utilizing Remote Sensing." *Journal of the Air & Waste Management Association* 43: 978–88.

Bishop, Gary A., et al. 2000. "Drive-by Motor Vehicle Emissions: Immediate Feedback in Reducing Air Pollution." *Environmental Science and Technology* 34: 1110–16.

Brooks, D. J., et al. 1995. "Real World Hot Soak Evaporative Emissions—A Pilot Study." Society of Automotive Engineers Technical Paper 951007, March.

California I/M Review Committee. 1993. *Evaluation of the California Smog Check Program and Recommendations for Program Improvements: Fourth Report to the Legislature.* Sacramento: California I/M Review Committee,.

Colorado Air Quality Control Commission. 1998. Report to the Colorado General Assembly on the Vehicle Emissions Inspection and Maintenance Program. Denver: Colorado Air Quality Control Commission, July.

———. 1999. Report to the Colorado General Assembly on the Vehicle Emissions Inspection and Maintenance Program. Denver: Colorado Air Quality Control Commission, September.

Gertler, A. W., et al. 1993. "Appointment of VOC Tailpipe vs. Running and Resting in Tuscarora and Fort McHenry Tunnels." Paper presented at the EPA/A&WMA International Conference on the Emission Inventory: Perception and Reality. Pasadena, CA, October.

Glazer, Amihai, Daniel Klein, Charles Lave, et al. 1993. "Clean for a Day: Troubles with California's Smog Check." Unpublished manuscript, University of California at Irvine.

Glazer, Amihai, Daniel Klein, Charles Lave. 1995. "Clean on Paper, Dirty on Road: Troubles with California's Smog Check." *Journal of Transport Economics and Policy* 29 (January): 85–92.

Hardin, Garrett. 1968. "The Tragedy of the Commons." *Science* 162: 1243–48.

Hubbard, Thomas. 1997. "Using Inspection and Maintenance Programs to Regulate Vehicle Emissions." *Contemporary Economic Policy*, April 1997, 52–62.

Klein, Daniel B., and Pia Maria Koskenoja. 1996. "The Smog-Reduction Road: Remote Sensing vs. Clean Air Act." Cato Institute *Policy Analysis*, no. 249, February 7.

Klein, Daniel, and Christina Saraceni. 1994. "Breathing Room: California Faces Down the EPA over Centralized Smog Checks." *Reason*, June, 24–28.

Lawson, Douglas R. 1993. "'Passing the Test'—Human Behavior and California Smog Check Program." *Journal of the Air and Waste Management Association*, December, 1567–75.

————. 1995. "The Costs of 'M' in I/M—Reflections on Inspection/Maintenance Programs." *Journal of the Air and Waste Management Association*, June, 465–76.

————. 1998. "The El Monte Pilot Study—A Government-Run I/M Program." *Proceedings of the Eighth CRC On-Road Vehicle Emissions Workshop*, April 20–22.

Lawson, Douglas R., et al. 1990. "Emissions from In-Use Motor Vehicles in Los Angeles: A Pilot Study of Remote Sensing and the Inspection and Maintenance Program." *Journal of the Air and Waste Management Association*, August, 1096–1105.

Lawson, Douglas R., et al. 1996. 1996. "Program for the Use of Remote Sensing Devices to Detect High-Emitting Vehicles." Desert Research Institute report to the South Coast Air Quality Management District, April 16.

Lawson, Douglas R., and Patricia A. Walsh. 1995. "Effectiveness of U.S. Motor Vehicle Inspection/Maintenance Programs, 1985–1992." Final Report, prepared for the California I/M Review Committee, Sacramento.

Lowi, Alvin Jr. 1996. "Exhaust Gas Particulate Instrument for Facultative Engine Control." Final Technical Report, NASA contract no. NA54-50068, report no. 95-1-03.08-8457-1, June 13.

Orski, Kenneth C. 1994. "Evaluation of Employee Trip Reduction Programs Based on California's Experience with Rule 1501: An Informal Report of the Institute of Transportation Engineers." Resources Papers for the 1994 ITE International Conference, January.

Pierson, W. R., et al. 1999. "Assessment of Nontailpipe Hydrocarbon Emissions from Motor Vehicles." *Journal of the Air and Waste Management Association* 49: 498–519.

Popp, Peter J., Gary A. Bishop, and Donald H. Stedman. 1999. "Development of a High Speed Ultraviolet Spectrometer for Remote Sensing of Mobile Source Nitric Oxide Emissions." *Journal of the Air and Waste Management Association* 49: 1463–68.

Rothbard, Murray N. 1982. "Law, Property Rights, and Air Pollution." *Cato Journal* 2, no. 1 (spring): 55–99.

Scherrer, Huel C., and David B. Kittelson. 1994. "I/M Effectiveness As Directly Measured by Ambient CO Data." SAE paper no. 940302, March.

Schwartz, Joel. 1998. "Remote Sensing of Vehicle Emissions: State of the Technology, Potential Applications, Cost Estimates, and Recommendations." Sacramento: California I/M Review Committee, September 9.

Stedman, Donald H. 1995. "Playing with Fire: Science and Politics of Air Pollution from Cars." The 1995 University Lecture. Denver: University of Denver, March 29.

Stedman, Donald H., et al. 1991. "On-Road Carbon Monoxide and Hydrocarbon Remote Sensing in the Chicago Area, ILENR/RE-AQ-91/14." Report prepared for the Illinois Department of Energy and Natural Resources, Office of Research and Planning, October.

Stedman, Donald H., et al. 1997. "On-Road Evaluation of an Automobile Emission Test Program." *Environmental Science and Technology* 31, no. 3: 927–31.

Stedman, Donald H., et al. 1998. "Repair Avoidance and Evaluating Inspection and Maintenance Programs." *Environmental Science and Technology* 32, no. 10: 1544–45.

Stedman, Donald H., G. A. Bishop, and P. Aldrete. 1997. "On-Road CO, HC, NO and Opacity Measurements," 8–25. *Proceedings of CRC 7TH On-Road Vehicle Emissions Workshop*, San Diego, April 11.

U.S. Environmental Protection Agency. 1992. EPA Guidelines. *Federal Register* 57, no. 215, November 5.

———. 1992. "EPA Responses to Questions." Prepared for the joint public meeting of the California I/M Review Committee, California Air Resources Board, and Bureau of Automotive Repair. Washington, DC: U.S. Environmental Protection Agency, July 29.

Wildavsky, Aaron. 1988. *Searching for Safety*. New Brunswick, NJ: Transaction Publishers.

Zhang, Yi, et al. 1996. "On-Road Evaluation of Inspection/Maintenance Effectiveness." *Environmental Science and Technology* 33, no. 5: 1445–50.

Part II

Quality Assurance and Consumer Protection

6

Technology and the Case for Free Banking

David Friedman and Kerry Macintosh

Central banking is a staple of conventional economic thinking. In this system, a single bank holds a monopoly over note issuance (Smith 1936, 168). One example of central banking is the Federal Reserve System, which is the sole issuer of currency in the United States.

Recently, an increasing number of economists have challenged the doctrine of central banking. These thinkers advocate free banking: a decentralized banking system in which any bank is free to issue notes (Selgin 1988, 3).

In this chapter, we identify some common arguments against free banking. We explain why the Internet, electronic payment systems, and other emerging technologies undercut those arguments and strengthen the case for free banking.

Three Models of Free Banking

Modern economic theorists have articulated at least three models of free banking (Selgin and White 1994, 1719). First, some economists have proposed an unregulated monetary and banking system that starts with a single base money. It can be gold or silver or even a government-issued fiat money as long as its stock is permanently frozen to eliminate any scope for discretionary monetary policy. Banks then issue money in the form of bank notes and transferable deposits made redeemable in the base money. The base money continues to serve as both the unit of account and the system's means of settlement (Selgin and White 1994, 1720–22). In our analysis, we identify this model as *traditional free banking*, since it is similar to the free-banking systems of the eighteenth and nineteenth centuries.

Second, Friedrich A. Hayek suggested that private companies issue their own base moneys. Although nonredeemable, each base money would be controlled in quantity so as to maintain its value in relation to a selected commodity bundle. Free competition among these base moneys would drive unstable brands out of the market (Hayek 1976). We describe this as the *competing base money* model.

Third, some economists argue in favor of a system that would separate the unit of account from the medium of exchange. In this "new monetary economics," there is no base money and no official medium of exchange. Instead, the market employs a common unit of account based on a fixed bundle of commodities that is diversified to safeguard against the destabilizing effects of shifts in the supply of or demand for any one commodity.

Thus, the unit of account is set by definition: the unit is simply the value of the defining bundle of commodities, so the value of anything else measured in that unit is the number of such bundles it exchanges for. Its value does not fluctuate any more than the length of the yard does. Obligations are denominated in the unit of account but can be satisfied with any medium. Individuals hold wealth accounts composed of liquid assets such as mutual funds or securities. Payments in the economy are effected through transfers to and from such accounts. For this reason, this system is sometimes called an *accounting system of exchange* (Greenfield and Yeager 1983). In this chapter, we refer to this model as *sophisticated barter*, since no money (in the sense of a medium of exchange) is involved.

How can someone make payments in a system with no medium of exchange? A debtor makes a payment by writing a check that the creditor deposits in her account. An amount of liquid financial assets whose market value is equal to the amount specified on the check is then transferred from the debtor's bank, where those assets were credited to his account, to the creditor's, where they are credited to her account; if the creditor prefers a different mix of financial assets than what she has just received, she makes whatever market transactions are necessary to readjust her portfolio. Amounts of value are defined by the unit of account—a thousand monetary units of securities means that this quantity of securities would exchange for a thousand of the commodity bundles used to define the unit—but the medium of exchange, what is actually transferred, need not be, and usually will not be, a collection of such bundles.

Electronic Money

Each of these three models can easily be transferred to the electronic realm. To see how, we first explain what electronic money is and how it works.

Today, entrepreneurs are experimenting with many different kinds of electronic money. One common technology is the "smart card," a plastic card in which a computer chip is embedded (Congressional Budget Office 1996, 10). Each card is loaded with "value" that represents a claim against the card issuer (Task Force on Stored-Value Cards 1997, 664). Cardholders can use their smart cards to purchase goods and services from merchants equipped with card-reading terminals. These terminals lift the information from the cards and store it in computer memory. Merchants transmit electronic claims to the issuer for redemption (Congressional Budget Office 1996, 11).

The range of potential applications is very broad. For example, banks could provide smart cards as a service to customers, transferring value from savings or checking accounts to computer chips that can be loaded, spent down, and reloaded. Other financial services companies that already provide stored value in other forms such as traveler's checks (e.g., American Express), might sell preloaded smart cards to the public. Major companies (e.g., Chevron, Barnes & Noble, Circuit City) might offer customers loyalty program cards that could be used only at their own franchises.

The smart card holds promise in virtual as well as real space. Already technology companies are developing smart card readers that can be connected to a computer's floppy disk drive. Thus equipped, cardholders can load cards with value from online bank accounts and go on an Internet shopping spree (Muller 1998, 410).

Most smart card systems are designed so that a unit of value can be spent only once before being redeemed by the issuer. However, Mondex, Inc., offers a more versatile technology that allows cardholders to transfer value directly from one card to another (Macintosh 1998, p. 735, n. 6).

As an alternative to smart cards, banks or other companies can issue electronic money, that is, redeemable claims that bear the digital signature of the issuer. Bank customers and others who purchase the money store it on the hard drives of their computers. When a customer decides to make a purchase, she transmits the money through her modem to the computer of a merchant. The merchant then returns the money to the issuer for redemption (Congressional Budget Office 1996, 28–29).

These advances in payment technology allow us to imagine exciting real-world applications of the three models.

1. Under the traditional free-banking model, banks and other financial services companies could issue electronic "notes" stored on smart cards or hard drives. Customers would spend the notes in the real and/or virtual world. Notes could be redeemed for a single base money, which could be a fiat money (e.g., the dollar) or a commodity (e.g., gold). If Mondex technology were employed, these notes could circulate for some time before being returned to the issuer for redemption.

2. Similarly, the competing base money model could be updated for a technological age. Banks and other financial service companies could issue competing name brands of electronic money stored on smart cards or hard drives. Unlike the traditional free-banking model in which notes are issued in terms of a single base money, each brand could be based on a different commodity bundle or standard. Thus, the system would generate competing units of account as well as media of exchange. Each issuer would manage the quantity of its electronic money to keep its value stable relative to the selected bundle or standard. Competition would force unstable moneys out of the market (Macintosh 1998, 747). Since what is being stored on the card is simply information, cards could and would be developed capable of simultaneously storing money from a variety of issuers.

Ultimately, this competition could produce two very different outcomes. One of us (Macintosh) believes that buyers and sellers in real and virtual space could reduce conversion costs by employing a common unit of account. Thus, competition would lead to a small number of currencies, perhaps only one (Macintosh 1998, 750).

The other (Friedman) points out that currency conversion is arithmetic and that computers do arithmetic rapidly and inexpensively. As the cost of currency conversion drops, so does the importance of having a common unit of account. Already, one can put a plastic card in an ATM in Toronto and draw Canadian dollars out of a U.S. dollar account. One country, Argentina, has actually incorporated the idea of multiple currencies into its legal system, thereby abandoning the principle of making its national money legal tender in favor of a legal rule of specific performance under which people are free to make contracts in any currency they like, with the courts enforcing performance in that currency.

In the near future we can expect to see currency-transparent browsers that read prices off a seller's Web page in the seller's currency and display them for the buyer in the buyer's currency, using a conversion rate read from the buyer's bank's Web page. Further in the future, we can imagine similar technologies for transactions in real space, although it is hard to predict their form: perhaps digital price tags that read each customer's monetary preference from a bar-coded lapel pin and display the price to him in his preferred currency at the current exchange rate, provided to the price tag via a wireless network. As such technologies improve, the world could accommodate dozens, hundreds, even thousands of base moneys.

3. Last, advances in technology would be instrumental in easing the transition to a system based on the separation of media of exchange from the unit of account. Such a system requires, and modern technology can provide, extensive price information readily available in order to eliminate any ambiguity about how many units of any particular commodity correspond to some specified number of monetary units. Fiber-optic cables and the digitalization of information could build an efficient high-speed communications network for the entire economy. Together with smart cards and other innovative payments technologies, this network would make it easier to implement sophisticated barter. Payments could be made cheaply and easily through electronic debiting and crediting of money-market mutual funds or other liquid wealth accounts. There would be no need for a common medium of exchange (Browne and Cronin 1995, 104, 108–9).

Bank Runs and Panics

Armed with this information about developments in technology, we now reconsider several common arguments against free banking.

The most serious charge leveled against free banking has to do with its susceptibility to runs and panics. The standard indictment goes something like this: a trigger event occurs, for example, rumors of mismanagement, insolvency, recession, or war. As a result, the public loses confidence in one or more banks. Customers besiege the banks, demanding that their notes or deposits be redeemed. Unfortunately, because the banks do not have enough commodity or fiat money to meet the demands, they are forced to close. These closures spawn a contagious panic as people stampede other banks. At this point, a free-banking system would be doomed to collapse. Only a central bank operating outside the limits of lost confidence could serve as a "lender of last resort" and preserve the stability of the monetary system (Goodhart 1988, 87; Selgin 1988, 134–37; Selgin and White 1994, 1725–26).

In part, this charge is based on a faulty understanding of history. Nineteenth-century America has become the poster era for the evils of free banking. Critics point to the runs, bank failures, and panics suffered during that time and insist that free banking is an unsafe system.

Recent historical studies have questioned this conclusion. Banking in nineteenth-century America was far from free. After the charter of the Second Bank of the United States expired in 1836, many states enacted laws that allowed banks to organize under general incorporation laws. However, the same laws often required the banks to secure note issues with state bonds, which prevented the banks from diversifying their assets. When the bonds declined in value, the banks became insolvent and suspended payments (Selgin 1988, 14; Solomon 1996, 61–62). Additional restrictions limited or prohibited branch banking, thereby preventing geographical diversification. In other words, it was regulation—not the lack of it—that doomed the state-incorporated banks.

In 1863, Congress authorized the establishment of federally chartered, note-issuing banks. That is, the notes of the national banks had to be secured by deposits of federal government securities. When those securities became scarce, the banks could not issue notes to meet cyclical increases in demand. Rather than acknowledge its own responsibility for the resulting problems, Congress established the Federal Reserve System as a lender of last resort to prevent panics and illiquidity in the banking system (Selgin 1988, 14, 123; Solomon 1996, 63–64).

There is historical evidence that free banking can function safely and soundly under a regime of true laissez-faire. In one of the best-known studies, Lawrence White demonstrated that Scotland enjoyed a stable free banking and monetary system in the eighteenth and nineteenth centuries (White 1984). This was so even though Scotland had no central bank, allowed banks to compete in note issue, and imposed few regulations on banks. Although individual banks failed, there were no panics in the Scottish system (Selgin 1988, 7, 138).

Despite this historical evidence, tradition holds that individual bank failures must inevitably spawn panics. Customers, lacking the information needed to determine which banks are affected by losses, feel the need to assure themselves of the safety of their balances, which they can best do by withdrawing them (Selgin 1988, 137).

However, as Selgin explains, in a competitive market for bank liabilities, exchange rates on bank notes would vary along with the risk of capital loss. A concerned bank customer could simply check the newspaper to see whether there was any discount on the notes he held. If not, he would feel no urge to redeem them (Selgin 1988, 138).

We can update this argument for the technological age. Today, the Internet provides a new tool for transmitting information instantaneously and across national boundaries. Search engines provide a powerful and inexpensive tool that ordinary people can and do use to sift out the information they need. Moreover, the market continues to produce a stunning variety of new technologies (ranging from fiber to cable modems to wireless) that could provide us with broadband telecommunication services in the near future (Shelanski 1999, 724–29). Speed and ease of communication and access to information are greater than ever before and will continue to increase.

Now consider what would happen if traditional free banking went electronic. Banks would issue electronic "notes" redeemable in a common base money. To reassure customers that the redemption promise was meaningful, banks could hire independent auditors to review and report on the adequacy and liquidity of bank assets, reserves, and insurance (Klein 1997).

Not all auditors are independent. In 2002, the value of stock in the Enron Corporation crashed after information surfaced regarding the company's questionable accounting practices. Arthur Andersen, LLP, a prestigious accounting firm, had audited the company but had failed to report that anything was amiss. This woeful tale raises the concern that audits may fail when auditors depend on income derived from a particular company and fail to report its problems. In light of the Enron debacle, customers may gravitate to banks that provide multiple audits from competing accounting firms or that employ firms with a well-grounded reputation for tough auditing. Also, customers may come to view private insurance as the most reliable proof that banks can redeem notes. Insurance companies could certify the existence and amount of the insurance.

In addition to auditors and insurance companies, competing financial news services would serve as watchdogs, reporting the exchange rates of the electronic notes on the Internet as well as in more traditional media like newspapers and magazines. Through improved access to such information, customers would be empowered to assess the financial stability of their own institutions. Even if one bank became insolvent, there would be no reason for customers of other institutions to demand redemption. The occasional bank failure need not produce a panic.

Despite modern information technology, if investors mistakenly instigated a run on the currency of a solvent bank, no serious problem would arise if the bank had taken the precaution of holding its interest-bearing securities in a sufficiently liquid form. The bank would simply contract liabilities (notes) and assets together, pay off all note holders in full, and go back to issuing notes with an enhanced reputation.

Modern technologies could also administer an old form of panic alleviation. In the eighteenth century, "the Bank of Scotland . . . inserted a clause into its notes giving it the option (which it did not normally exercise) of delaying redemption" and paying 5 percent interest during the delay (White 1989, 228). Under such an "option clause," note holders agree by contract to the bank's retaining its reserves during a panic. The availability of the option would quell note holders' impulse to panic. In the modern age, action taken under the option clause could be posted and mediated on an hourly basis while assessment and certification of the bank's solvency proceed.

Alternatively, the risk of runs and panics could be eliminated altogether by shifting from the traditional free-banking model to the sophisticated barter system. If most members of the public held their wealth as equity claims like money-market mutual funds, then any drop in the value of fund assets would be shared immediately by all holders. Runs would not occur because a shareholder would have nothing to gain by closing his account before others did (Goodhart 1988, 92; Selgin and White 1994, 1728).

As just explained, advances in technology could facilitate a move to a payments system based on sophisticated barter. Improved communications networks and sophisticated devices such as smart cards could make it easier for us to make payments by debiting and crediting mutual funds or other liquid wealth accounts (Browne and Cronin 1995, 104, 108). Presumably, the popularity of equity accounts would increase along with their utility. If so, the new technology could be one of the most important keys to realizing a run-proof system.

Hyperinflation

Bank runs and panics are only one charge leveled at free banking. Another complaint—also based on safety and soundness concerns—has to do with hyperinflation.

In theory, hyperinflation works as follows: A bank has a solid reputation for stability and reliability. Then one day, the managers cause the bank to release a large quantity of notes. The managers steal the assets provided in exchange for the notes and abscond to places unknown. Meanwhile, the public is left holding worthless money (Friedman 1989, 222).

The success of such a fraud depends on the ability of the perpetrators to act quickly and in the dark. The public must be induced to take the inflated money before the market lowers the value of the currency.

The principle of adverse clearings (Selgin 1988, 40) provides us with good reason to doubt the hyperinflation account. Suppose one bank seeks to expand the circulation of its notes at the expense of its competitors. Members of the public either deposit notes in their own banks or spend them. If the notes are spent, the merchants will deposit them. Either way, most of these notes will end up in possession of banks other than the issuer. These rival banks will quickly exchange the excess notes for their own notes or safer commodity money. As the reserves dwindle, the expansionary bank has no choice but to curb its issue (Selgin 1988, 40–42).

Under the principle of adverse clearings, competitive free-market forces serve as a brake on expansionary issues of currency. The faster that the notes are returned, the stronger the brake will be.

For this reason, the principle of adverse clearings should be particularly effective in curbing inflation when applied to smart cards and other forms of electronic money. Many of these products are designed so that they do not circulate. Each monetary unit can be spent only once before it must be returned to the issuer for redemption. Some other products, such as Mondex cards, permit transfer from one cardholder to another, enabling electronic money to remain outstanding for longer periods of time (Browne and Cronin 1995, 105–6). But either way, electronic money that is returned for redemption travels at the speed of light.

Moreover, hyperinflation works only if it is sudden and unpredictable. As we mentioned, in a free-banking system, honest issuers of electronic notes can reassure the public by releasing independent audits of company assets, reserves, and insurance. More generally, competing financial news services monitor and report on the actions, solvency, and stability of is-suers and their notes. As the Internet and broadband services continue to make communications faster and easier, such information will circulate more and more quickly, making it ever harder for fraudulent issuers to beat financial markets and the public to the punch.

The foregoing analysis assumes a traditional free-banking model. However, as we explained at the start of this chapter, that is not the only possible regime. Hayek envisioned a system of competing nonredeemable moneys, private fiat currencies (Hayek 1976). Other economists have crit-icized his vision on the ground that firms would engage in hyperinflation if the one-time profits of doing so exceeded the present value of staying in business (Selgin and White 1994, 1734–35). However, this problem can be avoided if issuers commit to redeeming electronic money in exchange for a minimum value equal to a specified percentage of the underlying commodity bundles (Macintosh 1998, 752–54). Moreover, the same ad-vances in telecommunications that promise to protect traditional free banking can also safeguard a system of competing base moneys. When the public has instantaneous access to up-to-date information regarding the stability of individual moneys, the risk of hyperinflation is greatly re-duced.

Natural Monopoly

Another common argument against free banking is that the issuance of money is a natural monopoly. According to this line of reasoning, a single bank is more efficient in providing currency than any group of banks could be. Thus a monopoly is inevitable. And because the monopoly bank might abuse its position by inflating the currency supply, either the mo-nopoly bank must be regulated or a central bank must take its place (Sel-gin 1988, 151).

Empirical evidence does not support the argument that money is-suance is a natural monopoly. As historical studies have documented, the experience of both Europe and America with competitive banking has al-ways been toward a plurality of note-issuing banks. Monopoly banks have appeared only when governments have passed laws to restrict, bar, or co-erce rival issuers (Selgin 1988, 151).

Economic theory accounts for this experience. Large firms face admin-istrative diseconomies of scale—too many layers of administration between top and bottom—with the result that once technical economies are exhausted, further increases in size increase rather than decrease costs. For this reason, most industries are not natural monopolies. Moreover, in a market in which free entry is possible, even a monopolist faces the prospect of potential competition. If the monopolist sets prices too high, smaller firms will find that they can compete profitably (Friedman 1989, 31–32). Applying this principle to electronic money, if a dominant issuer begins to inflate its currency, it will invite competition from other issuers who provide more stable moneys (Macintosh 1998, 750).

Another common argument holds that money production is a natural monopoly because consumers benefit from a common medium of exchange. But free-banking advocates contend that although a common unit of account may be efficient because it reduces the cost of currency conversions, this does not mean that a monopoly bank can produce the physical manifestations of that unit (e.g., coins and paper notes) most efficiently (Selgin 1988, 153; Friedman 1989, 222).

Today, we can take this counterargument one step further. As we explained, rapid improvements in computation could reduce the cost of currency conversion so that even a common unit of account might not be necessary. In an age in which hundreds, or even thousands, of competing base moneys are possible, the argument that money is a natural monopoly is no longer credible.

Finally, in a sophisticated barter system, concerns about monopoly vanish altogether. Since there is no currency, the question of whether one bank can produce currency more efficiently than another becomes irrelevant.

Counterfeiting

A final objection to free banking is that such a system would encourage counterfeiting (i.e., fraudulent note issue) (Selgin 1988, 149). This objection applies to both the traditional free-banking model and the competing base money model. It does not apply to a sophisticated barter system in which there is no medium of exchange to counterfeit.

Two technological developments may help reduce this risk. First, counterfeit notes are more likely to be detected when the issuer can review them frequently (Selgin 1988, 149). In an age of electronic money, notes can be returned to issuers with the click of a mouse. Ease and speed of return should increase the frequency of review and the likelihood of detection.

Second, the electronic age has brought us public key encryption and digital signatures. By allowing users to check the authenticity of any electronic note at any time, digital signatures should greatly reduce the risk of counterfeiting—and thereby further strengthen the case for free banking.

An example is instructive. Suppose a bank issues an electronic note. It can run the contents of the note through a hashing algorithm to create a message digest and then encrypt the message with its private key. The result operates as the bank's digital signature.

A user can check the signature by running the contents of the note through the same algorithm to create her own digest. Then she applies the bank's public key (as published in a directory) to decrypt its "signature" back into digest form. If the two digests match, she has verified that the note is authentic (Macintosh 1998, p. 789, n. 214).

A potentially dangerous kind of counterfeiting is called *double-spending*. An electronic note residing on a hard drive is simply a string of digits. A user might copy the original note and try to spend both copies. Technology has a solution for this problem as well.

The simplest solution couples single-use notes with online verification. Suppose a user tries to buy goods or services with an electronic note. Before her trading partner accepts the note, he first transmits it to the bank for review. The transaction does not go forward until and unless the bank confirms that that particular note has not been spent before. Once accepted and redeemed, the note is "retired" from service.

A more elaborate version of this model both prevents double-spending and protects financial privacy. When the bank verifies the note, it also alters its identifying information, so that control is transferred from user to recipient with no need to identify either (Chaum 1985).

Some electronic notes, including those stored on smart cards, are designed to be spent offline: that is, the product does not include the telecommunications necessary to contact the issuer for verification at the point of sale. Mondex technology allows stored value to circulate from user to user without immediate redemption. In such cases, there is a risk that the user may attempt to create and spend a second copy of a note before the original is returned to the issuer. One possible solution is a tamper-proof chip on the smart card. Another is legal action against users who double-spend. Finally, broadband telecommunication services will make online transactions easier, thereby reducing the opportunity to commit this kind of fraud.

Modern encryption technology even makes it possible to permit offline transactions while protecting the financial privacy of the individual spending the money. In one scheme (Brands 1993), a single interaction between the user of an electronic note and the recipient generates information sufficient to verify that the note was issued by the bank but insufficient to permit anyone, including the bank, to identify the user. However, if the user attempts to spend the same note twice, the bank can combine the information generated by the two transactions to identify the culprit.

In a more elaborate version of the protocol, the verification mechanism is built into a tamper-proof chip on a smart card. This prevents fraud in advance instead of punishing it after the fact. If a user breaks the card's protection, his double-spending generates information that allows the bank to identify him and take appropriate action.

How Might We Get There

Two different developments are necessary to move from a system of monopoly government moneys to a fully private system. One, replacing government money with private money as a means of payment, is already occurring. Smart cards, Eurodollars (dollar-denominated accounts in banks outside the United States), and traveler's checks all are forms of private money defined by public units of account. For reasons already discussed, this process can be expected to continue.

The second development, replacing government money as a unit of account by private alternatives, has not yet happened. The chief factor preventing the widespread use of private units of account is the advantage of standardization; it is convenient for people doing business with one another to measure prices in the same units. Currently, the standard units are government moneys and especially for international transactions, the dollar.

The development of a new unit of account could occur in two steps: first the creation of a new standard and then the adoption of that account for monetary purposes.

The first step could occur in the context of long-term contracting. If one is simply buying and selling goods, day-to-day fluctuations in the value of a reasonably stable money, such as the U.S. dollar, are usually insignificant. But unpredictable fluctuations over a period of years or decades present a serious problem for long-term contracts. A solution is to specify obligations in terms of the consumer price index (CPI) or some similar measure. One problem with that solution is the risk that a measure defined and maintained by a government may be manipulated for political purposes, especially if it is in widespread use. Hence parties might find it worth using a privately defined standard of value, such as the value of a particular commodity bundle, to define their long-term obligations. Once such a standard is in common use for that purpose, it is also available to be adopted as a private unit of account for monetary purposes.

The shift to using such a private unit of account as the basis for a monetary system, under any of our models, is a more difficult problem, because of the inherent advantages of an already established standard. One can imagine it happening through one or more of three different mechanisms.

1. Since national boundaries are irrelevant in online commerce, using a government money as the standard unit of account means that everyone may eventually use the same government money—probably U.S. dollars. That outcome may be unattractive, for reasons of national pride, to those who are not citizens of the issuing country, and once Internet access has reached saturation in the developed world and become substantial elsewhere, no single country's citizens will represent anything close to a majority of the online economy. One solution would be to shift to some neutral unit of account, such as a commodity bundle already in use as a standard of value for long-term contracting.

2. If, as one of us (Friedman) believes may happen, technological developments sharply reduce the importance of using the same unit of account as those with whom one does business, the problem described in the previous paragraph will disappear, along with the need for a standard unit of account. Americans can use dollars as their unit of account; French can use francs; and Japanese can use yen, with computers transparently translating in the background. In such a future, private moneys using private units of account that customers prefer to any of the existing units, perhaps for their superior stability, become practical.

3. Finally, a dominant unit of account based on a government currency might be destroyed by the collapse of that currency. While such a scenario seems unlikely at present, it is not, judging by the historical record, impos-

sible. If it happens, one or more private units of account might appear to fill the gap.

Conclusion

Few people are willing to entertain the possibility that a laissez-faire monetary regime could replace central banking. Even free-banking enthusiasts like Selgin and White have offered the caveat that such a switch would require a "revolution" (1994, 1745).

In fact, such a revolution is taking place today as we move from the industrial to the information age. This revolution invites us to rethink the doctrine that has been used against free banking during the past century.

In this chapter, we identified key technologies—including the Internet, electronic money, computers, broadband services, and digital signatures—that necessitate a reevaluation of traditional arguments against free banking. We conclude that in the information age, free banking need not lead to runs and panics, hyperinflation, monopoly, or counterfeiting. Private issuers are likely to play a major role in generating means of exchange and may also play a major role in defining units of account.

REFERENCES

Brands, Stefan. 1993. "Untraceable Off-Line Cash in Wallets with Observers." *Advances in Cryptology—Crypto '93*. Santa Barbara, CA, August.

Browne, F. X., and David Cronin. 1995. "Payments Technologies, Financial Innovation, and Laissez-Faire Banking." *Cato Journal* 15 (spring/summer): 101–16.

Chaum, D. 1985. "Security without Identification: Transaction Systems to Make Big Brother Obsolete." *Communications of the ACM* 28 (October): 1030–44.

Congressional Budget Office. 1996. *Emerging Electronic Methods for Making Retail Payments*. Washington, DC: U.S. Government Printing Office.

Friedman, David. 1989. *The Machinery of Freedom*, 2d ed. LaSalle, IL: Open Court Publishing.

Goodhart, Charles. 1988. *The Evolution of Central Banks*. Cambridge, MA: MIT Press.

Greenfield, Robert L., and Leland B. Yeager. 1983. "A Laissez-Faire Approach to Monetary Stability." *Journal of Money, Credit and Banking* 15 (August): 302–15.

Hayek, Friedrich A. 1976. *Denationalization of Money*. The Lancing, Sussex: Institute of Economic Affairs.

Klein, Daniel B. 1997. "Trust for Hire: Voluntary Remedies for Quality and Safety." In *Reputation: Studies in the Voluntary Elicitation of Good Conduct*, edited by Daniel B. Klein, 97–133. Ann Arbor: University of Michigan Press.

Macintosh, Kerry Lynn. 1998. "How to Encourage Global Electronic Commerce: The Case for Private Currencies on the Internet." *Harvard Journal of Law & Technology* 11 (summer): 733–96.

Muller, John D. 1998. "Selected Developments in the Law of Cyberspace Payments." *The Business Lawyer* 54 (November): 403–41.

Selgin, George A. 1988. *The Theory of Free Banking*. Totowa, NJ: Rowman & Littlefield.

Selgin, George A., and Lawrence H. White. 1994. "How Would the Invisible Hand Handle Money?" *Journal of Economic Literature* 32 (December): 1718–49.

Shelanski, Howard A. 1999. "The Speed Gap: Broadband Infrastructure and Electronic Commerce." *Berkeley Technology Law Journal* 14 (spring): 721–44.

Smith, Vera C. 1936. *The Rationale of Central Banking and the Free Banking Alternative*. Indianapolis: Liberty Press.

Solomon, Lewis D. 1996. "Local Currency: A Legal & Policy Analysis." *Kansas Journal of Law and Public Policy* 5 (winter): 59–92.

Task Force on Stored-Value Cards. 1997. "A Commercial Lawyer's Take on the Electronic Purse: An Analysis of Commercial Law Issues Associated with Stored-Value Cards and Electronic Money." *The Business Lawyer* 52 (February): 653–727.

White, Lawrence H. 1984. *Free Banking in Britain: Theory, Experience, and Debate, 1800–1845*. Cambridge: Cambridge University Press.

———. 1989. *Competition and Currency: Essays on Free Banking and Money*. New York: NYU Press.

7

Consumer Protection Regulation and Information on the Internet

John C. Moorhouse

> The real issue is whether [consumer] protection is best
> provided by "regulation" or by "free competition."
> —Manuel F. Cohen, *Can Regulatory Agencies*
> *Protect the Consumer?* 1971

> Just about everything we've ever done that has to do
> with communication and information has been digi-
> tized, and now we're going to start tackling stuff that
> hasn't been done because you can do it only with the In-
> ternet.
> —Steven Levy et al., "The Dawn of E-life," 1999

From apples to Z-cars, government regulation of consumer products
abounds. We read health warnings on cigarette packs, bake pies with sugar
rather than cyclamate, load nonflammable children's pajamas into our ef-
ficiency-rated dryers, brush no-lead paint on the walls of our low-radon
houses, serve less attractive apples because they have not been sprayed
with alar, and strap our children into certified car seats in the back so that
they will not be killed by mandatory airbags in the front.

   The announced goal of all such regulation—consumer protection and
the concomitant justification for regulation is everywhere the same—
consumer ignorance. Consumers do not and cannot know enough, it is
said, to make decisions that are in their own best interests.[1] Numerous
federal and state agencies promulgate a plethora of rules, regulations, and

standards meant to make life safer for consumers. At the national level these administrative agencies include the Consumer Products Safety Commission (CPSC), the Environmental Protection Agency (EPA), the Food and Drug Administration (FDA), the Federal Trade Commission (FTC), and the National Highway Traffic Safety Administration (NHTSA).

The asserted inability or unwillingness of the market to provide sufficient information justifies extensive government regulation of consumer products. But with few exceptions, the government provides not information[2] but restrictions on what can be sold, how it is to be sold, and how it is to be used. As Walter Oi (1977, 21) observed, "The [government] agency charged with reducing risk and accident costs . . . can produce and disseminate information. . . . Governments have almost universally rejected this informational approach. The National Commission on Product Safety asserted that consumer education has little if any impact on the accident toll."

But if a lack of information is a major justification for government consumer protection, the case for government intervention may be seriously weakened by the dramatic increase in the availability of consumer information on the Internet. This technology makes low-cost, up-to-date information readily available to consumers. This chapter explores how technological advancements affect the ability of free markets to deal effectively with consumer demand for product information and quality assurance. It discusses the alleged market failure to provide adequate consumer information, the multiplicity of ways in which consumers obtain and use information, the market devices employed to generate and distribute information, and the role that the Internet is increasingly playing in the dissemination of product and service information.

Justification for Government Intervention

To some, the necessity of government regulation of consumer products is obvious. For example, the former director of the NHTSA, Joan Claybrook (1978, 14), wrote, "In regulating for health and safety, government assumes what I believe to be one of its most basic functions, promoting the general welfare. Too many companies and industries refuse to recognize the multiple hazards of their technology and the government's legitimate interest in the public's health and safety." Others have developed theoretical arguments about the market's failure to provide the information necessary to ensure optimal consumer product quality and safety.

One of the more influential analyses of market failure was offered by Kenneth Arrow in 1962 (1972). In his essay, he contended that the market will not provide the optimal amount of information because information producers cannot appropriate a return on investment in information generation and dissemination. His argument, developed in a section of the essay entitled "Information as a Commodity," is that while the costs of researching, compiling, interpreting, and evaluating information can be substantial, they represent fixed costs at the time the information is to be disseminated. Because the marginal cost of distribution is frequently very low, anyone receiving the information can reconvey it cheaply, thus depriving the original producer of an appropriable return. "In the absence of special legal protection, the owner cannot, however, sell information on the open market" (1972, 225). Moreover, even if earning a return were possible, charging a positive price for the information that was commensurate with the necessary return, is likely to be inefficient. Arrow (1972, 225) noted that "if the [cost of distribution] were zero, then optimal allocation would obviously call for unlimited distribution of the information without cost." This public-good attribute of information, Arrow asserted, dooms its efficient provision by the market.

Arrow concluded that the market cannot provide information because it cannot offer a sufficient return and even that if it did, the allocation of information would be nonoptimal. His solution is to separate the reward for production of information from the charge to the users of information. This is accomplished by letting the government subsidize the production and dissemination of information. While Arrow originally was writing about the information surrounding invention, in principle his argument applies to any valuable information.

Writing nearly two decades later, Leland (1980, 268) observed, "As is well known, information on quality has many of the characteristics of a public good. . . . Under such circumstances inadequate resources will be channeled to providing information." Rothenberg (1993, 166, 172) argued similarly that

> perceptively safer versions of a commodity, or commodities, that can protect users against predictable hazards, will be profitable and hence likely to be produced through competitive pressure. Even some forms of precautionary information—for example, safety ratings on consumer goods—will be

generated by the market. But these will be inadequate where product performance is hard to monitor by users, where hazards are not widely or accurately perceived, or where people do not realize that they are uninformed. ... The market's myriad decentralized actions do not themselves ensure adequate safety. Centralized controls of various sorts are needed. These have been instituted in the form of regulations, constraints, information programs, licensing, and certification.

Building on Arrow's thesis, Akerlof (1970), Stiglitz (1979), and Carlton and Perloff (1994) offered models based on the assumption that markets fail to provide adequate consumer information. Given that assumption, Akerlof argued that in the absence of government regulation, low-quality products displace high-quality products, and Stiglitz predicted that prices rise higher than is compatible with competition.[3] In Akerlof's model, assume that a good comes in two qualities, high and low, and that while suppliers know the quality of their product, potential consumers do not. Moreover, customers cannot rely on the assurances of high quality from producers because such declarations would be seen as self-serving. Asymmetric information generates uncertainty among consumers who seek to purchase the high-quality good. They therefore offer a price, discounted by the uncertainty, that is below the cost of producing the high-quality good. At the prices offered, only low-quality goods survive in the market as suppliers refuse to sell high-quality goods at the discounted prices.

Stiglitz analyzed the price effects of incomplete information. Imagine an array of shops selling an identical consumer product. Searching among the stores for the best price is costly. For purposes of discussion, assume that under conditions of full information, the "competitive price" is $10 and that it costs $2 to search an additional store. With incomplete information, the owner of Arthur's Boutique believes that he can charge $12 for the good because it would cost a customer in his store $2 to check at Barbara's Smart Shop. Other storeowners come to believe that they can charge $12. But if other stores are charging $12, Arthur can now charge $14! Given the assumed initial conditions, the logic of the process leads to a monopoly price, even though a number of independent stores are competing for customers. Here, Stiglitz argued that the failure of the market to provide sufficient information leads to monopoly pricing.

Far from describing market pathologies, the models of Akerlof and Stiglitz provide insight into why the market produces and distributes so much consumer information. Consider the Akerlof lemon problem. It is because the consumer cannot accurately assess quality that the seller assures the consumer of high quality by selling brand-name merchandise coupled with guarantees, warranties, and a no-questions-asked return policy.[4] These widely employed devices reduce the risk associated with unknown product quality (Grossman 1981; Heal 1976; Viscusi 1978). Industry certification, franchise membership, and reliance on repeat buying are additional devices protecting the consumer against "lemons." The effectiveness of these devices in cultivating trust is built on the reputation of the seller, the manufacturer, and the independent certifier (Klein 1997). Even causal observation demonstrates that low-quality products do not drive high-quality products from the market. And in Stiglitz's marketplace, a single merchant need only advertise her prices to undercut overpriced competitors.

Ideas have consequences. One manifestation of the idea that markets fail to provide adequate consumer information was the passage of the Consumer Product Safety Act in 1973, which established the Consumer Product Safety Commission (CPSC). Its mission: "The CPSC is responsible for protecting the American public from unreasonable risks of injury and death from 15,000 types of consumer products" (*1999 Performance Report*, March 2000, ii). As originally conceived, the commission was to generate and disseminate information about consumer safety issues. But as Viscusi (1982, 36) found, "[The Consumer Product Safety Commission] has a positive mandate, stated clearly in the act, to pursue informational strategies as an alternative to command-and-control regulations. But it has largely ignored this mandate." Indeed, the commission quickly moved from general rule making and the promulgation of generic safety standards to adjudication and product bans and recalls.[5]

How does the CPSC identify unreasonable risk? According to Viscusi (1991, 51),

> The Consumer Product Safety Commission (CPSC) and other product safety agencies do not generally assess the presence of market failure. Typically, they do not even examine the frequency of injuries, but simply rely on injury counts that are unadjusted for intensity of activity. The existence of risk is often treated as being tantamount to evidence of the need for regulation.

Indeed, injuries are counted when an accident is associated with a product but not necessarily caused by the product (Rubin 1991, 61). In addition to employing a dubious measure of risk, Rubin (1991), Thomas (1988), and

Viscusi (1991) noted that the CPSC makes no effort to employ systematic cost-benefit analysis in its deliberations.

Did the CPSC abandon its informational function too quickly as it rushed to embrace a regulatory function? Paul Rubin (1991, 60) offered a suggestive example. Three-wheeled all-terrain vehicles are less stable, and hence more dangerous, than four-wheeled ATVs.

> When consumers learned that four-wheeled ATVs were safer, probably as the result of information put out by the agency and others, they ceased buying three-wheeled models. The CPSC negotiated a virtual ban on three-wheeled ATVs with the industry, but the ban had little, if any, effect. By the time of the ban, consumers had virtually stopped buying the three-wheeled variety.

In this instance, the informational approach appears more flexible and expeditious than a product ban. First, consumers can be informed more quickly than a ban can be put in place. Second, the dissemination of information preserves consumer choice, and third, as Rubin pointed out, it is less costly to correct errors in information than to undo the damage of an erroneous ban.

In addition, Rubin, Murphy, and Jarrell (1988) found that CPSC recalls are costly. Focusing on only one cost, the decline in a firm's value as measured by stock prices, the authors estimated that the average loss in equity value was 6.9 percent per recall. The CPSC issues about 300 recalls a year (*1999 Performance Report*, March 2000, ii). In contrast to the costs of CPSC regulations, Viscusi's empirical study (1985) found that the CPSC's bans, recalls, and mandatory standards have had no measurable effect on consumer safety. Rubin (1991, 59) reiterated that "there is no reliable public evidence that any of the CPSC's policies has saved any lives." The CPSC's own economist, in charge of the bicycle safety standards project, remarked that the agency's standards have had no statistically significant favorable effects on bicycle-related injuries. The CPSC first promulgated bicycle design standards more than 25 years ago (Petty 1994, 22).

In other words, the benefits of CPSC regulations have yet to be established. Perhaps this should not be surprising. Researchers studying the CPSC find that it devotes few resources to measuring risk, to performing rigorous cost-benefit analysis, or to generating and disseminating useful consumer information. While beyond the scope of this chapter, public-choice theory may explain why a government agency should prefer regulation and adjudication to the distribution of information to consumers.

But even if a federal agency pursues an informational function, is there any reason to think that consumers are more likely to obtain better or more timely product information from a government bureau than from a number of independent private sources operating on both sides of the market? Consider the following example. Recently, the federal government dropped saccharin from its list of cancer-causing chemicals after the release of new studies cited by the National Institute of Environmental Health that demonstrated "no clear association" between saccharin and human cancer. Before the government agency acted, the American Cancer Society, the American Medical Association, the American Dietetic Association, and the American Diabetes Association previously had given saccharin "a clean bill of health." The 2000 institute report also dropped from its list ethyl acrylate, which was used in the manufacture of latex paints and textiles (Associated Press, May 16, 2000).

The problem here is fundamental. When a state agency is vested with monopoly authority to certify, ban, or recall products, the incentives are perverse. If it fails to ban a dangerous product, the agency will come under attack, because the costs of the error are highly visible. Conversely, if the agency erroneously bans a safe product, the costs to consumers and manufacturers, though potentially large, are hidden and therefore much less likely to generate political scrutiny. Thus there is an asymmetry in the consequences to the agency of making regulatory errors. Failing to ban an unsafe product can pose a genuine threat to the agency, whereas banning a safe product occasions much less of a political risk. Prudent bureaucrats err on the side of issuing bans.[6]

The problem is compounded because products are not neatly divided into "safe" and "unsafe." The potential harmfulness of a product is measured in degrees. Such subtleties are lost on an agency put in the position of having to respond to political pressure from various constituencies "to protect the American people from unreasonable risk."[7] The agency has little incentive to perform sophisticated risk assessments or cost-benefit analyses.

By contrast, private certifiers, middlemen, and product testers competing in the market are much less likely to err systematically in one direction or to fail to provide information about the degrees of product hazard. The market process is an error-correcting process quite unlike that found in the political arena. Competition among these market participants rewards research into product quality and timeliness and accuracy in the information distributed. That private sources of consumer information are now online further reduces the likelihood that the CPSC's mandatory standards and product bans play a critical role in protecting consumers. In difficult, even controversial, cases, open exchange and debate are more likely in the private sector—leaving the final responsibility to weigh the evidence with the consumer.

How Consumers Acquire and Use Information

If we insist on elevating the static, textbook conditions of "perfect competition" to a normative standard for evaluating market performance, the market will fail by definition. Efficiency, properly understood, must include the transaction costs of gathering information, market search, product evaluation, and negotiation. Like the frictionless plane of physics, "perfect information" may be a useful fiction when answering certain economic questions, but the assumption does not help us evaluate policies for a world in which gathering and assessing consumer information are costly.

An honest assessment of alternative policies must include an analysis of the costs of regulation and the potential for regulatory failure. Even a world in which markets perform with less than textbook perfection, regulation does not win by default. A number of recent studies have demonstrated that product quality and safety regulations either have failed to protect the consumer or have deprived the consumer of desirable, sometimes lifesaving, products.[8]

The nature of information may represent less a source of problems than a set of opportunities for sellers to win customers. To understand the role of information in market exchange, it is useful to consider the sources of consumer information and how individuals actually use information when making consumption choices.

Consumers use a wide variety of sources of product information, including personal experience, friends and acquaintances, manufacturers and vendors of goods, and independent suppliers of consumer product information. For example, repeat business is based on the experiences of satisfied consumers. Not only must producers supply a satisfactory good, they also must reduce the cost to the consumer of identifying and finding the good again. The latter is achieved through branding and advertising. Friends, colleagues, and acquaintances can be a rich source of information based on market experiences. All of us have asked friends to recommend an auto mechanic, a dentist, or realtor or about their experiences with house paint, an automobile, a grocery chain, or a private school. In addition, we ask friends to recommend sources of consumer information. The personal experiences of friends remain a major source of consumer information because of their low cost, prompt acquisition, and trust in their accuracy.

Producers provide information about goods and services through electronic and print advertising and consumer trade fairs. Because advertising is understood to be self-interested, its credibility must be vouched for by reputation. In turn, commercial reputation is established by citing the duration of a firm's history; by conducting business in an attractive facility; by selling brand-name goods; by displaying memberships in trade associations, including the local Chamber of Commerce and the Better Business Bureau; and by hiring celebrity spokespersons to grace advertisements.

Hiring Michael Jordan as a spokesperson and conducting business in a well-appointed facility are meant to convey substance and commitment. Consumers intuit that such sunk investments, which produce neither direct product quality nor specific consumer information, can be recovered only if the firm remains in business. These investments are hostage to continuing good consumer relations. Such investments signal an intention to conduct business with an eye to the long haul and suggests that an ongoing enterprise will offer quality products at competitive prices and follow up with acceptable consumer services.[9]

Determining the quality of different types of goods uses very different approaches to gathering information. For example, only by eating a breakfast cereal, drinking a particular wine, or wearing a certain perfume will an individual learn whether or not he or she likes the product and wants to purchase it again. An advertisement picturing a beautiful woman putting on a particular fragrance may associate the perfume with glamour and sex appeal, but it cannot inform a consumer as to how the fragrance will interact with her body chemistry. While critics of advertising scold about the emptiness of such advertising, it is precisely the case of experience goods that there are no sources of useful consumer information ex ante. All such advertisements can do is attempt to get consumers to try the product (Nelson 1974; Telser 1974).

Agglomeration economies make full use of consumers' reliance on sellers' reputations. Department stores offer a vast array of goods and services within a single store. Added shopping convenience is only a partial explanation. A store known for its good dress and fine china departments is unlikely to have a poor beauty salon and men's furnishings department. Thus, a store can leverage established reputations into other departments and product lines. Such strategies have value precisely in those cases in which reputation and consumer service matter the most.

The golden arches sign along the highway instantly conveys information to the traveler about the array, quality, and price of the food offered by the restaurant, whether the McDonald's is in Winston-Salem or Bozeman. The establishment of national and regional store chains allows a retailer's reputation to be established quickly, at low cost, and in new locations. This enhances competition while permitting the retailer's reputation to redound to the products, including the unbranded ones that she sells. Conversely, national product brand names may be a substitute for investing in establishing a local business reputation (Png and Reitman 1995). Standardized, prepackaged brand products, from Del Monte canned corn and Titleist golf balls to Imation computer disks and Camel cigarettes can be purchased with confidence about quality from a full-service shop, a local discounter, or a corner mom-and-pop convenience store.

Finally, independent sources of consumer information abound. *Consumer Reports, Consumer Digest*, plus literally hundreds of specialty magazines, books, newspaper columns, and radio and television programs disseminate information about products, services, and businesses to consumers. Trade associations, consumer groups, special-interest clubs, *Good Housekeeping*, Underwriters Laboratories, and J. D. Power all stand ready to certify the quality of products and services. Agents supplying independent certification have an incentive to remain objective and fair because the authenticity of their recommendations is all that keeps them in business. By the same token, manufacturers and retailers have an incentive to acquire good ratings and publicize them.

Consumers do not need to be *generally* knowledgeable about the multiplicity of consumer products. Instead, they need and seek *pointed information* in the initial stage of acquiring a particular good or service. A consumer need not be generally knowledgeable about 18-speed mountain bikes, digital cameras, or gas grills if he does not bike, take pictures, or cook out. Only when a good shows up on their radar screen do consumers seek specific and timely information to assist them in making sound consumption choices. Thus evidence that consumers are not well informed about consumer products in general has no implications about the adequacy of the market in providing information or the wisdom of the consumer in remaining ignorant (Klein 2000, 32–33).

Furthermore as Klein (1997) argued, consumers may need only *assurance* of product quality and safety, not comprehensive information. Technical information may be of little use to the consumer. Consumers need not understand the intricacies of lens alignment in a pair of binoculars to make a sound selection and are rarely put in a position in which they must repair a product or explain the side effects of a prescription medicine. Indeed, the market may simplify the knowledge required to make a sound decision. In turn, that can reduce the costs of acquiring and interpreting useful information. Brand names, reputation, warranties, and seals of approval all are assurances that substitute for detailed technical knowledge.

In many cases in which information about products or product characteristics is difficult to obtain and assess, the market offers ex post protection that reduces consumer uncertainty at the time of purchase. Guarantees, warranties, and return policies provide this assurance. The value of these devices is enhanced by the use of brand names that permit consumers to draw on direct product experience. Their use is also made more valuable when employed by established retailers.

How the Internet Has Changed the Equation

In 1999 an estimated 80 million Americans had direct access to the Internet (Levy et al. 1999, 40). A communications revolution is under way that includes not only growth in e-commerce and an altogether new means for the direct delivery of digitized goods and services but also the Internet as a prompt, low-cost, convenient source of up-to-date consumer information.

Indeed change is coming so quickly in the way retailers conduct business and in the growth of Web firms that specialize in providing independent consumer information that there is no way of cataloging the informational services currently available on the Internet. Instead I can only suggest the types of informational services offered. Jacob Schlesinger (1999, A1) pointed out that with the advent of the Internet, "shoppers have two powerful new weapons—information about what competitors around the country are charging for goods, and easy access to those goods online if the nearby merchant won't deal."

The technology exists today to transmit data, images, and text from any Internet site to any other designated site or sites and to do so at high speed and low cost. Any information good that can be reduced to a string of digital code can be transmitted over the Internet. These information goods include books, scholarly journals, magazines, reports, maps, graphic images, pictures, data, test results, service bulletins, software, financial analyses, educational materials, and the evaluation of legal, medical, and other professional services.

Internet technology has shifted the margin of effectiveness between private and public sources of consumer information. The Internet provides up-to-date consumer information about an incredible array of goods and services at very low cost. Perhaps its singular advantage is the breadth of consumer products covered. A person need only access the Internet to find information about virtually any good or service. The Internet is a one-stop source of consumer information.

In addition, different types of information are readily available from technical reports and product reviews to certification lists and personal experiences reported by members of specialized user groups. A bad product review posted on the Internet can quickly reach tens of thousands of consumers. The Internet is magnifying the adverse consequences concomitant with marketing uncompetitive low-quality and unsafe products.

Household names such as *Consumer Reports, Consumer Digest,* and the Better Business Bureau have gone online to provide consumer information. The first two charge a fee for service. PriceSCAN is one of a number of sites that displays the prices and shipping charges of suppliers of hundreds of consumer products, from books to videos, affording the Internet user the opportunity to make side-by-side comparisons. Hundreds of specialized user groups, chat rooms, support groups, and clubs exist that permit Internet users to draw interactively on the experiences of others with consumer goods and services. Such sources of information are convenient, inexpensive, and continually updated. CoinUniverse lets prospective buyers determine market prices of rare coins before contacting dealers. The Professional Numismatic Guild protects buyers of rare coins by offering online arbitration should a dispute arise between buyers and Guild member dealers (*Barron's,* July 19, 1999, 24). The latest version of vendor catalogs are routinely placed on the Internet and offer timely information about merchandise, prices, warranties, return policies, and ordering security. Many Web sites publish reviews and test results. The Internet has given new meaning to the notion of comparison shopping.

Consumers are turning in increasing numbers to a growing variety of professional services offered on the Internet. At least 170 firms offer online brokerage services, some of which are full-service brokerage houses offering stock reports and market analysis. As Edward Iwata (1999, B1) observed about Internet financial services, "There's a goldmine of information out there and much of it is free." Besides brokerage services, interactive family financial-planning programs are available on the Internet. By supplying personal data, customers can use these programs to assess the adequacy of their insurance coverage, portfolio diversification, saving rate, and risk management. A growing number of households are doing their banking via the Internet. E-banking permits customers to check account balances, transfer funds, pay bills, and apply for loans, all with a high level of security. A number of Internet firms specialize in brokering consumer and real estate loans. The Internet facilitates the canvassing of a large number of lenders, thereby allowing consumers to secure more competitive terms than those offered by local financial intermediaries. Better information and heightened competition—both made possible by the Internet—afford consumers more protection than does periodic government certification.

E-shopping also permits individuals to purchase real assets. Increasingly, real estate and major consumer purchases, including automobiles and appliances, are being made over the Internet. In an economy of high labor mobility, the Internet affords the opportunity to explore the full range of real estate offerings in local and distant communities before actual traveling there for firsthand assessment. Additional information about a community's climate, schools, and taxation, for example, is readily available on the Internet. Real estate tours on the Internet enhance the effectiveness and reduce the expense of finding a home. Such readily available information undermines the rationale for licensure of real estate agents.

CARFAX provides a measure of protection to consumers purchasing used automobiles by allowing individuals to trace the title of any automobile sold in the United States. No federal or state government agency provides such information. Millions of families regularly plan their vacations and make hotel, automobile, and airline reservations over the Internet. Again, the chief advantage of using the Internet is the ease with which people can identify and sort through a long list of options, selecting those that come closest to meeting their price and service demands. By facilitating such comparison shopping, the Internet reduces the need for state business regulation of public accommodations and public transportation. How can state certification and regulations compete with assessments, updated daily, from actual users of travel agents, hotels, and transportation services?

With Internet financial advice as a model, national and regional professional associations are planning Web sites for offering legal and medical advice. Such services could permit a local attorney to consult with distant specialists or access a reference library in which case precedents are updated daily. Already Law.com provides information about legal processes free and e-law services for a fee (Lublin 1999, B1). Similarly a physician can obtain specialized diagnostic assistance or tap into a frequently updated database. From there it is but a small step to develop Internet services offering consultation to those seeking health care advice. HealthSurfing and WebMD permit customers to obtain medical information. Intel's e-Medicine links physicians directly with their patients and facilitates timely consultation and the exchange of medical test results. Privacy is protected by information security firms (Kornblum 1999, A1). MVP provides health information (Lublin 1999, B1). The latest in medical research is available to the layperson on HealthGate Data's Web site. The site publishes articles from the *New England Journal of Medicine* (Johannes 1999, B1).

HealthAxis, eHealthInsurance, and QuickenInsureMarket are, according to Marilyn Chase (1999, B1), "among the companies letting consumers take a more active role in choosing their health insurance coverage, a process that has traditionally been mediated by agents." Better pricing is the result because consumers are better informed, there is more competition, selling costs are reduced, and customers make more comparisons. Furthermore, consumers are using these sources of health information. Jupiter Communications reports that 45 percent of Internet users have sought health care information on the Web (Kornblum 1999, A1). The low-cost availability of such information reduces the need for licensing professionals as a means of protecting consumers.[10]

New companies such as NetEffect are helping existing Web companies improve their consumer services by setting up help buttons, e-mail linkages, and facilities for answering consumer questions in real time (Meyers 1999, B1). BigStep, an Internet mall, provides a well-advertised location for new Web start-up companies. The companies tend to be small and deal in retail consumer products and services. By screening companies before they set up a site at BigStep, the latter provide at least a modicum of consumer protection and the reputational economies usually associated with bricks and mortar shopping centers (Weber 1999, B1).

An array of useful information awaits the consumer online: reading reviews, test results, or consumer reports; identifying alternative products and associated options; engaging in comparison shopping; auditioning a product; and exchanging views in a chat room. The Web's comparative advantage lies in its low costs of organizing, storing, retrieving, and transmitting information. The information can take the form of text, pictures, graphic images, data, audio, and video. User groups provide access to highly specialized information bringing together sometimes thousands of individuals in a coordinated exchange of information and opinions. Much of the information available on the Internet is free—perhaps an ironic market answer to Arrow's optimal pricing criterion.[11] In addition, Internet technology ushers in a new era of competition because thousands of new online firms have been created and because e-commerce is conducted on world markets. The welfare-enhancing effects of Internet information on competition follow even if only a fraction of consumers avail themselves of and act on that information. Competitive responses are triggered at the margin. Products and firms earning bad reviews on the Internet lose customers. Those losses occasion improvement in product quality and consumer service or business failure. It is simply not the case that most or all consumers must access the Web in order for the Internet to contribute to consumer protection in general.

Market processes are not ideal. Information remains costly to obtain and evaluate. Mistakes will be made. The point is that the Internet drastically reduces consumer information costs and therefore improves consumer choice. In addition, common-law remedies against misrepresentation and fraud may provide legal redress.

Conclusion

Markets exist for the generation and dissemination of consumer information. Entrepreneurs attempt to economize on the amount and complexity of the information desired by consumers in order to make cogent choices. The burgeoning use of the Internet as a tool of consumer research reflects the first phenomenon, while the substitution of assurance, reputation, and trust for detailed consumer information reflects the second. In addition, after-purchase remedies reduce consumer risk associated with unknown product quality. Such ex post devices as warranties, return policies, and pay-only-if-satisfied sale terms reduce transaction costs by economizing on costly ex ante information. To the extent that consumer protection regulation is based on the claim that consumers lack adequate information, the case for government intervention is weakened by the Internet's powerful and unprecedented ability to provide timely and pointed consumer information.

NOTES

1. An argument that is widely accepted is that consumers systematically underestimate the risk of death from activities that have a relatively high hazard rate and overestimate the risk from sources with low hazard rates. New evidence, however, finds to the contrary that consumers gather and use information efficiently in estimating risk (see Benjamin and Dougan 1997; Benjamin, Dougan, and Buschena 1999).

2. From my examples of regulations, only the warning on a cigarette pack and the energy efficiency rating for a clothes dryer constitute government-provided information.

3. See, for example, the intermediate microeconomic theory textbooks by Landsberg (1999) and Perloff (1999).

4. Akerlof mentions some of these "counteracting institutions" like guarantees, brand names, and franchises.

5. For a more complete discussion by a former commissioner on how the CPSC operates, see Scanlon and Rogowsky 1984.

6. On a related issue, Thomas's empirical study finds that CPSC regulations are "excessively stringent" (1988, 113).

7. Political pressure can compromise the quality of consumer decisions in other ways. Organized pressure by highly interested regulated firms can prevent a government agency from releasing potentially useful consumer information. For example, until recently the Federal Aviation Administration refused to release data on airline flight delays, baggage losses, or accident rates even though the FAA collects such data.

8. Often the threat to consumer welfare is exaggerated by regulatory agencies. For examples, see Abelson 1991 on radon; Adler 1992 on lead; Avery 1998 on pesticide standards; Blevins 1997, Higgs 1995, Hudgins 1997, and Ward 1992 on the FDA; Gough 1997 on the EPA; Kazman 1997 on airbags; Levy and Marimont 1998 on deaths from smoking; McKenzie and Shughart 1987 on airline safety after deregulation; and Whelan 1999 on cyclamates.

9. For more discussion of the economics of signaling product quality, see Allen 1984; De Alessi and Staaf 1992; Ippolito 1990; and Shapiro 1983.

10. Also see Ginsburg and Moy 1992 on other new technologies that reduce the benefits of physician licensure and, more generally, Carroll and Gaston 1983 and Rottenberg 1980 on occupational licensure.

11. Usually firms posting advertisements on a Web site pay for the information made available to consumers.

REFERENCES

Abelson, Philip H. 1991. "The Radon Threat: The Role of Flimflam in Public Policy." *Regulation* 14, no. 4: 95–100.

Adler, Jonathan H. 1992. "Is Lead a Heavy Threat?" *Regulation* 15 (fall): 13–15.

Akerlof, George A. 1970. "The Market for Lemons: Quality Uncertainty and the Market Mechanism." *Quarterly Journal of Economics* 84: 448–500.

Allen, Franklin. 1984. "Reputation and Product Quality." *Rand Journal of Economics* 15 (autumn): 311–27.

Arrow, Kenneth J. 1972. "Economic Welfare and the Allocation of Resources for Invention." In *Readings in Industrial Economics*, vol. 2, edited by Charles K. Rowley, 219–36. New York: Crane, Russak.

Associated Press. 2000. "Government Takes Saccharin off List of Cancer-Causing Chemicals." *Winston-Salem Journal*, May 16, A3.

Avery, Alex. 1998. "Pesticide Pole Vaulting." *Regulation* 21 (spring): 8–9.

Benjamin, Daniel K., and William R. Dougan. 1997. "Individuals' Estimates of the Risks of Death: Part I—A Reassessment of the Previous Evidence." *Journal of Risk and Uncertainty* 15: 115–33.

Benjamin, Daniel K., William R. Dougan, and David Buschena. 1999. "Individuals' Estimates of the Risks of Death: Part II—New Evidence." Unpublished manuscript.

Blevins, Sue A. 1997. "FDA: Keeping Medication from Patients." *Regulation* 20 (winter): 13–14.

Carlton, Dennis W., and Jeffrey M. Perloff. 1994. *Modern Industrial Organization*. 2d ed. New York: HarperCollins.

Carroll, Sidney L., and Robert J. Gaston. 1983. "Occupational Licensure and the Quality of Service: An Overview." *Law and Human Behavior* 7 (September): 139–46.

Chase, Marilyn. 1999. "An E-Shopper's Guide to Health Insurance As It Moves to the Web." *Wall Street Journal*, October 22, B1.

Claybrook, Joan. 1978. "Crying Wolf." *Regulation* 2, no. 6: 14–16.

Consumer Products Safety Commission (CPSC). 2000. *1999 Performance Report*. Washington, DC: Consumer Products Safety Commission.

De Alessi, Louis, and R. J. Staaf. 1992. "What Does Reputation Really Assure? The Relationship of Trademarks to Expectations and Legal Remedies." *Economic Inquiry* 32 (July): 477–85.

Demsetz, Harold. 1972. "Information and Efficiency: Another Viewpoint." In *Readings in Industrial Economics*, vol. 2, edited by Charles K. Rowley, 237–62. New York: Crane, Russak.

Ginsburg, Paul B., and Ernest Moy. 1992. "Physician Licensure and the Quality of Care: The Role of New Information Technologies." *Regulation* 15 (fall): 32–39.

Gough, Michael. 1997. "EPA's Sham Science Reveals Political Agenda." *Regulation* 20 (winter): 15–16.

Grossman, Sanford J. 1981. "The Informational Role of Warranties and the Private Disclosure about Product Quality." *Journal of Law and Economics* 24: 461–83.

Heal, Geoffrey. 1976. "Do Bad Products Drive out Good?" *Quarterly Journal of Economics* 90 (August): 499–502.

Higgs, Robert. 1995. *Hazardous to Our Health? FDA Regulations of Health Care Products.* Oakland, CA: Independent Institute.

Hudgins, Edward L. 1997. "Kessler's FDA: An Autopsy." *Regulation* 20 (winter): 10–12.

Ippolito, Pauline M. 1990. "Bonding and Nonbonding Signals of Product Quality." *Journal of Business* 63: 41–60.

Iwata, Edward. 1999. "The Web Becomes Rich Resource for Investors." *Winston-Salem Journal*, October 18, B1.

Johannes, Laura. 1999. "Medical Journal Faces Questions over Web Deal." *Wall Street Journal*, October 26, B1.

Kazman, Sam. 1997. "NHTSA Air Bag Mandate Misfires." *Regulation* 20 (winter): 17–18.

Klein, Daniel B. 1997. "Trust for Hire: Voluntary Remedies for Quality and Safety." In *Reputation*, edited by Daniel B. Klein, 97–133. Ann Arbor: University of Michigan Press.

———. 2000. *Assurance and Trust in a Great Society.* Irvington-on-Hudson, NY: Foundation for Economic Education.

Kornblum, Janet. 1999. "Intel Seeks to Protect E-medicine." *USA Today*, October 12, A1.

Landsburg, Steven E. 1999. *Price Theory.* 4th ed. Cincinnati: South-Western College Publishing.

Leland, Hayne E. 1980. "Minimum-Quality Standards and Licensing in Markets with Asymmetric Information." In *Occupational Licensure and Regulation*, edited by Simon Rottenberg, 265–84. Washington, DC: American Enterprise Institute.

Levy, Robert A., and Rosalind B. Marimont. 1998. "Lies, Damned Lies, & 400,000 Smoking-Related Deaths." *Regulation* 21, no. 4: 24–29.

Levy, Steven, et al. 1999. "The Dawn of E-life." *Newsweek*, September 20, 38–78.

Lublin, Joann S. 1999. "To Find CEOs, Web Firms Rev up Search Engines." *Wall Street Journal*, October 26, B1.

McKenzie, Richard B., and William F. Shughart II. 1987. "Deregulation and Air Travel Safety." *Regulation* 11, nos. 3 and 4: 42–47.

Meyers, Bill. 1999. "Service with an E-smile." *USA Today*, October 12, B1.

Nelson, Philip. 1974. "Advertising as Information." *Journal of Political Economy* 81: 729–54.

Oi, Walter. 1977. "Safety at Any Price?" *Regulation* 1, no. 3: 16–23.

Perloff, Jeffrey M. 1999. *Microeconomics*. Reading, MA: Addison-Wesley.

Petty, Ross D. 1994. "Bicycle Safety: A Case Study in Regulatory Review." *Regulation* 17, no. 2: 22–24.

Png, I. P. L., and David Reitman. 1995. "Why Are Some Products Branded and Others Not?" *Journal of Law and Economics* 38: 207–24.

Rothenberg, Jerome. 1993. "Social Strategy and the Tactics in the Search for Safety." *Critical Review* 7: 159–80.

Rottenberg, Simon, ed. 1980. *Occupational Licensure and Regulation*. Washington, DC: American Enterprise Institute.

Rubin, Paul H. 1991. "Why Regulate Consumer Product Safety?" *Regulation* 14, no. 4: 58–63.

Rubin, Paul H., R. Dennis Murphy, and Gregg Jarrell. 1988. "Risky Products, Risky Stock." *Regulation* 12, no. 1: 35–39.

Scanlon, Terrence, and Robert A. Rogowsky. 1984. "Back-Door Lawmaking at the CPSC." *Regulation* 8, no. 4: 27–30.

Schlesinger, Jacob. 1999. "New E-economy." *Wall Street Journal*, October 18, A1.

Shapiro, Carl. 1983. "Premiums for High Quality Products as Returns to Reputations." *Quarterly Journal of Economics* 98: 659–79.

Stigler, George J. 1961. "The Economics of Information." *Journal of Political Economy* 69: 213–25.

Stigler, George J., and Manuel F. Cohen. 1971. *Can Regulatory Agencies Protect the Consumer?* Washington, DC: American Enterprise Institute.

Stiglitz, Joseph E. 1979. "Equilibrium in Product Markets with Imperfect Information." *American Economic Review* 69: 339–45.

Telser, Lester G. 1974. "Advertising and the Consumer." In *Advertising and Society*, edited by Yale Brozen, 25–42. New York: NYU Press.

Thomas, L. G. 1988. "Revealed Bureaucratic Preference: Priorities of the Consumer Products Safety Commission." *Rand Journal of Economics* 19: 102–13.

Viscusi, W. Kip. 1978. "A Note on 'Lemons' Markets with Quality Certification." *Bell Journal of Economics* 9: 277–79.

———. 1982. "Health and Safety." *Regulation* 6, no. 1: 34–36.

———. 1985. "Consumer Behavior and the Safety Effects of Product Safety Regulation." *Journal of Law and Economics* 28: 527–54.

———. 1991. " Risk Perceptions in Regulation, Tort Liability, and the Market." *Regulation* 14, no. 4: 50–57.

Ward, Michael R. 1992. "Drug Approval Overregulation." *Regulation* 15 (fall): 47–53.

Weber, Thomas. 1999. "Instant Web Stores Herald a Dizzying Era of Desktop Retailing." *Wall Street Journal*, October 4, B1.

Whelan, Elizabeth. 1999. "The Bitter Truth about a Sweetener Scare." *Wall Street Journal*, August 26, A27.

8

Medical Licensing
Existing Public Policy and Technological Change

Shirley V. Svorny

Medical licensing is required in all fifty of the United States. State medical boards may deny individuals the right to practice medicine if they (1) do not meet state-defined standards for training or (2) are found to be incompetent or malfeasant. Licensure is thought to provide information to consumers about physicians' training and competence. It is also thought to deter malpractice by physicians who offer services they are not competent to perform or inappropriately prescribe controlled substances.

With technological change—primarily innovations in computer hardware and software—the rationale for public-sector intervention in the form of physician licensing has weakened. It is now feasible to provide consumers with direct, online access to information about physicians' education, training, and specialty certification. At the same time, consumers may be made aware of a physician's history of malpractice claims and settlements, hospital disciplinary actions, and fraudulent behavior.

Even more important to consumer protection is the fact that in health care provider organizations, technology has made the practice of medicine observable through software that allows providers to profile the practice patterns of individual physicians. Physicians are compared with others in the same field. This innovation, teamed with increased liability on the part of institutional health care providers, protects consumers. Practice outliers are identified, counseled, and, if necessary, "deselected."

In regard to the incentive effects of licensing—those that discourage opportunistic behavior on the part of physicians—technology has made existing deterrents redundant. We no longer need the loss of license hanging over physicians as the proverbial stick to deter malfeasance. Instead, the access to information in databases has created a new, substantial penalty for malfeasance: public knowledge. For example, the ability to make judgments public has upped the ante in malpractice cases, as physicians want to avoid the loss of reputation that results from public disclosure.

Improvements in computer hardware and software likewise have made it possible to limit the inappropriate prescription of controlled substances, an area of abuse that has been a major cause of state medical disciplinary actions over the years. Prescription activity can now be monitored on a nearly real-time basis. In several states where prescriptions are monitored, forgeries and falsifications have been virtually eliminated.

This chapter documents the progress in monitoring physicians and providing consumers with direct access to information about physicians and other service providers. As these efforts increase, the case for state spending on medical licensing and discipline weakens. Where information is widely available, it is hard to argue that state medical boards add to quality assurance in the market for physician services.

Arguments Supporting Government Regulation of Medical Professionals

A popular view is that consumers need the guidance of a public agency to assess the quality of physicians' service.[1] Licensure is defended as guaranteeing minimum quality in a situation in which risk cannot be sufficiently insured and information is imperfect (Arrow 1963).

Opponents of licensure have long argued that certification (under which training is verified, but uncertified practitioners are not barred from providing care) gives consumers the same information but is less restrictive and intrusive.[2] Furthermore, some people have suggested that the government need not intervene at all, that in a purely market system, if individual and institutional reputation did not offer sufficient protection to consumers, private credentialing agencies could be expected to emerge (Friedman 1962).

A justification for licensing over certification is that licensing increases the penalties for malfeasance (Svorny 1987). By limiting entry and reducing competition from nonphysician service providers, licensing inflates physicians' incomes. Physicians who engage in opportunistic or fraudulent behavior face a substantial loss if their behavior is discovered and their license is revoked.[3] In this view, state licensing adds to market penalties (such as loss of reputation) to deter malfeasance.

In summary, state licensing has been defended as a means of assuring consumers and discouraging physician malfeasance. With the advent of the computer age, state efforts in this regard are increasingly redundant to market outcomes. Computer hardware and software offer wide access to information, which serves both to inform consumers and deter physician malfeasance. Technological change has led to the real-time assessment of physicians' performance, which offers health care consumers substantially increased protection from physicians' malfeasance.

Public Knowledge

Innovations in computer software and hardware have dramatically changed the market for physicians' services by increasing the amount of information available to consumers. Information was once so sparse as to encourage some economists to argue that medical markets in large, densely populated communities did not have the information transmission mechanisms to support competition among practitioners: "Consumers cannot accurately catalog in their minds what they hear about thirty different physicians . . . therefore, as the number of physicians within the community increases, the quality of information consumers have concerning physicians' relative qualifications and prices declines" (Pauly and Satterthwaite 1981, 490). Today, however, a great deal of information is available, much of it on the Internet. For example, Los Angeles's Cedars-Sinai Hospital maintains a Web page (www.csccc.com/physicians) that lists physicians' training, fellowships, board certifications, faculty positions, and clinical expertise. Consumers interested in a physician's specialty board certification can access this information through the American Board of Medical Specialties' Web site (www.certifieddoctors.com). The Web site includes information on physicians certified by the American Board of Medical Specialties' twenty-four member boards. More detail on certification is available for a fee: "Official Certification Data Reports" include the date on which a physician received his or her specialty certification and the date on which the certification expires.

This access to information about a physician, which includes his or her area of specialization, length of specialty training, and experience, is superior to the simple verification of medical training provided by traditional licensing. But where consumers have access to such information, it is not clear why they should desire assurance in the form of a state-granted license.

In addition to checking a physician's training and certifications, consumers can now judge the quality of the provider group to which that physician belongs. For example, a private provider, PacifiCare, posts performance indexes on its Web site (www.Pacificare.com/california) for the physician groups in its network (Chesanow 1999). Along the same lines, United HealthCare has announced its intention to make performance-related information about doctors and hospitals available to millions of patients across the United States (Butler 1998).

Information is available on health plans as well. The Web site of the Pacific Business Group on Health (www.healthscope.org)—a coalition of West Coast employers—provides information about the quality of preventive care and patient satisfaction for specific health maintenance organizations (HMOs). It includes statistics on health plan accreditation, physician groups' opinions of health maintenance organizations, and health maintenance organization quit rates.

Besides access to information on physician groups and health plans, consumers can also surf the Web for information about diseases and methods of treatment.[4] A patient suffering from a rare disease has access to medical information relevant to his or her condition. Through various Internet sites and libraries, patients have direct and free interface with MEDLINE, the software that physicians use to search medical journals (www.ncbi.nlm.nih.gov/PubMed). And patients can interact with one another directly online. For example, the Association of Cancer Online Resources information system (www.acor.org) offers access to approximately one hundred electronic mailing lists and direct links to patient sites (Smith 1998). If a physician fails to offer a range of treatment options, a patient is more likely to know what questions to ask. With the emotional support of those who have been in the same situation, the patient may seek a second opinion, offering protection from physician incompetence, and is more likely to learn about successful unconventional approaches.

An important consequence of this access to information is that the penalty for malfeasance has increased. The magnitude of the disciplinary function generated by public access to information is evidenced by physicians' efforts to defend against malpractice claims that, at one time, would have been settled (Goodman 1999). As information technology improves, market penalties for malpractice grow, and the justification for public intervention in the form of state medical licensing and discipline diminishes.

Public versus Private Data Provision

To date, a significant portion of collecting data on individual physicians has been mandated and controlled by the federal and state governments. Established by the Health Care Quality Improvement Act of 1986, the National Practitioner Data Bank (NPDB) was set up as a central source of information on physicians (Setness 1996). The data bank is supported by user fees and essentially enjoys a monopoly position, as hospitals and other health maintenance organizations are required to check periodically on the physicians with whom they have contracted. The data bank includes reports on medical malpractice payments, adverse licensure actions, adverse clinical privilege actions, and adverse professional society membership actions (NPDB 1999). It is the utmost irony that politicians have withheld access to the database from consumers and that legislation to remedy this has failed to garner sufficient support in the U.S. Congress (Rogers 1998).

The NPDB does not offer comprehensive coverage of physician malpractice. Consequently, some physicians have been able to keep their names out of the NPDB by bargaining out of settlements at the last minute, leaving their professional corporations to shoulder the liability (a "corporate shield") (Guglielmo 1996; NPDB 1999). Also, the adoption of alternative dispute resolution by managed care organizations, which requires members to agree to arbitrated settlements, has kept some physicians out of the data bank. Under this arrangement, a managed care organization, rather than the doctor who provided the service, is named in a malpractice complaint (Guglielmo 1996).

Federal and state efforts presume that physicians would not be privately credentialed in an unregulated market, but to some extent, they have been. As discussed earlier, hospitals, managed care providers, and other agencies make information about physicians' training, specialty certification, and expertise available to the general public.

What would the situation be if there were no government-mandated data banks or any government-mandated reporting requirements? For most physicians, the reputation of the managed care organization with which they contract might be sufficient to offer consumers assurances about service quality. If the reputation of the managed care provider were not sufficient assurance, physicians would have an incentive to reveal information about themselves voluntarily.

Without state licensing or public credentialing, we would expect private associations of physicians to be formed. Such groups would have an incentive to review all possible information, including information that could be hidden from the NPDB, when determining which physicians to include. As with organizations that offer specialty certification, these groups would work to enhance the market value of member physicians by setting standards and admitting only those physicians who met their standards.

Physicians who chose not to reveal information or who were rejected on the basis of group standards would be notable for their absence. Certainly, the weakest quality assurance would surround those physicians who either would not open their records for verification and review or who were not associated with a reputable hospital or managed care provider.

It is likely that new or existing private companies will assume the task of recording public information and selling it to interested parties. More informally, as the Internet reaches more libraries and homes, the access to knowledge of other patients' experiences with particular physicians may prove to be the best private credentialing of all.

Mandated, subsidized public-sector Web sites suggest the type of data that might be voluntarily provided and certified on private Web sites in the absence of government intervention.[5] In Massachusetts, the information provided includes demographics of the physician's practice, education and training, awards received, participation in peer-reviewed publications, disciplinary history, and paid malpractice claims and settlements. Some states disclose criminal convictions, serious misdemeanors, and final disciplinary actions by a state licensing board or hospital. California, for example, offers information on license status, out-of-state discipline history, felony convictions, accusations filed by the attorney general, malpractice judgments, and loss of hospital staff privileges.

Monitoring

One of the reasons that consumers have increased access to information about physicians is that for both economic and quality-of-care reasons, providers have begun to monitor individual physicians. Computer software allows organizations to gather data and compare physicians' practice patterns.

Physician profiling looks directly at patterns of care and resource use. A profile might show how a physician's treatment of a specific diagnosis compares with those of his peers, based on length of stay, cost per case, and tests and procedures administered. A study of physicians who are part of the United HealthCare network made front-page news when it found scores of physicians failing to prescribe essential prescription drugs and failing to order appropriate diagnostic tests (Butler 1998).

Ahwah and Karpiel (1997) described the software available for profiling emergency room physicians and reported on an effort by the American College of Emergency Physicians to develop clinical practice guidelines against which physicians can be measured. Similarly, the American Medical Association's Accreditation Program is working on a long-term project to set criteria by which physicians' performance can be evaluated on a disease-by-disease basis (Chesanow 1999).

One encouraging, even remarkable, observation is that physicians do respond when given information about their own behavior. When told that they practice outside the norm or that certain procedures are ineffective, there is anecdotal evidence that they change their practice patterns (Chesanow 1999; Montague 1994). One hospital administrator is quoted as saying, "Physicians are extremely responsive to getting good information. We have already seen a significant improvement in care quality" (Gilbert 1998). When physicians don't respond, managed care organizations use profiling to decide which ones will participate in its network (Krentz and Miller 1998).

The ability to monitor physicians' actions increases the probability of identifying incompetence or malfeasance. By shortening the lag time on identifying incompetence and malfeasance, the computer-aided monitoring of physicians offers patients more protection than the disciplinary function of licensing ever could. The importance of license suspension and revocation thus diminishes in the overall effort to ensure physicians' service quality.

Incentives for Peer Review

In the past, it was not uncommon for physicians to be criticized for maintaining a "code of silence," that is, for being unwilling to report incidents of peer malpractice (Crane 1999). Recent changes in the health care industry, however, have contributed to a willingness to engage in peer review. The first is the move toward managed care, in which institutional providers of health care contract with large numbers of physicians for patient care. Managed care is an increasingly important source of pressure for physician profiling and peer review, as managed care providers, induced by the market to promote quality and reduce unnecessary spending, evaluate the performance of their physicians.[6] Capitation payment schemes—under which the financial risk of patient care is shifted from insurers to provider groups—are thought to further motivate efforts toward physician profiling and peer review.

On the judicial side, changes in how people perceive the role of hospitals and managed care providers have led courts in the United States to shift the liability for physician malpractice toward the institutions with which the physicians contract. This shift in liability has strengthened the incentives to review physicians' practice patterns.

Market-Based Incentives for Peer Review

The greater interest in peer review is, to some extent, the result of competition among health care insurers and providers. For example, it is now common for large corporate employers and public-sector employee organizations to request information on hospitals' success rates and physicians' practice patterns from the managed care plans with which they contract. The National Committee for Quality Assurance, a private, nonprofit agency that assesses managed care organizations, has been working for nearly a decade on its Health Plan Employer Data and Information Set, which ranks managed care providers (Grimaldi 1997). On its Web site (www.ncqa.org), the committee advertises the names of major employers who have requested reports.

Firms that purchase insurance for a large number of employees have the clout to force providers to gather information on physicians and to make it available on a timely basis (Slomski 1995). Chesanow (1999) reported on efforts to assess quality. For example, in December 1998, Health Net, California's second largest HMO, released a report card rating its physician groups on their treatment of asthma patients. Poor compliance with established asthma treatment guidelines led Health Net to tie bonuses to their physicians' report card ratings. Since 1993, PacificCare of California has made quarterly assessments of its member providers' performance.

PacificCare examines both clinical quality (for example, rates of cervical cancer screening) and member satisfaction.

A new industry, taking advantage of computer technology to provide health care performance measurement services, offers providers assistance in surveying consumer satisfaction. One firm, for example, advertises to potential clients its ability to pull together "real-time data about individual departments, units or physicians" within hospitals, health systems or provider networks (National Research Corporation; www.nationalresearch.com).

The pressure from employer groups that motivates efforts to gather data about managed care is just one of the factors creating incentives for physician profiling and peer review. A second pressure comes from the very nature of physician associations within managed care organizations. In managed care, physicians become associated with the managed care provider for which they work, and individual physicians do not want to see their reputations tarnished by underperforming colleagues.

One lingering problem is the fear of physicians on peer review committees of legal consequences, that is, lawsuits by disciplined physicians hoping to overturn judgments against them. But the federal Health Care Quality Improvement Act of 1986 provides immunity for physicians who serve on peer review committees (Baxter 1997).

Capitation

Providers that assume the risk associated with payment on a capitated basis are especially interested in software that profiles individual physicians' resource use (Krentz and Miller 1998). Under capitation arrangements, managed care organizations or groups of physicians assume the risk of patient care normally held by insurance companies. The providers receive a predetermined payment to cover the care of an individual for a fixed amount of time. Unlike traditional payment schemes, in which care is reimbursed on a cost basis, if a group accepting capitation payments is unable to control costs, it must bear the consequences. Capitation has become popular for just that reason: it creates incentives for health care providers to consider the cost along with the efficacy of alternative treatment patterns.

Where reimbursement for claims is made on a capitated basis, a physician's actions influence his or her peers' compensation. For example, if one doctor spends too much on unnecessary tests, there will be less money left for other uses. The result is an incentive to closely monitor physicians' practice patterns with respect to individual disease processes (Crane 1999; Montague 1994).

As a result of capitation, "economic credentialing" has become popular. Physicians whose costs exceed normal practice patterns are identified and scrutinized for excessive and/or unnecessary procedures. The purpose is to discourage physicians from recommending costly methods of care that are not recognized as appropriate, with the goal of saving money for the insurer or health care organization. Physicians' practice patterns are accordingly the subject of intense scrutiny. Lowes reported that "observers of the group practice scene are virtually unanimous in predicting that physician evaluation will become more commonplace and more sophisticated as capitation gains ascendancy" (Lowes 1995).

Liability

One of the biggest changes with respect to incentives in medical markets is that the courts are holding hospitals and other health care providers and insurers liable for the actions of physicians working under their auspices, whether or not they employ those physicians directly.[7] This change in the courts' interpretation of liability reflects the growing perception among consumers that hospitals and managed care organizations are care providers, even when the hospital or organization does not have a direct employment relationship with its doctors. Because the large providers are assumed to vouch for the skills of physicians within their umbrella of care, the courts have dropped previous interpretations that directed liability solely to individual physicians.

Because hospitals, managed care organizations, IPAs (independent practice associations), and other entities are now directly liable for the actions of their physicians, careful examination of their practice patterns has become a necessary business practice. Liability creates incentives to assess a physician's ability, as well as his or her inclination toward fraud, before establishing a formal relationship. Once a relationship has been established, peer review committees assess the efficacy of practice patterns. Physicians whose practice patterns lead to undesirable outcomes can be identified and instructed to improve their performance. Managed care organizations have an incentive to drop physicians who practice in ways that leave the organization open to liability (Liner 1997). Similarly, hospital peer review committees have an incentive to limit or deny hospital privileges when necessary to protect against adverse legal judgments. In this fashion, affiliation with such an organization increasingly becomes a "seal of approval," a form of private-sector, voluntary certification.

Prescription Drug Abuse

State medical licensing has played a role in curbing prescription drug abuse, a significant share of all disciplinary actions against physicians. In this respect, advances in technology have reduced, if not eliminated, the need for licensing. In several states, electronic substance-tracking programs have proved successful in reducing the number of inappropriate prescriptions; other states successfully track prescriptions with a heavy paper trail by using triplicate prescription forms (Gebhart 1997).

Triplicate prescription arrangements track "schedule II" drugs, those medications with a high potential for abuse.[8] Not only do these arrangements reduce forgery and illegal sales by doctors (Colan 1991), but they also allow regulators to identify drug-dealing professionals, prescription thefts, and people who trick physicians and pharmacists into prescribing drugs (Weikel 1996).

Weikel (1996) found that triplicate prescription requirements in Michigan and New York had virtually eliminated prescription forgeries and falsifications. Before adopting the prescription-monitoring system, both states recorded more than 100,000 forgeries and falsifications a year.

Conclusion

It is reasonable to ask whether in the face of all of the innovations noted here, it makes sense to preserve licensing restrictions and disciplinary activities. The advent of computer technology and innovative software programs have made information on physicians and practice patterns available to health care providers and their patients. Because liability for physician malpractice has shifted, hospitals, health maintenance organizations, insurers, and even employers (who purchase insurance for their employees) who do not take advantage of the new technology to check physicians' qualifications are open to costly judgments in court. Prescription fraud can be reduced by means of electronic tracking. For all these reasons, it becomes ever more difficult to justify state licensing and the continued funding of state medical boards.

Fraud and malpractice are by their very nature difficult to discover or identify, and they will never be eliminated. But the issue today is whether state medical boards are redundant to market mechanisms borne of advances in computer technology.

Many economists argue that licensing hurts society by restricting supply and offers little, if anything, beyond the quality assurance provided by certification, referrals, and reputation. With recent advances in technology, consumers—and the institutional providers who serve them—are allowed direct access to physicians' performance records. The result is a greater base of information from which to make intelligent health care decisions.

NOTES

1. Derbyshire 1969 outlines the history of medical licensing regulation in the United States. On justifications for licensure, see Leffler 1978.

2. Certification offers patients additional legal options for care outside traditional medicine.

3. The incentive effects of this arrangement are similar to those described in Lazear 1981 and Klein and Leffler 1981.

4. Examples of sites with health information include the Cable News Network's www.cnn.com/HEALTH/; Lycos's Webmd.lycos.com; AOL's www.aol.com/Webcenters/health/home.adp; and the Health on the Net Foundation at www.hon.ch.

5. See, for example, www.docboard.org; also Osheroff 1997; Rogers 1998.

6. By 1995, more than 83 percent of all U.S. physicians had at least one managed care contract.

7. This is discussed in Svorny 1992.

8. Controlled substances are "scheduled" under the Federal Controlled Substances Act according to their potential for dependence and abuse (Nowak 1992).

REFERENCES

Ahwah, Ian, and Marty Karpiel. 1997. "Using Profiling for Cost and Quality Management in the Emergency Department." *Healthcare Financial Management* 51 (July): 48–53.

Arrow, Kenneth J. 1963. "Uncertainty and the Welfare Economics of Medical Care." *American Economic Review* 53 (December): 941–73.

Baxter, Michael J. 1997. "A Potent Weapon: Federal Peer Review Immunity under HCQIA." *Defense Counsel Journal* 64 (July): 364.

Butler, Thomas M. 1998. "Self-Examination: An HMO Checks up on Its Doctors' Care and Is Disturbed Itself." *Wall Street Journal*, July 8, A1.

Chesanow, Neil. 1999. "Your Report Card Is about to Go Public." *Medical Economics*, April 12, 220–35.

Colan, Michael F. 1991. "New Push for Tracking Controlled Substances Looms; Pharmaceutical Products Legislation Introduced by Rep. Pete Stark." *Drug Topics*, August 5, 56.

Crane, Mark. 1999. "Peer Review: Breaking the Code of Silence." *Medical Economics*, May 10, 158–71.

Derbyshire, Robert C. 1969. *Medical Licensure and Discipline in the United States.* Baltimore: Johns Hopkins University Press.

Friedman, Milton. 1962. *Capitalism and Freedom.* Chicago: University of Chicago Press.

Gebhart, Fred. 1997. "California, Nevada Move on Electronic Triplicate to Prevent Prescription Abuse." *Drug Topics*, April 21, 82.

Gilbert, Jennifer A. 1998. "Physician Profiling: Using Software to Refine the Art." *Health Data Management*, June.

Goodman, Richard D. 1999. "The Use—and Misuse—of the National Practitioner Data Bank." *Medical Malpractice Law & Strategy* 16 (January): 4.

Grimaldi, Paul L. 1997. "HEDIS 3.0 Advances Health Plan Accountability." *Healthcare Financial Management* 51 (May): 48–52.

Guglielmo, Wayne J. 1996. "Are Doctors Evading the Malpractice Data Bank?" *Medical Economics*, May 28, 52.

Klein, Benjamin, and Keith B. Leffler. 1981. "The Role of Market Forces in Assuring Contractual Performance." *Journal of Political Economy* 89 (August): 615–41.

Krentz, Susanna E., and Thomas R. Miller. 1998. "Physician Resource Profiling Enhances Utilization Management." *Healthcare Financial Management* 52 (October): 45–47.

Lazear, Edward P. 1981. "Agency, Earnings Profiles, Productivity, and Hours Restrictions." *American Economic Review* 71 (September): 606–20.

Leffler, Keith B. 1978. "Physician Licensure: Competition and Monopoly in American Medicine." *Journal of Law and Economics* 21 (April): 165–85.

Liner, Richard S. 1997. "Physician Deselection: The Dynamics of a New Threat to the Physician-Patient Relationship." *American Journal of Law & Medicine* 23: 511.

Lowes, Robert L. 1995. "Groups Get Serious about Judging Their Doctors." *Medical Economics* 72 (9): 51.

Montague, Jim. 1994. "Profiling in Practice." *Hospitals & Health Networks*, January 20, 50–52.

National Practitioner Data Bank (NPDB). 1999. http://www.npdb.com/welcome.htm, July 2.

Nowak, R. 1992. "Cops and Doctors: Drug Busts Hamper Pain Therapy." *Journal of NIH Research* 4: 27–28.

Osheroff, Jerome A. 1997. "Online Health-Related Discussion Groups: What We Should Know and Do." *Journal of General Internal Medicine* 12 (8): 511–12.

Pauly, Mark V., and Mark A. Satterthwaite. 1981. "The Pricing of Primary Care Physicians' Services: A Test of the Role of Consumer Information." *Bell Journal of Economics* 12 (autumn): 488–506.

Pinkowish, Mary Desmond, Ace Allen, Mark Edwin Frisse, and Jerome A. Osheroff. 1999. "The Internet in Medicine: An Update." *Patient Care* 33, no. 1: 30.

Rogers, Carolyn. 1998. "Physician Profiling Legislation." *Bulletin of the American College of Surgeons*, December 1, 34–39.

Setness, Peter A. 1996. "What Do You Know about the NPDB?" *Post Graduate Medicine* 100 (July): 15.

Slomski, Anita J. 1995. "Employers to Doctors: It's Time for Real Savings." *Medical Economics* 72, no. 14: 122.

Smith, Jennifer. 1998. "'Internet Patients' Turn to Support Groups to Guide Medical Decisions." *Journal of the National Cancer Institute*, November 18, 1695–97.

Svorny, Shirley. 1987. "Physician Licensure: A New Approach to Examining the Role of Professional Interests." *Economic Inquiry* 25, no. 3: 497–509.

———. 1992. "Should We Reconsider Licensing Physicians?" *Contemporary Policy Issues* 10, no. 1: 31–38.

———. 2000. "Licensing. Market Entry Regulation." *Encyclopedia of Law & Economics*, vol. 3, ed. Boudewijn Bouckaert and Gerrit De Geest. Cheltenham: Edward Elgar.

U.S. Department of Health and Human Services, Office of Inspector General, Office of Evaluation and Inspections. 1995. "National Practitioner Data Bank Reports to Managed Care Organizations: Their Usefulness and Impact." PIC ID: 4616.5.

Weikel, Dan. 1996. "Prescription for an Epidemic; Drug Firms Battle Rule on Prescription Forms." *Los Angeles Times*, August 19, A1.

Part III

Natural Monopoly?

9

Technology and Electricity
Overcoming the Umbilical Mentality

Alvin Lowi Jr. and Clyde Wayne Crews Jr.

Supplying electricity to a community is ordinarily a three-stage process: generation, transmission, and distribution. Electricity generators running on fossil fuel, wind, solar, hydro, or nuclear energy spin magnets inside copper wire coils to generate a flow of electrons. The current is sent through high-voltage, high-capacity transmission lines to local regions. There it is transformed to a lower voltage and sent through local distribution wires to final users. The electricity is transmitted and distributed through a network of cables and wires traversing steel towers, wooden poles, and underground vaults that make up a system often referred to as *the grid*.

The so-called deregulation of electricity has focused on introducing competition—but only in its generation and only among restrictively authorized high-tension wholesalers. For its transmission and distribution, reformers have called for "open access" to the power grid: commercial, residential, and industrial customers must be allowed to choose any electricity provider they prefer, and the local utility must be required to distribute the new provider's electricity for a fee. In the new setting, electricity producers—whether the conventional vertically integrated utilities or newer and smaller generators—must be able to sell to whomever they chose via the grid. Utilities would be required, however, to relinquish control of their lines to regulatory agencies.

But few would invest in grid technologies and innovations if authority over such investments were surrendered and the fruits of their efforts were divided according to the machinations of a political authority or a regimented, nonprofit industry association. That is, what is politically possible often diverges from what is really desirable, and vice versa.

Although few political players favor full-scale decontrol, such a policy is, in our assessment, the most desirable one. Full-scale decontrol would mean the elimination of exclusive territorial franchises. It would mean the de-regimentation and de-politicization of distribution as well as generation. The resources used for generation and distribution would be deemed the private property of the owners, and freedom of contract would be granted. In conjunction with a free-enterprise policy, governments could allow reasonable and fair access to the public's right of way. Problems of emissions, noise, vibrations, and risk could be treated by tort action, negotiation, or, especially in the case of emissions, by simple and fair pollution charges based on direct measurements of emissions at each exhaust pipe or smokestack. Such an approach differs substantially from many current regulations.

The root of utilities' monopoly is usually found in such legal devices as "certificates of convenience and necessity" requiring permission to compete in the marketplace. The law from the state of Colorado is typical: "No public utility shall begin the construction of a new facility, plant, or system or of any extension of its facility, plant or system without first having obtained from the [public utilities] commission a certificate that the present or future public convenience and necessity require or will require such construction" (Colorado Revised Statutes). Here we can clearly see the exclusion of competition, the attenuation of authority over supposedly privately owned resources, and the pretense of knowability (of "present and future public convenience").

We believe that the case for free-enterprise electricity has always been strong. Technology, however, is making the case even stronger, in two ways. First, technology is making less and less tenable the notion of natural monopoly in electricity. Decentralized generation and distribution are increasingly economically viable. Second, technology is opening up so many new possibilities that the field has become more complex and hence unknowable to regulatory authorities. Now more than ever, policymakers should recognize that complex productive activities call for experimentation, heterogeneity, spontaneity, and flexibility, which are especially the virtues of private property rights and the freedom of contract.

A central failing of industry regulation and regimentation, a failing that pertains to much of what follows in this chapter, is the almost complete neglect of time-of-use pricing. In Atlanta in the middle of August, the price of electricity at 5:00 A.M. is the same as the price during the peak usage at 5:00 P.M. Varying the price with time of use, however, would avoid peak crunches and level the load. Price changes mobilize the help and co-operation of electricity users. These benefits are well known to telephone companies, airlines, hotels, and movie theaters. In electricity, it would be easy for each end user to have LED displays at hand, like those on digital alarm clocks, showing the price of electricity right now and the price later on. This type of pricing would be easy technically, since the power line could also serve this informational and metering function. In the middle of a hot summer afternoon, the householder would then have a strong financial incentive to refrain from running the electric clothes dryer until an hour when electricity were less scarce. The householder might decide to turn down the air conditioner, take a cold shower, or go for a swim or to the shopping mall. In a thousand different ways, people substitute one option for another when given an incentive to do so (Borenstein and Bushnell 2000, 48). Businesses and large-volume customers would, of course, respond assiduously to time-of-use pricing. Electricity suppliers then could better optimize their build-versus-buy choices and other decisions. But for political and bureaucratic reasons, the regulators and utility monopolies have forsaken a simple, practical innovation that, by itself, would be a huge leap forward in managing load and capacity.

The regulators seem to have an obsession with price controls stemming from a tradition of trying to control a monopoly of their own creation. As a result, they act as if their policies are exempt from the consequences of supply and demand, which they cannot control.

The neglect of time-of-use pricing is just one of the travesties of industry regimentation. We will highlight others in making two central points about how technology enhances the case for de-regimenting the industry. The first part of the chapter deals with dispersed generation, and the second deals with heightened complexity.

Dispersed Generation: Now More Than Ever

Unnatural History, Unnatural Doctrine

For decades, the market for electricity delivery has been said to be a natural monopoly, that is, a service featuring a high fixed cost and an ever declining cost per unit, so that a single large firm could produce and sell output more cheaply than two or more smaller ones could (Stiglitz 1993: 411, 455–60). The theory of natural monopoly implies that a free market naturally gravitates toward dominance by one firm (a summary of this theory may be found in this volume's introduction).

Historically, however, electric utilities never achieved natural monopoly status before the advent of the state public utility commissions that arose to regulate them. According to economist Richard Geddes, "State regulation was instituted not to correct private market failure and to increase social welfare, but to provide firms with a way to insulate themselves from the discipline of competition" (1992, 76). The idea that it is optimal to have a solitary power grid under unitary administration really has no solid grounds, especially considering the inefficiencies that result when authority and residual claimancy are divided and politicized.

If regulation really helped consumers, prices should have fallen and the quantity of power supplied should have increased after the transition to regulation. Instead, as an article by economist Greg Jarrell (1978) demonstrates, customers paid more for electricity under the rate of return regulation than they did under the prior competitive environment. Jarrell found that the states in which utilities were first subjected to rate-of-return regulation were those that had been charging the *lowest* prices, rather than those charging "monopoly" prices. Furthermore, following regulation, the prices in the early-regulated states were higher relative to those of the late-regulated states (Jarrell 1978, 287). Also following regulation, the output of electricity fell while the return on assets rose (see also Stigler and Friedland 1962).

One of the common pitfalls of electricity-policy discourse has been to overemphasize the distinction between generation and transmission/distribution. Intellectuals and regulators try to impose order on the world just to get a handle on it. But the strong distinction really presumes a natural-monopoly fate for electricity. Joseph Stiglitz's textbook says: "The electricity industry could be divided into electric power generation and distribution. Some competition may be viable in electric power generation" (1993, 460). But of course, not distribution. As the distinction determines the course of policy, monopoly, though *un*natural, becomes a predetermined outcome.

Consider what a natural-monopoly presumption would imply for the delivery of restaurant meals. There would be central sources of meal generation and a monopoly grid of distribution to dining points everywhere (somewhat like WebVan or the frozen dinners distributed through supermarkets). Such a distinction between generation and distribution is highly artificial. Restaurant-meal production is a complex process that melds and mixes various stages of generation and distribution, that is, *dispersed generation*.

Of course, there are important differences between restaurant meals and electricity, differences that make it much more natural in the case of electricity to distinguish generation and distribution. The dispersed-generation model has long been economically viable, however, and technology is making it more so.

Generator Sets ("Gensets")

A *genset* is a self-contained, stand-alone, usually transportable electric power plant consisting of a prime mover (engine), a dynamo, and some controls. The word *plant* as used here should not be construed as a grand industrial installation. Rather, it implies merely that the unit is located, installed, and hooked up for usage. Gensets are capable of producing electricity for use in isolated, local applications, in team with other gensets, or in parallel with large central stations via the power grid.

A diesel locomotive is a genset on rails. A hybrid automobile is an electric car fitted with a genset (and getting 80 miles to the gallon in all-around driving). Other familiar gensets are the small units that make electricity for motor homes, boats, and other independent facilities. Available for ordinary household installation, many gensets are equipped with automatic starting and grid isolation transfer switching for standby or emergency service, such as when the grid service is interrupted by weather and the household needs secure power for medical appliances such as respirators (for a selection of such devices, see www.mcmaster.com).

A typical genset consists of a combustion engine mechanically coupled to a self-excited synchronous generator or permanent magnet alternator mounted on a rigid base. Also mounted are the control console, fuel supply, and cooling provisions, including a radiator. The combustion engines, whether piston ("internal combustion") or turbine ("external combustion"), can use diesel, gasoline, kerosene, alcohol, propane, or natural gas. Gensets are usually enclosed in weatherproof housings for outside location on the ground, in parking lots, or on rooftops. For mobility, they may be mounted on skids, wheels, or barges. They offer low setup and operating costs with a high reversibility of investment. For most locations, their emissions are very manageable and acceptable to all reasonable people. Noise pollution is rendered insignificant by ordinary engineering measures such as sound-absorbing construction, sound insulation, mufflers, baffles, and considerate and prudent siting ("prudent" because any operator would be liable for nuisance).

A Glimpse at the Current Genset Catalog

Mass-produced engines from various fields (automotive, aviation, marine, and railroad propulsion) are available with a wide range of heavy-duty power ratings suitable for genset application. Such engines, suitable as genset prime movers operating on gasoline and propane, cost as little as $30 per horsepower rising to more than $50 per horsepower for operation on diesel and natural gas. Diesel and natural gas engines dominate the 100- to 3000-kW output range.

Natural-gas burning gas turbines are new to the genset field. Two new entrants into this field of engine power deserve to be mentioned here.

Although their purchase price is ten times that of internal combustion engines of equal power output, engines popularly known as *microturbines* or *microturbogenerators* are being manufactured and marketed by several firms, both recent startups and those long established in the field (e.g., www.capstoneturbines.com, www.honeywell-des.com, www.distributed-energy-solutions.com). The advantages of these microturbines over internal combustion engines for dispersed power application are their much lower size, weight, vibration, noise, and maintenance requirements. Weighing only a few hundred pounds and often with only a single moving part, these small self-contained units are about the size of a large refrigerator. They are designed for unattended operation nearly maintenance free to produce from 25 to 75 kW—adequate to power a 7-Eleven store, a McDonald's restaurant, a group of homes, a condominium complex, or an apartment building. These units capitalize on recent developments in materials, turbomachinery design, heat exchangers, electromagnetic machinery design, automatic controls, and microprocessors to form a package that is highly efficient, durable, compact, lightweight, and portable. Their high reliability and long service life are attributed to the development of foil bearings that support the turbogenerator shaft on a film of air rather than oil. Because of the recuperation technology employed, the operating costs of these units are reputed to be competitive with conventional engine-powered units (www.microturbine.com).

The developers of the microturbine products have incorporated certain new technologies to improve their competitiveness. One such innovation is the recuperation of waste heat in the heat-engine cycle, a process that significantly increases fuel efficiency. Recuperated turbine engines approach the fuel efficiency of internal combustion engines. Another innovation is the use of foil bearings that eliminate dependence on lubricating oil and thus the requisite maintenance and wear.

One "microturbine" example is AlliedSignal's 75 kW TurboGenerator, which sells for $40,000 to $50,000, or almost $670 per kW. At 1998 fuel prices, operating costs are 4.5 cents per kilowatt-hour (kWh), while total costs, including recovery of capital, are 6.7 cents per kWh (see www.worldbusinessreview.com/underwriters/AlliedSignal/).

New Energy Ventures is marketing this system widely in the western states (see www.newenergy.com/press/detail.cfm?nid=445&sid=2). McDonalds is a prominent customer (www.wbrtv.com/underwriters/unicom). Allison Engines (now part of Rolls-Royce) and Capstone Turbine Corporation also produce microturbines (www.capstoneturbines.com, www.honeywell-des.com, www.distributed-energy-solutions.com).

In 1996 the Electric Power Research Institute of Palo Alto, California, predicted reliable, low-maintenance commercial applications of these units could be available for under $300 per kW within three to five years (Preston and Rastler 1996, 15). Given the five years already passed, what are the facts today? After shipping its first unit for commercial installation in December 1998, Capstone Turbine Corporation of Tarzana, California (www.capstoneturbine.com), announced on November 27, 2000, that it had shipped its one thousandth microturbine unit. This unit was one of a "six-pack" sold to Peoples Energy PLC for installation in the Fulton Street Brewery of the Goose Island Beer Company of Chicago. These natural gas–fired cogeneration units are dedicated to critical production equipment and processes that must be protected from utility blackout.

It is easy to envision hospitals, commercial firms, shopping malls, and real estate developers embracing microturbine technology and setting up single or stacked units in buildings, on roofs, in parking lots, in basements, and along new streets. Banks of such turbines could be stacked in key locations, ensuring reliability because any turbine that fails is rapidly replaced with a new one or electrically switched to an idle one. A new turbine repair industry can be expected to emerge, much like the independent photocopier, fax machine, and computer repair businesses that emerged to complement those technologies. Such developments could displace utility and distribution lines.

Areas that lack distribution lines are also likely to lack natural-gas lines, but the microturbines can be modified to run on diesel, gasoline, propane, kerosene, and other fuels that can transported by truck or railroad as well as pipeline. Thus, gensets can easily adapt to installations beyond either the electricity grid or the gas main.

Recently, gas turbines derived from commercial aviation propulsion engines (turbojets and turbofans) have been adapted to industrial shaft power drives. These "aero-derivative" engines have spurred the development of a new class of very high output, highly mobile gensets useful for peaking service. Such engines, operating on natural gas, are beginning to compete with diesels in the 10- to 60-mW range. While they consume somewhat more energy per unit of electricity output, they are lightweight and compact enough to be integrated into highly mobile intermodal containers easily sited in most neighborhoods.

Living Proofs of the Genset Alternative

Generators and controls are available for local domestic and isolated building service as well as for paralleling on the grid. Most of the on-site applications are for standby or emergency power units but are capable of continuous operation under load. Such units are installed in numbers at nearly every major hotel, hospital, and high-rise building in the country, in conformance with prudence, fire insurance policies, and numerous, complex layers of governmental codes and permits. Even if they run only occasionally, they pay for themselves in terms of fewer interruptible utility rates and lower insurance premiums. Some such installations that operate continuously generate both heat and air conditioning.

The response of the genset industry to Hurricane Hugo in 1989 illustrates the robust capability and potential of this technology and industry. At this time, major genset manufacturers such as Stewart and Stevenson Services of Houston (www.ssss.com) and Penske Power of Hoboken, New Jersey (www.penske.com), had stocked various types and sizes of gensets for short- and long-term lease as well as sale. When the hurricane struck, the Carolina utility system went down because substations were flooded; generating furnaces were extinguished; and power poles were toppled. Emergency service agencies and private companies expedited the delivery of thousands of gensets from Stewart and Stevenson, Penske, and other suppliers by truck, rail, and barge. With competent field support from the suppliers, they succeeded in powering up isolated buildings and serviceable parts of the grid well before central service was restored. By the time the interstate power intertie system was ready to resume service, the dispersed power units on temporary loan were providing about 500 mW of electricity, or almost 10 percent of the normal utility load (Fox 1992).[1]

Recent Technological Developments in Gensets

Although dispersed generation by independent gensets has been technically feasible for many years, recent technological advancements have considerably enhanced the economic viability of dispersed generation. Significant improvements have been made in engines, combustion, materials, microprocessors, instrumentation, controls, automation, and electronics by which gensets can produce power, either inside or outside the grid, and compete with central stations on the basis of reliability, unit cost of power, and cost of contracting. Accordingly, the market for gensets now is huge (see www.dieselpub.com).

Significant technology developments in the community electricity supply field include the following:

Technological Advancements in Internal Combustion Engines:
LEAN-BURN NATURAL GAS. This is a technique for using natural gas in a homogeneous charge spark ignition engine with an excess of air over chemical correctness in order to improve fuel efficiency.

LOW-EMISSION DIESEL. Regenerative particulate traps and selective catalytic reduction units have been developed to permit stationary diesel engines to operate at low emission levels of carbon soot and nitrogen oxides.

DUAL-FUELED DIESEL-NATURAL GAS. This is a technique for substituting a major fraction of the fuel energy in a compression ignition diesel engine by fumigating cheaper, cleaner-burning natural gas. Besides lowering the cost of fuel, the process reduces the emissions of particulates, carbon, and nitric oxide as well as noise.

EBULLIENT COOLING FOR STEAM COGENERATION. Engine cooling can be a source of heat for other uses. When heat from the engine oil and structure is removed by conventional liquid cooling, it is dissipated via radiators and the like. New technology has been developed to generate low-pressure steam within the engine as a consequence of controlling the engine's temperature. The steam produced is a valuable commodity for heating purposes, and the engine is cooled more efficiently.

EXHAUST HEAT RECOVERY. Improved materials and heat exchanger technology permit the development of more effective means for recovering useful heat from otherwise wasted engine exhaust. This heat can be delivered at somewhat higher temperatures than that recoverable from engine cooling jackets. However, exhaust heat recovery requires sophisticated design measures using highly durable materials.

INDUCTION ALTERNATORS. Most electric motors used nowadays for industrial purposes are polyphase "squirrel-cage" induction types. This machinery is rugged, inexpensive, and free of the sliding electrical contacts that account for most of the maintenance cost for electrical machinery. With certain advances in electrical engineering know-how, induction machines are being used as asynchronous alternators. These machines must be operated on the grid to be loaded synchronously with other generators, but they provide power-factor correction to the grid. In an alternating-current distribution system, inductive reaction in certain loads causes the current to lag the voltage in phase, resulting in a loss of available electrical power. Induction generators deliver their current at leading phase, which tends to correct the power factor. Many small such generators dispersed about the grid could recover some of the nearly 10 percent of the otherwise unavailable reactive power in the grid.

This technology is not only useful for building economic capacity, but it should also be considered an important conservation technique.

EMISSION CONTROLS. Automotive emission control technology developments can be economically transferred to stationary engines of the spark ignition type. These are the genset engines that run on natural gas, propane, or gasoline. The most important and valuable of these technologies are the closed-loop electronic engine controls, exhaust gas–oxygen sensors, electronic fuel injectors, nonselective three-way catalysts, and exhaust gas recirculation controls. Turbochargers, wastegates, and intercoolers developed for heavy-duty on-highway truck application are important and economical emission-control features of stationary diesel engines.

NOISE CONTROL. Advancements in acoustic controls and materials now enable the construction of genset enclosures for stationary engines to run in virtual silence. Sound and vibration absorption as well as acoustic wave cancellation by electronic means are being used to eliminate noise objections in most neighborhood installations.

Technological Advancements in External Combustion Turbine Engines
RECUPERATION. In their simplest form, external combustion gas turbine engines cannot compete with internal combustion engines for fuel economy. However, recent developments in materials and heat exchanger technology recover internal heat during the cycle to significantly improve the engine's thermal efficiency. Such thermal recuperation consists of cooling the underexpanded combustion gases leaving the turbine and transferring the heat recovered to the cooler air leaving the compressor before entering the combustor. Less fuel is thereby required to maintain the turbine's inlet temperature and power output.

FOIL BEARINGS. Lubrication is a high-maintenance item in all machinery because wear determines the useful life of the equipment. The invention and development of foil bearings for gas turbine application have extended the equipment's service life and lowered its maintenance cost. Such bearings permit the lightweight, very high speed shaft to be supported by a film of air that reduces friction, wear, and maintenance. This achievement enables an otherwise prohibitively expensive machine to compete on the basis of its life-cycle cost.

HIGH-SPEED BRUSHLESS PERMANENT MAGNET ALTERNATORS. The development of new high-coercive-strength magnetic materials and high-speed microprocessor-based electronic controls has yielded a new generation of synchronous generators that can be driven at very high shaft speeds. This permits direct turbine drive and eliminates gear reductions and attendant machinery costs and lubrication problems. In addition, the generator is small and lightweight. These generators can be run at any speed with synchronization with the grid provided by external rectification and inversion using solid-state controls.

EMISSION CONTROLS. Although emissions standards are more easily met by gas turbines than by internal combustion engines, control measures are often required to meet local codes. Water and steam injection has been perfected to minimize the emission of nitric oxides. In addition, selective catalytic reduction processes have been developed to reduce these ozone-forming emissions even further.

NOISE CONTROL. Advancements in acoustic controls and materials also apply to the soundproofing of gas turbine engine enclosures. However, additional acoustic controls are required for these engines to deal with high-frequency emissions from their intakes and exhaust stacks. Control of such noise is now routine using a combination of materials, baffles, and electronic acoustic wave cancellation.

Does Dispersed Generation Forsake Scale Economies?

Central plants can capitalize on the so-called six-tenths power law (Chilton et al. 1967). Originating in the chemical industry, this loose maxim describes the relationship between the cost of production and plant capacity. It maintains that the cost of producing a quantity of plant output is proportional to the plant capacity raised to the 0.6 power. Thus, if plant 2 has twice the capacity of plant 1, the larger plant's output (say, 200 units) should cost only 1.52 times as much as that of the smaller plant (100 units). Thus, plant 2's average cost would be only about 75 percent of plant 1's average cost. This maxim applies to raw materials, labor, and capital.

For small-scale producers, however, scale economies apply to the mass-produced capital component only. The heat engine prime mover for a genset may be sourced from automotive or aviation production volume. The genset assembly itself may well justify volume production to serve a multitude of applications. Thus, genset production itself exhibits economies of scale.

An outstanding bargain in engine power is the 350-horsepower Chevrolet Mark V ("Big Block") truck engine that can be purchased complete in boxcar lots from the factory in Tonawanda, New York, for less than $1,500 per engine (1990 dollars). (The current automobile dealer price complete is about $2,000, depending on accessories.) Once the truck engine is prepared and equipped to run on natural gas and drive a 200-kW generator at constant speed, this engine costs about $5,000, or $25 per kW (Lowi 1991).

Technological developments are making small-scale generation even better at producing power closer to the customer and transporting it over shorter distances at lower voltages.

Improvements in engine performance and durability are reducing the costs of on-site generation to such an extent that small plants can now compete with large central stations on the basis of energy consumption and direct operating cost. Small-scale electricity production on site eliminates the costs of the grid and power transmission. Those costs include organization, land use, amortization of capital, maintenance, and voltage dissipation in transmission lines and substations.

In addition, on-site production facilitates the cogeneration of heat from a single source of fuel energy for such processes as laundry and climate conditioning. Such heat is necessarily wasted by remote central plants.

These developments favor a competing model of "subgrids" or self-contained loops. Although these subgrids might make deals with incumbents to connect themselves to the main grid, on-site generation could bypass the grid altogether. Just as mainframe computing technology has given way to "desktop" computing, with suitable liberalization we could see a flourishing of dispersed power generation.

Portability and the Reversibility of Investment

The traditional power plant is site specific and largely nonsalvageable, so the investment that it represents is largely irreversible, or "sunk." But advances in generator design are changing the situation significantly, even for generators that are quite large. The capability has long existed for water-transportable power plants designed to float atop barges. Used to serve places lacking adequate infrastructure, such plants eliminate a great deal of default risk. On land or water, gensets and microturbines can often be installed, uninstalled, transported, and reinstalled. Such portable stations will, according to Donald Smith, president of the Smith Corporation, "be liquid assets like a tanker or a 747" (quoted in Bulkeley 1996, B1). Thus, in a liberal regime, electricity delivery would enjoy not only a large measure of free entry but also what has been called *free exit*, meaning the ability to recover the costs of market forays that don't pan out or that have run their course. The ability to recover makes the foray more appealing and more likely in the first place. Markets would be more competitive and more "contestable" (Baumol, Panzar, and Willig 1982).

Obstacles to On-Site Power

The operation of local gensets is not as common as their economics would presume, because of the administrative hurdles facing a small power producer in contracting with a regulated utility company to connect to the grid for either base load or peaking service. However, since the early 1980s, a growing number of cogenerators and small power producers have been so connected. A few have managed to secure arrangements under the rules of the Federal Energy Regulatory Commission (FERC) and the 1978 Public Utility Regulatory Policies Act (PURPA), according to which they are permitted to sell their excess power to major utility companies for retail distribution.

Many regulatory barriers stand in the way of dispersed generation (whether or not they are grid connected). Regulators do not like to see a multiplication of regulatees with whom they must interact. In other words, they much prefer a system in which they regulate a small number of large sites, rather than a large number of small sites. Thus, they tend to drag their feet and throw roadblocks in the way of small-scale permitting.

The following list of difficulties is based on the situation in California, but the description may be generalized to the rest of the country.

Permit to Construct

In seeking to install a small-scale plant on site, a business must apply for a construction permit from the local government. The construction-permit process delves into the health, safety, environmental, and economic impacts of the proposed project. Deposits on fees are not refunded if the application is withdrawn or the permit is denied.

Permit to Operate

After the plant is permitted, constructed, and approved again by the relevant building and safety agencies, a separate permit to operate must be obtained from state and local government agencies. All this must be done in the proper sequence before the plant can be used for its intended purpose. Further costs in time, expenses, and fees are then incurred while EPA, OSHA, state and district air-quality authorities, and local housing and safety agencies inspect facilities, observe operations, and look over the test data. At any point along the way, a single bureaucratic office can kill the project, making the entire effort for naught. Thus, aside from the delays involved, the process entails enormous uncertainties.

Grid Connection Difficulties

If the small-scale producer wishes to connect its on-site system to the grid, it must meet the utility's connection specifications. It must obtain certain "utility grade" relays, switches, and circuit breakers that must be procured at grossly inflated prices from the utility company and installed under the supervision of the utility company's engineers. The utility company's charges for these special parts and services are not known in advance (somewhat like military specifications). Accordingly, allowing competition at the local level by ending the franchise would make utilities more inclined to make a deal.

Moreover, if the grid-connected enterprise wishes to obtain lower rates in exchange for its willingness to disconnect when ordered (during which time it would rely on its own generating facilities), it would face extraordinary charges in the event that it did not disconnect when ordered. Among the reasons that it might not be able to disconnect when ordered are the following: (1) its generator is down for maintenance or repair; (2) it is out of fuel (possibly owing to gas service interruption); or (3) the enterprise may have run out of emission credits to operate, in which case it would face heavy emission fines. These connection difficulties discourage those who need to maintain a grid connection from developing on-site generation.

Avoided-Cost Contract with the Franchised Utility

Small-scale producers who want to use the grid to sell their excess power and capacity must obtain a contract with the local franchised utility. Under federal law (PURPA), the sales price schedule for the power sold is based on the so-called avoided cost of the franchised utility receiving the power. This "avoided cost" is to be determined and approved by the state's public utility commission. For the small-scale producer, the bureaucratic framework means a loss of time, huge uncertainties, and back-and-forth bargaining in the "avoided-cost" determination—and the PUC bureaucrats, who usually protect the franchised monopoly, have the final word. PURPA also contain bureaucratic rules regarding "energy utilization" to qualify for such a contract. Even if a contract is secured, if spot-check inspectors (from FERC, the state PUC, or the utility company) find that a contracted producer is cogenerating electricity and heat year-round at rates less than 50 percent of the fuel burned, the utility can claim an "energy utilization" disqualification and refuse payment or rescind the contract. Thus, bureaucratic uncertainties and transaction costs suffuse any such agreement with the franchised local monopoly. To make matters worse, when the franchised utilities became insolvent at the onset of the electricity crisis in early 2000, the PUC bureaucrats allowed their clients to renege on avoided-cost contracts with small-power producers (Tamaki 2001).

Tribute Extracted by the Franchised Utility
In California, if a customer with its own on-site generators wishes to exit the grid to generate its own electricity independently or to buy electricity through the grid from a supplier other than the franchised utility company, it must pay tribute of up to $6.40 per kW of its own generating capacity per month (even after it has left the system). Backed up by the PUC, the utilities rationalize this tribute as continued payment for historic investments to serve the customer—never mind that the customer may not want the service (Hirsch 2001). The arrangement is rather like a restaurant extracting monthly tribute from local residents on the grounds that it had to invest in building the restaurant and that it incurs current costs in continuing to provide residences with the option of going to the restaurant.

The existing bureaucratic conditions can make it very difficult for hospitals, hotels, factories, and homeowners' associations to generate power on-site, especially if they wish to connect to the external grid as a backup or an avenue to the retail electricity market. In a freer market, many more would do so because of favorable terms and reliability. In a free market, the dispersed-power option competing with the electricity-generation establishment would quickly deliver more generating capacity in response to demand, shave peaks, reduce costs, and enhance reliability and price stability. In a setting of secure and certain property rights and freedom of contract, users would have many options—connecting to competing loops (not a monolithic grid), buying power from a neighbor, and self-generating. Entrepreneurship would be the prime mover.

Free-Enterprise Dispersed Generation Would Increase Stability

The stability of the alternating-current electrical utility grid is reckoned in terms of constancy in voltage and frequency at whatever location within the rating of the service connection. The frequency must be maintained at given level (60 hzÅ1/8 wavelength in the United States). Otherwise, generators would not synchronize and share the load, and many clocks would not keep time. Voltage surges cause appliance failures. Low voltage (a brownout) damages loaded-induction motors such as those in refrigerators. Obviously, blackouts—whether of the deliberate load-shirking rolling type or inadvertent breakdowns—are the ultimate instability.

Grid instabilities may be local or general. Local instabilities occur when local power demand exceeds the current carrying capacity of the grid conductors, causing a drop in the local voltage. In that case, no amount of excess generating capacity at a distance can stabilize the grid; only additional conductors or locally generated current will suffice.

General instabilities of the grid are attributable to deficiencies in the overall generating capacity connected to the grid. When the connected load exceeds the generating capacity—as when some of that capacity is impaired by equipment problems, fuel shortages, or emission quotas—there is a risk of overload. In that case, distributed or dispersed generation can stabilize the grid not only locally but also generally.

New technology in computer controls and automation enables dispersed generators to operate unattended on the grid in perfect harmony with established central utility stations. The necessary voltage and frequency regulation performance of PC-based computer controls are well within the state of the art.

Heightened Complexity, or Other Reasons to Be Humble

Besides the technological advancements that make dispersed generation more viable, other technological developments enhance the viability of grid competition, including parallel transmission and distribution, and cogeneration. All told, technology is making electricity experts and regulators aware of the vast diversity of options and opportunities. Because of their extreme complexity, the results of alternative policies are unknowable. But these technologies can be reduced to decentralized practice at the hands of private owners and entrepreneurs with predictable results.

Aggressive Cogeneration

An additional incentive for adopting dispersed generation is the recovery of heat. Heat recovery is valuable only if it can be used locally before it dissipates into the environment. Central plants offer no reasonable access to such heat. If electricity is its only useful product, the typical heat engine–powered generating plant squanders 60 to 70 percent of the fuel's energy.

Companies like Trigen Energy Corporation (www.trigen.com) produce standardized, mass-produced modular "trigeneration" systems (hence the name Trigen), which burn fuel once to make three energy products: heating, cooling, and electricity. How's that for energy conservation?

This process serves offices, universities, and hospitals. Through such a system, the utilization of the fuel energy rises from approximately 30 percent to 85 percent. In Trigen's case, a key is an assembly line–produced gas-fired cogenerator that can be trucked to a site from order to operation in two months. The cogeneration factor makes it more complex and exacerbates the regulator's unknowability problem.

The Potential for Parallel Transmission and Distribution

In 1997, America was crisscrossed by about 600,000 miles of high-voltage transmission lines and about 2.5 million miles of distribution wire (Collins 1997). Ending franchises would allow at least the right to build one's own infrastructure alone or in alliance with other network industries such as telecommunications firms, pipeline companies, and railroads. Potential partners in private infrastructure development would include competition-minded utilities, real estate developers, long-distance and local telephone companies, cable companies, water utilities, natural-gas companies, railroads, private landowners, and authorities governing interstate highways and Amtrak corridors.

Contrary to natural-monopoly doctrine, it is common to have duplication, overlap, and active competition in distribution services. Network industries other than power utilities are spending billions of dollars to expand their systems. During the Internet boom, fiber-optic cable was being deployed at the rate of 4,000 miles per day. Even though some of today's most sophisticated fiber optics can carry all the calls on Mother's Day on a single strand, numerous firms are building overlapping networks. The research company KMI predicted that by 2001 the amount of fiber-optic cable deployed would be equivalent to 82 round trips between the earth and the moon (GaAs Net). Installing fiber-optic line is much simpler than installing power distribution line. Nonetheless, the fiber-optic bonanza may suggest that the dreaded inefficiencies of "duplication" are vastly overstated. Eighty percent or more of fiber optics' costs are incurred before any customers are signed up (Gilder 1997, 2). If the telecommunications industry can manage both the costs and the coordination of investors and customers, so can electric power entrepreneurs. Working together, the two industries could be even more successful.

In a free market, hungry electricity entrepreneurs would make good partners with those intent on wiring America for voice, data, and video. Distribution line installation could piggyback on the installation of cable modem wiring and other home-wiring options. Most fiber-optic cables come to an end a few yards or a few hundred yards from homes, but the current layout cannot sustain growth, since none are fast enough. For example, to download the film *Titanic* (about 4.7 gigabytes), it would take a 28,800 bps modem sixteen days, an ISDN line (128,000 bps) about three and a half days, and a cable modem about one hour. The demand for greater bandwidth will be without limit as people become increasingly accustomed to live interactive video conferencing. The demand is likely to be such that even homeowners' associations might pay to dig up their own streets to "fiberize" if real estate developers have not already done so. Clearly, cross-industry alliances are critical here.

Another promising avenue that may induce new electric firms to justify the expense of adding to or modifying wire networks is the development of techniques for allowing phone calls and high-speed Internet access to be offered through electricity lines. Access is obtained through the standard electric outlet. Electricity and information travel through the same wires. As the capability matures and engineering problems are worked out, electricity entrepreneurs will look anew at the value of their wire networks.

Horizontal Directional Drilling

Computer-controlled technology called *horizontal directional drilling* allows oil and gas companies to drill sideways, flexibly snaking under streets and buildings with no disturbance aboveground, while sensors read surrounding conditions and allow lines to be installed (www.direction-aldrilling.com/). High-tech drilling can also be used to bury low-voltage electric distribution lines in towns, and using it in that way could eventually bring down the costs of all applications. Burying lines in this way may be highly attractive compared with digging up a crowded city or residential street or stringing more unsightly wire overhead on poles.

One can envision fiber-optic installers such as Qwest and cable TV and fiber-to-the-home innovators being invited in to run their lines down the conduit in exchange for shouldering some of the costs. They could buy a guaranteed slot for future generations of higher-speed fiber, much as Qwest has done in leaving an empty conduit for itself along railroad tracks (Diamond 1998).

Integrating Centralization and Dispersion

Several technologies, not discussed here, raise the value of central generation and transmission by enhancing efficiency, capacity, reliability, and stability. Such developments make central-station generation and long-range transmission more valuable relative to dispersed generation. But regulation cannot determine the proper balance and integration of the two approaches. Voluntary processes based on property and contract would best discover balance in a competitive environment. Private control would permit prices to fluctuate to reflect relative scarcities. Free-enterprise forces would send the signals to upgrade the grid at key bottlenecks and avoid the possible stagnation of new-generation technologies. As noted, electricity and information can flow along the same wire, leading to potentially interesting and unpredictable alliances between power producers and telecommunications, Internet, and software firms. It is important for analysts to recognize the richness of potential relationships and consumer benefits.

Other developments are just starting to change the nature of power transport. A newly developed superconductive film can carry many times the electricity of current wire technology. Such innovations combined with silicon switching technology change the nature of the grid and undermine utopian visions of its being managed efficiently by regulators. Modular flywheel energy storage devices targeted at cable and telephone markets provide power during outages and can provide backup power at hospitals and schools (*Electricity Daily* 1996b, 2). These portend new alliances with independent generators that lessen dependence on the power company for reliability. And although solar power is currently above market prices at its cheapest, photovoltaic cells do provide "a competitive peaking power option" (*Electricity Daily* 1996a, 1).

Intellectuals cannot know the local undulations of opportunity, just as they cannot chart and predict the specific patterns of skating in a roller rink. The skaters carry on, nonetheless, profitably and without difficulty. The regulator who would direct and control activities is like the perambulator who would accompany the skater.

Conclusion

Dispersed generation has long been economically viable, with technology making it even more so. Natural monopoly is a myth. Furthermore, the continuum between central generation and dispersed generation must be mediated in each particular context by parties with appropriate authority and local knowledge. Not all the answers about the shape of tomorrow's power markets are locked in some imagined set of initial conditions, as planners assume. Knowledge and opportunity are created as we go along. Technology has delivered conditions and alternatives that recommend a system whose success no longer depends on regulators making the right decisions.

NOTE

1. The best corroborative references available for the 500 mW statement are verbal communications with Eric Gozer, president, Certified Electric Distributors, York, SC (802) 684-0058; and Herbert Whittall, technical adviser, Electrical Generating Systems Association, Boca Raton, FL (561) 564-2641. The exact numbers were originally obtained by phone from Corporate Marketing (Barbara), Stewart and Stevenson Services, Inc., Houston, TX (713) 898-7700.

REFERENCES

Balzhiser, Richard E. 1997. "Technology to Play Hand in Future Power Market." *Forum for Applied Research and Public Policy*, fall, 25.

Baumol, William J., John C. Panzar, and Robert Willig. 1982. *Contestable Markets and the Theory of Industry Structure*. New York: Harcourt Brace Jovanovich.

Bayless, Charles. 1994. "Less Is More: Why Gas Turbines Will Transform Electric Utilities." *Public Utilities Fortnightly*, December 1, 21.

Borenstein, Severin, and James Bushnell. 2000. "Electricity Restructuring: Deregulation or Reregulation?" *Regulation* 23, no. 2: 46–52.

Brown, Stuart F. 1996. "Here Come the Pint-Size Power Plants." *Fortune*, April 1, 64D.

Bulkeley, William M. 1996. "Building Power Plants That Can Float." *Wall Street Journal*, May 22, B1.

Casten, Thomas R. 1995. "Electricity Generation: Smaller Is Better." *Electricity Journal*, December, 67.

Chilton, Cecil H., et al. 1967. *Cost Engineering in the Process Industries.* New York: McGraw-Hill.

Collins, Jim. 1997. "The Power Grid." *U.S. Airways Attache,* November, 43–45.

Colorado Revised Statutes. Title 40, (Utilities), Article 5, New Construction—Extension, Section 40-5-101.

Diamond, David. 1998. "Building the Future-Proof Telco." *Wired,* May, 124–26.

The Economist. 1998. "Stand and Deliver." April 18, 65.

Electricity Daily. 1996a. "Largest PV Farm Set for Nevada Test Site." November 6, 1.

Electricity Daily. 1996b. "Satcon Spins out Flywheel Uninterruptible Power System." October 10, 2.

Electricity Daily. 1998. "Big Future for Distributed Generation." September 30, 1.

Fox, William Price. 1992. *Lunatic Wind: Surviving the Storm of the Century.* Chapel Hill, NC: Algonquin Books.

Geddes, Richard. 1992. "A Historical Perspective on Electric Utility Regulation." *Regulation* 15, no. 1 (winter) (Internet address: http://www.cato.org/pubs /regulation/reg15n1-geddes.html).

Gilder, George. 1997. "Fiber Keeps Its Promise." *Forbes ASAP,* April 7, 92.

Hirsch, Jerry. 2001. "Declaring Energy Independence: Path Blocked to Truly Deregulated Power Network." *Los Angeles Times,* February 10, C1, C3.

Houston, Douglas A. 1995. "The Case for Deregulating Electric Transmission: The Virtues of Self-Governance." Paper prepared for the Cato Institute/Institute for Energy Research Conference, New Horizons in Electric Power Deregulation, Washington, DC, March 2.

Hutheesing, Nikhil. 1997. "The Last Furlong." *Forbes,* October 6, 72.

Jarrell, Greg A. 1978. "The Demand for State Regulation of the Electric Utility Industry." *Journal of Law and Economics* 21: 269–95.

Karlgaard, Rich. 1997. "Digital Warriors Want Baby Bells' Blood." *Wall Street Journal,* December 8, A24.

Kriz, Margaret. 1996."Power Brokers." *National Journal,* November 30, 2596.

Kupfer, Andrew. 1997. "Son of Internet." *Fortune,* June 23, 120–22.

Lowi, Alvin Jr. 1991. "Stewart and Stevenson's 100kW/15 PSI Steam Packaged Cogeneration System Development." Chicago: Gas Research Institute.

"9 Things to Watch in 1997." *GaAs Net: The GaAs Electronics Industry Resource* 3, no. 1 (Internet address: http://www.gaasnet.com/CompSemi/3-1/).

Preston, George T., and Dan Rastler. 1996. "Distributed Generation: Competitive Threat or Opportunity." *Public Utilities Fortnightly,* August, 13.

Schuler, Joseph F. Jr. 1996. "Generation: Big or Small?" *Public Utilities Fortnightly,* September 15, 31.

Stigler, George J., and Claire Friedland. 1962. "What Can Regulators Regulate? The Case of Electricity Regulation." *Journal of Law and Economics* 5 (October): 1–16.

Stiglitz, Joseph E. 1993. *Economics*. New York: Norton.

Tamaki, Julie. 2001. "Power Crunch's Ripples Hit Small Supplier, Others." *Los Angeles Times*, February 10, A16.

Tullock, Gordon. 1971. "Public Decisions as Public Goods." *Journal of Political Economy* 79, no. 4: 913–18.

10

Avoiding the Grid
Technology and the Decentralization of Water

Alvin Lowi Jr.

Traditional Water Facilities

During the twentieth century, American communities depended mainly on public utility monopolies for their water supplies.[1] Textbook expositions of "natural monopoly" might suggest to an unsuspecting reader that such local monopolies evolved in a free market (Musgrave and Musgrave 1993, 51–53; Rosen 1988, 322–25; Stiglitz 1993, 411–60; a summary of the argument may be found in this volume's introduction). However they may have originated, monopoly waterworks practices are now so entrenched that nearly all local governments have them and hardly anyone gives the matter a second thought. Water is so essential to a community's life and well-being that few seriously consider leaving its delivery to the vagaries of free enterprise in a market economy that has even the slightest possibility of high prices, conspiracy, and segmentation. So, to preempt such an outcome, the public has allowed municipal water and sewage works to be monopolized under political control. The costs and revenues of government-operated utilities tend to become commingled with the other costs and revenues of government. Taxes cover any operating deficits and debt service, and even if the water is metered, the patrons pay a rate that bears little relation to water's actual cost or value. As a result, municipal utilities have little incentive to conserve, and payment for the system is left to the vagaries of politics.

Once utility operations are taken over by the government, the real cost of the water supplied is buried in arcane municipal funding and accounting practices. In the new city of Rancho Palos Verdes, California, for exam-

184

ple, the local franchised water monopoly charges the householder from $3 to $4 per 1,000 gallons delivered, depending on his monthly usage as metered plus a surcharge based on the size of his meter. In addition, the householder's share of the county property tax is about $13 per year per $1,000 of assessed valuation, with about 10 percent going to the various water supply, sewerage, and drainage agencies. This levy adds about $1 per 1,000 gallons (25 to 33 percent) to the average household's direct cost of water.

Political monopoly arrangements are generally assumed to be in the public interest. Accordingly, their privileges by law and taxation are rarely questioned. But is a monopoly really inevitable in providing a community's water supply? It might seem so by looking only at the bargains in metered charges for raw tap water.

Is the political administration of communitywide waterworks really desirable? What are the real costs of the buried assets, wasted resources, environmental insults, immunity from liability, and postponement of progress? The answers to these questions depend in part on the state of relevant technologies.

A Qualified Laissez-Faire Regime

To address the question of whether technology is enhancing the case for free enterprise, we need to specify what laissez-faire would mean in the delivery of water. Assume that it is possible to remove all but a residue of constraints left over from preexisting government operations. We might then have a "qualified" laissez-faire regime applicable to the community's water business. Such a qualified laissez-faire regime might be characterized as having

- Free entry into and exit from any and all businesses subject to contractual commitments freely entered into.
- No regulation of pricing, product quality, or operations.
- No guarantees of return on capital invested or protection against operating losses from any cause whatsoever.
- Equal and fair access to government rights-of-way and reasonable easement rights.
- Equal and fair access to all government-controlled water-related facilities for any and all purveyors of water. Those facilities would

include lakes, rivers, canals, bays, beaches, aqueducts, aquifers, and the like, as well as such government-sanctioned privileges as easements, eminent domain powers, and other exclusive or subsidized access to government-controlled rights-of-way.

The difference between a qualified laissez-faire policy and a fully laissez-faire regime for water supply and delivery is that the latter would have no government-held resources, eminent domain powers, or regulations.

Which community utility paradigm benefits the populations served more—government or free enterprise? Some actual historical experience in less developed regions of the world seems to contradict the conventional wisdom favoring politically monopolized water utilities. In the less developed countries where political government has been relied on exclusively to provide utilities, these places are notoriously deficient, almost without exception, in hygienic water supplies accessible at affordable cost to the general public. Recent experience has found private enterprise to be decidedly superior to a traditional government monopoly in bringing water accessibility, quality and service to a community (Cowen and Cowen 1998).

Policy and technology are mutually dependent. Private ownership is motivated, flexible, and forward looking. According to the economic historian Werner Troesken, "about 20 percent of all private water companies had installed filters by 1899. Only 6 percent of all public companies had installed filters by 1899" (1999, 946). Private enterprise uses more technology, but outside our window we find a water sector dominated by government. Although many water supply and treatment technologies are available "on the shelf," few are widely used. Indeed, the implementation of technological advancements by political jurisdictions moves so slowly as to be imperceptible. Fully 100 years after bell-and-spigot cast-iron pipe was developed, the municipal water bureaucracy in Philadelphia still used bored logs, and the city was hit by a typhoid epidemic lasting for 50 years while its officials pondered a relatively newer innovation called filtration (see Steel 1947, 3). We can only speculate how, under an alternative regime, currently underutilized technologies might be used more efficiently, but such is the task at hand.

In a qualified laissez-faire environment, a private enterprise producing and distributing water to a community would have to be innovative. It could not rely on price protection, taxes, or assessments to cover its operating deficits or obtain certain traditional economies of scale available to

government-controlled central facilities. It could not be compelled to connect unlimited numbers of customers to large central plants by networks
of pipelines. Without the ability to resort to eminent domain powers to
condemn and traverse property lines, centralizing facilities under a privately owned monopoly would be difficult. However, a laissez-faire rendering of community utilities would not be restricted to a centralized approach but would also allow a decentralized, *on-site* approach. Rather than
examine the notion of competing private water grids, therefore, we will
explore the viability of on-site water systems.

The On-Site Alternative

On-site utilities operated as private enterprises can be economic units of
significant size. Even though they are generally deprived of the economies
of scale available to central utilities under political administration, they
can serve major realty operations like multiple-tenant income properties
under undivided ownership without any multiple transits of property
boundaries.

The on-site approach allows an entrepreneur to compensate significantly for scale-related costs by providing opportunities to minimize initial and recurring costs. On-site utilities offer an incentive for recycling
valuable materials, thereby avoiding additional transportation costs and
adding value in the form of by-products. In addition, by using new technologies for the intensive treatment of wastewater on the site, additional
potable water can be made available to consumers without further exploiting natural resources. By avoiding such development costs, the initial
costs facing a new homeowner would be sharply reduced, and the transaction costs associated with permitting and connecting to existing utility
networks might be eliminated altogether.

Localizing waste treatment on the site where the waste is produced
could significantly curtail the volume of water used and the sewage to be
removed and collected at some large, remote treatment site. A community's dependence on large-scale public works for reservoirs, pumping stations, water lines, sewerage, and treatment plants could, therefore, be minimized if not eliminated altogether. Realty operators and homeowners
using on-site utilities would have no reason to deal with public utility
commissions, city public works departments, county utility districts, sanitation districts, consolidated sewer works, groundwater recharge agencies,

waste recovery and recycle agencies, metropolitan water districts, and standby water reserves. Avoiding the politics, uncertainties, and strings-attached might, alone, be an enormous cost savings.

The on-site utility approach would not rely on the regimentation of property owners. Technological developments have now matured to the point that on-site utility arrangements can be competitively marketed, economically constructed, and reliably operated. Such facilities can offset all the so-called market-failure problems, real or imagined, used to justify central utility monopolies. Technological means are now available to support a full spectrum of affordable on-site water services.

The Cogeneration Factor

Cogeneration refers to the utilization of a single source of energy to "cogenerate" a multiplicity of utility functions. For example, fuel oil may be burned in a heat engine (such as a diesel) to generate electric power, and the otherwise wasted heat generated in the process may subsequently be used to produce hot water, space heating and cooling, and water treatment as by-products.

Let us assume that our laissez-faire regime would also permit the on-site supply and delivery of electricity on an entrepreneurial basis (a scenario explored by the chapter by Wayne Crews and me in this volume). Heating and cooling as well as other energy uses like water supply and waste disposal could be packaged to obtain significant additional cost reductions and profit opportunities. An integrated on-site utility systems scenario is appealing because it can combine a variety of domestic energy uses in a cogeneration hierarchy to maximize energy utilization and service potential.

The technologies that make integrated energy systems practical in domestic residential applications are not esoteric but are actually quite familiar to engineers. However, their use thus far has been limited to larger-scale commercial and industrial applications for which the cost of obtaining building and operating permits from local political authorities is smaller in relation to prospective gains from the installation.

An Alternative to Turning up the Heat: Closing the Windows

Water that is found in nature can have such widely varying properties that some sources of it may even be overlooked. Thus, Coleridge's Ancient Mariner anguished, "Water, water, every where, Nor any drop to drink."

On a raft cast adrift on the ocean, a shipwrecked mariner may not stop to consider that the medium supporting him is 96.5 percent pure water. For him, it may as well be concrete unless he is prepared to extract the potable quantities he needs to drink in order to survive. How much does he need, and how can he extract it? The "how much" depends on how he behaves and how he uses the crude water supply he finds at hand. The "how to extract it" involves physics and engineering. In any case, although the answers to both questions may not be common knowledge, they are not complicated.

The shipwrecked mariner's essential intake of pure water for metabolic purposes depends on the water content of his diet as well as the rate of water loss from his skin, gut, and kidneys. If he suffers from colic, his infected bowel will pretty surely doom him to death by dehydration. If he is exposed to tropical summertime sunshine and air temperatures, his skin will lose more water to the air than he may find suitable to drink. However, if he understands that he can immerse himself in the aqueous medium that his raft is floating in and allow his skin to mitigate this loss, he can subsist on substantially less drinking water.

Similarly, conditioning the air of buildings can reduce the residents' essential water consumption requirements by reducing their transpiration losses. Moreover, the water transpired by the inhabitants of buildings can be recovered by condensation on the air conditioner cooling coil surfaces where it must be condensed to maintain a comfortable equilibrium in the ambient humidity level.

Hierarchy of Water Qualities

The details of and the possible choices among the many kinds of water-refining technologies are manifold, and most are beyond the scope of this chapter (see Ingram et al. 1969). Complicating this matter further is the question "what for?" Obviously, getting drinkable water from seawater is a problem different from getting suitable supplies for firefighting or lawn irrigation—or from getting drinking water in turn from such supplies. Indeed, it may be appropriate to apply different standards of water quality to a community's various water uses (see *Treating Farmstead* 1972). A hierarchy of standards can facilitate significant economies in serving the common demands for utilities without threatening public health and safety.

The value of a water-quality hierarchy is exemplified in the chemical engineering technology known as *continuous countercurrent decantation* (Perry 1941, 1600). Countercurrent washing and rinsing procedures are used in pulp mills, plating plants, and other water-intensive industries to conserve water consumption per unit of output. The electroplater knows, for example, that to rinse a given batch of his product to a certain level of cleanliness in the highest-quality water available to him requires a volume of water that is 100 times greater than the volume of parts. He finds that he can clean the same quantity of parts to the same level of cleanliness by rinsing the dirtiest parts in the dirtiest water and progressing in a countercurrent manner from dirtiest to cleanest in successive steps. As a result, he finds he needs only a tenth as much water for the job. The analogous household situation might be to use dishwashing, laundry, and bath rinse water as toilet-flushing water. Thereby, the most stringent cleaning stage (dishes, persons, clothing, etc.) is accomplished in the "cleanest" water, and the least stringent wash (the toilet bowl) uses the same water after it has leached out, dissolved, and entrained the solid wastes from the antecedent operations.

Nonetheless, the traditional pattern of public utility service is burdened with a single quality standard for all domestic water supplies because the political establishment is obliged to provide water to all users for all purposes through a common piping system. If the quality supplied is adequate for the most demanding purposes, most of the water will have been treated beyond necessity. The greater part of the treatment outlays will have been inappropriate, if not outright wasted. At the same time, the small fraction that is destined for heath-sensitive usage will most likely be undertreated.

Typically, municipal utility systems serve a mosaic of users connected in common via piping networks run in dedicated rights-of-way and easements from an exclusive provider. In the case of water supply and sewage, the provider is usually the political establishment itself.

An all-purpose system will be held liable for personal injury from infection or toxicity, because it must provide water quality that is safe for the most biologically and physically sensitive uses and users, even though the least sensitive uses comprise the bulk of the community's demand for water. Furthermore, all users are served by an extensive piping network that is vulnerable to infiltration by the pathogens and toxins that reside in the subsurface environment through which the pipes must pass. Moreover, because the political establishment is obliged only to serve all alike, the people most vulnerable to waterborne disease cannot be any better protected than the least vulnerable.

Treatment Processes

It is clear that those water treatment technologies applicable to all-purpose central utility systems will differ from those that will be most effective and economical in an on-site setting. The mission of the conservative administrators of central utility systems is to satisfy the public's thirst for water without complaint. But the only approach available to them is establishing a sufficient quantity and quality of water in a reservoir and then attempting to maintain that quality as the water flows from the reservoir throughout the system all the way to the end users. The administrators focus on technology advancements in pipe materials, piping practices, bulk treatment facilities, chemical methods, and the like. The gradual introduction of plastic pipe, "hot-tapping" tools, horizontal-drilling machines, and chemical agents with residual bacteriostatic properties has helped maintain the status quo in community services provided by central plants, notwithstanding the significant growth in population and groundwater pollution in recent years. However, these technologies have nothing to do with water quality and quantity improvement.

Small-scale and on-site utilities marketed, constructed, operated, and managed by entrepreneurs represent bona fide alternatives to the traditional water service monopolies. Private ownership of water treatment facilities demands a degree of specialization that is alien to bureaucratically administered central plants. Private ownership in a laissez-faire environment demands profit-seeking management under which the owner/provider is personally liable for damages. Therefore, the most appropriate technologies for this approach must be both economical and reliable. Although true private enterprise is relatively rare in the field of community utilities, there is, nevertheless, an inventory of assorted technologies waiting to be used in individual and on-site utility systems.

In recent years, various new water treatment techniques have been advanced and perfected. Some are new processes using existing materials. A few are old processes refined with the application of new materials and apparatus. Others use new processes involving new materials, processes, and apparatus. The most common of these processes, each of which has its virtues and limitations, are listed next, presented in approximate descending order of the severity of water treatment performed and the rigor of quality control attainable. The quantity and quality of energy used by these processes are approximately in the same order when the chemicals and controls required to implement them are taken into account.

Distillation: Nature's own method of water purification and recycling. Distillation is a thermal process. It is the oldest, most complete, and most reliable method available for extracting pure water from raw sources. During the past thirty years, significant refinements have been made in the methods and means for large-scale recovery from saline-water sources like the ocean. One example is given at the end of this treatment (Lowi 1983). Small distilling units of varying design, size, and energy efficiency have been developed and available since about 1970 for household, laboratory, and marine applications.[2]

Deionization: Inorganic ion separation by chemical means. This is a relatively recent advancement of the old-fashioned "zeolite" cation (positively charged ion) exchange process in which certain natural minerals called *zeolites* arranged in porous granular beds substitute sodium ions for calcium and magnesium ions in a stream of water flowing through the bed. Such ion substitution improves soap solubility and has become known popularly as *water softening*. New ion exchange resins have been developed since World War II using new methods of chemical synthesis. By combining these new materials in the same bed, both anions (negative ions) and cations can be captured to remove virtually all ionizable material from water, including most dissolved polar solids and liquids. This process is widely used in research laboratories to prepare mineral-free water. Like all related though less severe ion exchange processes, including water softening and chelation, deionization requires consumable chemicals for regeneration.[3]

Electrodialysis: The process of using an ion-selective membrane to demineralize water. Electrochemical technology developed after World War II

produced ion-selective membranes or electrodes capable of demineraliz-
ing water as with ion-exchange resins but without any chemical regeneration. In the early 1960s, anticipating cheap electric power from atomic energy, electrodialysis was seen to offer an improvement in the economics of
large-scale water demineralization. Like a storage battery, electroplating
bath, or other electrochemical cell operation, electrodialysis requires large
quantities of expensive direct-current electricity.

Reverse osmosis: A physical membrane process for the partial separation
of dissolved solids in water. The selective permeation of larger molecules
in solution, whether or not ionized, can be accomplished with a thin film
of certain plastic materials, provided that sufficient pressure is applied in
excess of and in opposition to the osmotic pressure of the solution. Membrane and cell construction have developed rapidly in recent years to reduce the cost and improve the durability and range of separation. Some
products are available at reasonable cost for undersink installation in a
household to purify tap water using service pressures only. These are now
widely available through water-conditioning services (see www.culligan
.com). Purification of exceptionally mineralized water requires somewhat
higher pressures than available from domestic service, which calls for
pumping and expensive membrane support. A less expensive alternating
current is used to drive the pumps.

Chelation: Selective inorganic ion modification. Selective ion exchange
such as the softening processes for reducing "hardness" (increasing soap
effectiveness) is familiar and used in many households. Numerous advancements have been made since the early 1900s, and many products and
systems are now widely available through water-conditioning services like
Culligan. However, there are many other applications for chelating agents
in water such as increasing the solvation in laundry machines or forming
filterable precipitates and flocculating and coagulating them for clarifica-
tion purposes. Chelation involves the use of disposable chemicals.

Anaerobic digestion: A culture of anaerobic organisms used to reduce the
mass and concentration of dissolved and suspended organic materials in
aqueous wastes. Certain bacteria are cultivated in a body of aqueous waste
containing digestible organic material. These anaerobes obtain their
metabolic oxygen from chemically bound oxygen in the material in solution rather than from air. Since organic ash is formed as a result of biotic

digestion, the process is analogous to submerged incineration. Subsequently, the ash can be flocculated, coagulated, precipitated, and settled using chemical aids (see Chelation). This is the type of treatment process that takes place in common septic tanks. The process requires periodic sludge removal and possibly inoculation and culture boosting.

Aerobic digestion: A culture of aerobic organisms used to reduce the mass and concentrate the bulk of aqueous organic waste. A stream of aqueous organic waste is treated by aeration to allow air-breathing microbes to digest the organic material, reducing it to filterable inorganic solids and gases like carbon dioxide and water. This process is carried out in aeration ponds, cascades, and trickling filters. A trickling filter is like a cooling tower but is usually constructed as a porous rock pile. This process requires pumping power, filtration, and sludge removal. It is generally known in the municipal sanitation field as *secondary treatment*.

Filtration: A solids-laden stream of water is passed through a porous solid medium that presents a large surface area to the fluid. A bed of so-called sharp river sand through which water is made to flow represents perhaps the oldest engineered water treatment process. Beds of activated carbon particles (charcoal) are used to trap odorous chemicals like chlorine and sulfur compounds as well as inert particles. Diatomaceous earth, the filter medium of preference for swimming pools, is used to improve clarity and remove sediments. Silver-bearing materials may be included in the media to improve bacteriostasis. Some filters may be reconditioned by back flushing to remove trapped material. Others require replacement of the filter media themselves. Filters have been produced in myriad forms ranging from whole-house units to cartridges fitted to the faucet (see www.culligan.com).

Disinfection: Live microscopic and possibly pathogenic organisms are killed in solution. Dousing water-containing microorganisms with molecular chlorine, ozone, or other chemicals that liberate these molecules in solution denatures the live organisms, rendering them nonpathogenic. The effective level of concentration of the disinfectant varies with the organism and the chemical. Irradiation of the infected water stream with ultraviolet radiation of certain wavelengths also is effective, both from the generation of ozone in situ and by direct germicidal radiation. The effectiveness of any of these methods of disinfection depends to a large degree on prior filtration to reduce competition from noninfectious matter and to improve clarity.

All these processes have been investigated at one time or another under government auspices, usually with significant involvement in the research by the various, grant-funded, nonprofit universities and government laboratories. Rarely have private businesses with vested interests in the results, such as realty enterprises, participated in this work. Nevertheless, the greater usage of these water treatment technology developments is to be found outside government utility establishments that rely on exclusive, single-purpose central stations serving an extended geographical area in which there is diverse ownership and activity.

The appropriate technical approach for establishing and maintaining engineered and managed energy systems on an entrepreneurial basis is likely to be as integrated and flexible as possible. A wide assortment of technologies are considered in order to minimize costs and liabilities while maximizing marketable benefits because the entrepreneur has no access to taxes or other noncommercial sources of funds to cover his operating deficits or his liabilities for damages. Self-containment combining all appropriate technologies carries a high premium for private enterprise because of the high cost of transporting bulk commodities like water and aqueous wastes from a distance and across property lines. The integration of utility services on site leads to technical divergence in utility practices from those that now dominate centralized systems.

Application to a Typical Community Situation

The Existing Problem

In a front-page article, the *Pahrump Valley* (Nevada) *Times* highlighted a common problem with Nevada tap water, stating that "75 to 80 community water systems in this state are contaminated with arsenic and as much as $525,000,000 will be required to remedy the situation" (June 9, 2000). The article went on to state that to finance an unspecified government remedy to this so-called toxic contamination problem, water rates might have to be quintupled in the near future.

The use of the word *contamination* implies blameworthy human mischief calling for government action to protect property owners and the public from injury. However, what is actually happening to the public water supplies in Pahrump and other Nevada communities is a natural local environmental phenomenon, and one that has long been familiar to geologists and hydrologists.

Instead of sensationalizing the matter, the *Pahrump Valley Times* might have simply informed its readers what a fine solvent water is and how it naturally leaches soluble elements and salts from local mineral deposits existing in and around the local aquifer that is the source of their supply. As a result, readers might have learned that their tap water could very well contain unsavory concentrations of salts and elements because the soil in the state of Nevada is exceptionally rich in arsenic as well as silver and other heavy metals. Then, they might have informed their readers of alternative, more wholesome sources of water available, indicating that some of these might even be available at the local supermarket for mere pennies a gallon. They might have pointed out that still other alternatives might be available delivered at the door or produced on-site with available appliances at an adequate level of reliability and affordable cost. So informed, the public might realize that they have in their own hands technically and economically feasible alternatives to the proposed government action.

The minerals in community water sources such as Pahrump's were present long before the water was tapped for human use. And since it was tapped from the ground, generations of consumers have used it in ignorance of its chemical composition. Until recently, almost all water consumers and many waterworks managers had no better idea of water quality than what they could surmise from its color, odor, and taste. Even so, by the beginning of World War I, waterborne diseases were already on the wane, largely as a result of improving personal hygiene practices like hand washing, cooking, bottling, and canning.

The government's actual technical prospects for cleaning up the general water supply to cooking-and-drinking-quality standards are quite unrealistic. While it might technically fulfill its promise to purify the water to wholesome levels at the reservoir, whether it could do so without excessive cost to the taxpayers is another question. Maintaining reservoir quality as the water passes through antiquated delivery systems buried in public easements and in defective piping embedded in private buildings is an unrealistic expectation. The Romans were doing about as well two thousand years ago without the benefit of spectroscopy, bacteriology, chlorination, and PVC pipe. Nowadays, new technology makes central utility practices mimicking the Romans anachronistic.

A New Approach: Public Water as a Bulk Commodity

The proliferation, elaboration, and refinement of water treatment and reuse technologies make it timely to look at public water supplies from a wholly new perspective. Technical information, products, and services available directly to water consumers are rapidly expanding and increasingly accessible via the Internet.[4] Countertop and undersink appliances integrate filtration, reverse osmosis, or distillation with ultraviolet radiation and refrigeration for continuous antisepsis. Some of the water purification appliances combine hot and cold dispensers. Such products are readily available and becoming better and cheaper every day.

Curiously, the water treatment technologies and products that are practical and economical for in-home and on-site applications are already more sophisticated than those found in most central plants. Moreover, high-quality, germ-free, and palatable water is widely distributed in bottles at supermarkets at low retail prices. So, instead of depending on the government to do the impossible, to treat the community's whole water supply as a refined commodity, more and more people are taking their water supply into their own hands and becoming healthier in the process.

It is a fact that the great bulk of the water in a mixed-use community is for cooling, sanitation, firefighting, and landscaping purposes. Since none of these uses is for persons, a communitywide water supply might better be considered as just a bulk commodity, a raw material supplied to consumers for further processing for particular needs as they wish. Consumers might use such a supply directly out of the pipe or ditch for sanitation and landscaping purposes and then refine only a small part, as needed, for cooking, drinking, and bathing.

On-Site Refining

To minimize the dependence on instant access to municipal water supplies or receding water tables of whatever quality, a homeowners' association or individual homeowners could either install their own engineered treatment system and storage tanks or else convert their septic tanks and drain fields to such. They could then maintain an inventory of bulk water to be replenished at will using various economic sources, whether they be city water mains, tank trucks, rainstorm runoff catchments, or reclaimed water from certain prior uses like laundry and bathing.

Water is already commonly refined in the home. For example, many households use water softeners to improve the cleaning power of their laundry water using less soap. Then they install reverse-osmosis or distillation units to remove the excess minerals in their cooking and beverage water. Charcoal filters are commonly installed at the tap to improve the hygiene and taste of the water they use for drinking, cooking, and ice making. Modern refrigerators are connected to a source of filtered and sometimes also demineralized water under pressure to operate the ice and chilled-water dispensers.

Distillation is the ideal process for preparing water for personal consumption because it is a complete and reliable method of water purification regardless of raw water quality or composition. Nevertheless, distillation appliances are not yet common in households, even though they can be designed for permanent installation and connected to plumbing like a water heater or made into a cord-connected countertop appliance like a coffeepot. Both types are available on the market, and neither requires any particular skill or talent to install and operate successfully.[5]

A properly designed distiller can produce pharmacologically pure water inexpensively.[6] The energy required to evaporate a pound of cold tap water at sea level is about a third of a kilowatt-hour (Keenan 1936). If the water can be evaporated and subsequently condensed back into liquid form without a significant loss of steam or heat, the production of a gallon of pure water in a simple still would consume about 3 kilowatt-hours of electricity. At prevailing domestic electricity rates, the energy cost would be about $0.30 per gallon. That gallon of genuine distilled water may be purchased in a supermarket for about $2.50. The retail price for a gallon of bottled water of lesser purity ranges from about $0.50 from a coin-operated dispenser up to $2.00 on the beverage shelf, container included.

Pharmacological purity is the water purity required to prepare solutions for safe intravenous injection. To be pharmacologically pure, water may contain no more than 2 parts per million (ppm) total dissolved solids.[7] By contrast, the total dissolved solids carried in most public water supplies ranges from 100 to 5000 ppm and has been increasing year by year as subsurface aquifers, lakes, and streams are drawn down and replaced by drainage laden with sewage, fertilizers, insecticides, solvents, detergents, and the like (*Environmental Quality 1982*). However, to put this situation into some kind of meaningful perspective, recall that seawater contains approximately 35,000 ppm of total dissolved solids (Sverdrup et al. 1942).

Managing an Inventory

To gain independence and safety in their lifestyle in regard to their water supply, homeowners will face, among other things, some plumbing changes in their household drainage piping to inventory raw water and recover gray water. Although local building codes, laws, or regulations may prohibit such changes in many locations at the present time, such restrictions would not exist in a free-enterprise regime. Be that as it may, if homeowners recognize the realities of their hierarchy of uses, they can learn to create a bulk water supply separate and distinct from their particular end-use water needs. They can segregate and store relatively large volumes of so-called gray water, the residue of their most voluminous usage, like dishwashing, laundry, and car washing. Recovered gray water is satisfactory for most sanitary flushing and landscaping purposes. Where it is not, only minor treatment is required, depending on the amounts and kinds of soaps, bleaches, conditioners, and detergents used in the household. With additional treatment, such water may also be used in swimming pools, wading ponds, fish ponds, and the like, in which case the household may already have abundant raw water storage capacity on site.

Sanitary flushing produces relatively small volumes of "black water." Low-flush toilets can reduce the volume of black water by an appreciable fraction and increase the concentration of organic waste being transported by a comparable amount. This not only conserves water and reduces sewage volume; it also enables greater efficiency in subsequent waste-treatment processing. (Black water can even be eliminated from the household altogether by the use of chemical toilets or waterless earth closets; see www.envirolet.com).

Black-water drains contain relatively large fractions of solid organic waste. Such drains may be intensively treated to produce a smaller volume of safely reusable water, resulting in a comparable amount of septic aqueous waste. This liquid waste may, in turn, be de-watered by evaporation in a pond and then composted for use as organic fertilizer, or it can be stored in a septic tank for microbial digestion. The clarified and disinfected water may be decanted for gray water makeup. The sludge may be composted or disposed off-site via sewerage if a connection already exists or hauled off by a vacuum truck if not. On the basis of the solid-waste content, kitchen garbage disposers are also black-water dischargers. Accordingly, their drains should be piped in common with toilets to simplify the subsequent collection, treatment, and disposal of fluidized solid waste.

Households would acquire and maintain an inventory of gray water by recovering as much as they can of the water they use. The water used for metabolic consumption and outdoor plant irrigation is difficult to reclaim, however, because most of it ends up evaporating into the air, percolating into soil, or fluidizing organic waste for subsequent transportation off-site. To make up for these various losses, householders must periodically replenish their raw water inventory. Inventorying water on-site is the key to improving a community's water supply.

Recycling gray water involves the familiar technologies of filtration and disinfection as a minimum. That portion of the gray water to be used for metabolic and bathing purposes is best extracted by distillation to ensure the removal of those organic contaminants in domestic water supplies that are as readily absorbed into the body through the skin as through the gut. By such means, the water for the household's most sensitive uses would be far purer than that flowing from the ordinary kitchen tap today. Indeed, today's tap water is laden with toxic chloramines that are formed in the basic water supply by chemical reactions between the dissolved organic compounds and the chlorine dose applied at the central plant for disinfection prior to distribution (McDaniel 1972). But germs can grow in distilled water as well or better than in tap water without residual chlorine compounds. To deal with this dilemma, the John Ellis Company developed its Electron Water/Air Machine (www.johnellis.com). Various companies offer ozonation and ultraviolet irradiation treatment products for this purpose as well.[8]

Even those who might not care to treat their own water have readily available alternatives. A growing number of enterprises cater profitably to householders.[9] No doubt, many more such enterprises will form in the future.[10] Whether or not such water is of the purity achieved by distillation, such commercially refined water nevertheless meets the needs of discriminating consumers. Doubtless in time such products will be prepared by distillation, if only to minimize liabilities.

A Specific Implementation for Pahrump

How would the on-site utility scheme work out in the case of Pahrump, a community still using individual septic tanks? First, to protect the health of their neighbors as well as their own, Pahrump residents would install gray-water storage tanks or convert their existing septic tanks into cisterns with separate black-water clarifiers. They would want to abandon the use of haphazard drain fields, which, though legal in many areas, run a high risk of exposing the neighborhood to infectious and toxic materials. Once established, the inventory of gray water would be recycled after being treated and rendered aseptic and clear by local trickling filters.[11] After sediment filtration in sanitary diatomaceous earth, the clarified water would be disinfected by ozonation or ultraviolet irradiation. Chlorination should be used only if the amount of dissolved reactive organic materials is minimal and there are no aesthetic objections to the residual gas, which is toxic in relatively low concentrations. Consumers could then subject that part of the water destined for more personal use such as cooking, drinking, and bathing to a more intensive treatment like distillation. Or they could obtain such refined water on the market, as many households already do for their cooking and drinking needs.

The water inventory contained in the cistern would consist of recovered gray water, possibly a smaller amount of recovered black water, and imports of doubtful quality from external sources such as a municipal water system. As already noted, some replenishment would be required from time to time because of local water losses. The heaviest losses would come from landscape irrigation, but here again, technological advances in the form of drip irrigation and underground soakers are dramatically reducing the amounts of water required for gardening and general landscaping.[12] Drip watering requires less than 30 percent of conventional sprinkling. Drip has been found to reduce plant stress from over- and underwatering, resulting in earlier production and up to 49 percent faster growth. Healthier and more beautiful plants are cultivated with up to 84 percent greater yields of flowers and fruit. Drip also reduces weed growth by watering only the base of the desired plants and eliminating water runoff. Subsurface soaking feeds only the roots. Both prevent excessive soil moisture, expansion, and erosion. Whatever makeup water of sufficient quality and quantity that remains to be obtained may come from the public water system. If not available from that source, it could be trucked in by private water companies like General Water Club of Southern California.

Developments in Distillation Technology

Since we have cited distillation as a key component in the on-site approach to community water supplies, we should discuss the state of the art of that technology.

Distillation is the most comprehensive and reliable method of water treatment known. Although various other water treatment processes are less energy intensive, they are somewhat more specialized than distillation in their community applications. When water recycling, inventory, and reuse is contemplated, distillation is essential because it is the only fail-safe method of producing pure water from almost any available source.

Whereas many different and ingenious engineering methods have been devised for boiling-type distillation, many applications have certain economic disadvantages, including the need for descaling heat-exchanger surfaces and for high-temperature heat. Mineral-scale deposits must be removed periodically to maintain thermal performance, and such maintenance is labor intensive. While boiling at lower temperatures may reduce scaling, this requires subatmospheric pressures entailing the use of costly pressure vessels, which must be manufactured and transported from factory to site at some expense.

Supplying heat at high temperatures for boiling-type distillation typically uses high-pressure steam. Such heat is expensive because it requires sophisticated steam-generation equipment with licensed and unionized operators around the clock. In addition, steam commands a higher value for generating power than for heating.

Curiously, these disadvantages are absent in nature's distillation process in which water evaporates from the surface of the ocean at ordinary atmospheric pressure and condenses back again as rain without ever approaching the boiling point. Mineral-scale deposits are nowhere in evidence. This scale-free, natural-distillation phenomenon sharply contrast with the experience with conventional water distillers on naval vessels at sea, a comparison that led to the conception of an all-direct-contact, vapor-staged, multieffect process called *absorption distillation* (Lowi 1983).

The object of this innovation was to devise a suitable process and apparatus for large-scale seawater desalination to support a mixed-use real estate development on a seacoast location having good accessibility to everything but municipal or other suitable water supplies. However, an unanticipated result of this new development in distillation technology was to make the cogeneration of water in integrated, on-site utility systems economically attractive.

By perfecting the means for carrying out partial evaporation and condensation in the presence of a noncondensable medium such as air, which is the absorption distillation technique, a number of advantages could be realized and drawbacks avoided while retaining the basic virtues of distillation. For example, absorption distillation is carried out in a structure very similar to an ordinary and familiar cooling tower. In fact, a cooling tower is representative of the evaporative portion of the absorption distillation apparatus. A similar tower located adjacent to the evaporative tower is used for direct-contact condensation, which is essentially a spray dehumidification process.

Some salient attributes of the absorption distillation process and apparatus include the following:

- Site-constructed facilities using only locally available building materials can be scaled to suit any size application and modularized for flexible uprating to suit future growth.
- An all-direct-contact heat and mass transfer arrangement eliminates scaling, corrosion, expensive construction materials, and expensive pumping and piping machinery.
- A nonboiling evaporation process carried out in stages entirely at atmospheric pressure eliminates expensive, fabricated pressure vessels and uses low-level heat input to heat water without boiling.
- The low-level heat requirement facilitates the operation on waste heat from electric power generation plants without penalty to them, thereby inviting cogeneration arrangements.
- The bona fide distillation process implemented provides a robust and reliable separation of water from contaminants ranging from radioactive salts to septic organic matter.
- Concurrent aerobic digestion of organic matter as a result of the intimate contact of the raw water with the oxygen in the transport medium (air) reduces the residual mass of that form of contamination to inert mineral ash.

Experimental results support these attractive characteristics of absorption distillation (see Lowi 1983). By using economical energy and facilities, this innovation in distillation technology can provide the comprehensive water treatment needed to facilitate integrated, on-site utility systems. The economic advantage of absorption distillation over other distillation methods is attributable to its low-cost construction and effectiveness in utilizing low-grade heat.

Conclusion

This chapter has touched on the extensive range of water treatment techniques and complex combinations of them that are accessible to private enterprise for providing on-site utilities. It questioned the natural-monopoly arguments justifying single-purpose, indefinitely expandable, centralized water, sewer, and power grids under political jurisdiction.

Progress invariably depends on the introduction and application of new technology, which always brings change and risks. Government is bound to be conservative because it must be seen to be avoiding taking risks with the commonwealth it controls. Hence government is not only noncompetitive; it is antiprogressive.

Entrepreneurial activity in this arena of community service can accelerate technological initiative combined with financial responsibility. The value of such alternatives is clearly illustrated in the case of Pahrump, Nevada. The residents of Pahrump would be well advised to look at their water situation from a fresh technological perspective before they agree to government projects that, with very questionable chances of success, may in the near future quintuple their water rates.

Unlike centralized municipal utility bureaus, proprietary on-site utilities are inclined to use a wide assortment of technologies, especially for serving the community's water demands. This approach recognizes a quality hierarchy in serving various uses. Emphasizing the economies of water reuse on site, the on-site approach substantially reduces the demand for water supplies from the environment as well as the overall burden of aqueous waste disposal into the environment.

The existence of proprietary utility systems like the on-site alternatives described depends on the existence of a qualified laissez-faire social environment. Such dependence implies a substantial independence of regulation by municipal and county governments, which have long relied on their ability to grant or withhold permission to connect to "the grid" as a major tool for controlling land development and generating revenues. So the challenge of engaging in the utility business under present circumstances should not be minimized. But this challenge is political, not technological or economic.

When researchers consider the recent technological advancements in the provision of utilities, they will realize it is not nature that creates monopolies. As technologies overcome previous limits, decentralized and competitive water systems will become more attractive and economical. Technological advancements in water supply and delivery would allow the natural competition of many substitutes and alternatives, if permitted by law.

NOTES

1. Most nineteenth-century waterworks were privately provided. See Crocker and Masten 2000. On the history of private waterworks in London, see Tynan 2000.

2. See "Home Appliance Makes Pure Drinking Water," *Waterwise Catalog*, www.waterwise.com, *Popular Science* Magazine Showcase, December 2000, 107. Another example is the 1997–98 catalog for the Cole-Parmer Instrument Company, Vernon Hills, IL, 1997-98 Catalog, 1318–25, www.coleparmer.com.

3. Also see the Chelation section; *Engineers Catalog*, Culligan International Company, Northbrook, IL, 1973; and www.culligan.com for an extensive, up-to-date selection of domestic water treatment products and services.

4. See the product and service catalogs at www.culligan.com, www.waterwise.com, www.envirolet.com, www.watergeneral.com, www.filterdirect.com, www.puritywater.com, www.johnellis.com, www.clearwater-az.com, www.ecosoft-engineering.com.

5. *Home Appliance Makes Pure Drinking Water*, Waterwise Catalog, www.waterwise.com.

6. Brochure for *Quench* Portable Water Distillers, Terraqua, Inc., San Pedro, CA 1972.

7. U.S. Pharmacopeia, ISBN 1889788031, Bk. & Suppl. ed., January 1, 2000.

8. The *1999 Regional Industrial Buying Guide* of the Thomas Regional Directory Company lists hundreds of sources of such water treatment products. See www.thomasregional.com.

9. See product and service listings in the Product Showcase section of any issue of *Popular Science* or *Popular Mechanics*.

10. The *Los Angeles Times*, Saturday, June 3, 2000, advertised on p. C3 an offer to residents of Southern California by the General Water Club to dial 800-440-4048 to arrange to have quality drinking water delivered to their home in unlimited amounts for $10 a month.

11. A trickling filter consists of a porous bed of rock in which water is con-
tacted by a countercurrent of air to promote the aerobic digestion of organisms
and to remove the resulting ash.

12. James Dulley, "Update Bulletin No. 598," James Dulley List, P.O. Box
54987, Cincinnati, OH 45254; www.dulley.com. (The Web site lists manufacturers
and suppliers of various types of drip watering systems and components.)

REFERENCES

Cowen, Penelope Brook, and Tyler Cowen. 1998. "Deregulated Private Water Sup-
    ply: A Policy Option for Developing Countries." *Cato Journal* 18, no. 1
    (spring/summer): 21–41.
Crocker, Keith J., and Scott E. Masten. 2000. "Prospects for Private Water Provi-
    sion in Developing Countries: Lessons from 19th Century America." University
    of Michigan, June. Available online at http://www.isnie.org/isnie00/papers
    /crocker-masten.pdf.
Culligan International Company. 1973. *Engineers Catalog.* Northbrook, IL: Culli-
    gan International Company.
Environmental Quality 1982. 1982. Thirteenth annual report of the Council on
    Environmental Quality. Washington, DC: U.S. Government Printing Office.
Ingram, William T., et al. 1969. *Water and Wastewater Control Engineering Glos-
    sary.* Joint publication of the American Public Health Association, American
    Society of Civil Engineers, American Waterworks Association, and Water Pol-
    lution Control Federation. Washington, DC: American Public Health Associa-
    tion.
Keenan, Joseph H. 1936. *Thermodynamic Properties of Steam.* New York: Wiley.
Lowi, Alvin Jr. 1983. "Direct-Contact Absorption Distillation System." U.S. Patent
    Office Disclosure Document Deposit no. 123638, December 20.
McDaniel, Allen. 1972. *Water—What's in It for You.* San Pedro, CA: Heather Foun-
    dation.
Musgrave, Richard A., and Peggy B. Musgrave. 1993. *Public Finance in Theory and
    Practice.* 2d ed. New York: Norton.
Perry, John H. 1941. *Chemical Engineer's Handbook.* 2d ed. New York: McGraw-
    Hill.
Rosen, Harvey S. 1988. *Public Finance.* Homewood, IL: Irwin.
Steel, Ernest W. 1947. *Water Supply and Sewage.* 2d ed. New York: McGraw-Hill.
Stiglitz, Joseph E. 1993. *Economics.* New York: Norton.
Sverdrup, H. U., et al. 1942. *The Oceans, Their Physics, Chemistry and General Biol-
    ogy.* Englewood Cliffs, NJ: Prentice-Hall.
Treating Farmstead and Rural Home Water Systems. 1972. Farmers Bulletin no.
    2248. Washington, DC: U.S. Department of Agriculture.

Troesken, Werner. 1999. "Typhoid Rates and the Public Administration of Private Waterworks, 1880–1920." *Journal of Economic History* 59, no. 4 (December): 927–48.

Tynan, Nicola. 2000. "Private Provision of Water in London: Re-Assessing the Externalities." George Mason University, Department of Economics.

11

Technological Change and the Case for Government Intervention in Postal Services

Rick Geddes

In 2001, the United States Postal Service (USPS) employed more than 891,000 workers, processed more than 200 billion pieces of mail, and earned revenues of more than $63 billion (*2001 Annual Report of the United States Postal Service*). If the U.S. Postal Service were a private company, in 2000 it would have been the eleventh largest in the country. Until World War II, it was the largest department of the federal government and remains the largest civilian employer. Although it was "reformed" through the Postal Reorganization Act of 1970, the USPS still is owned by the government.

The Postal Service enjoys a legally enforced monopoly in letter delivery. Most of its revenues are derived from mail that is monopolized under the private express statutes of 1845.[1] In 2001, 57 percent of its revenues were derived from monopolized first-class mail, and more than 24 percent came from partially monopolized standard mail (A) (formerly third-class mail).[2] For much of the mail it delivers, the USPS is required to provide universal service within the United States at uniform rates for a particular weight/class category.

The rationales for government involvement in postal services have evolved over time. I first address the traditional "universal service" rationale, which asserts that government must intervene to ensure that customers in rural areas will receive service. I then look at the more recent "natural-monopoly" rationale, which suggests that there are social gains from this legally enforced monopoly. Whatever validity the rationales may have had in the past, technological advances have made the government's monopoly of mail service obsolete.

The Universal Service Rationale
for Government Intervention in Postal Services

Government intervention in postal services in North America predates the United States itself. British colonials imposed a postal monopoly so that insurgents communicating treasonous plans either had to pay for an expensive private messenger or risk capture when using the Royal Mail. Continuing the government's involvement, the Continental Congress was concerned about national security but also about dependable communications and the security of messages during wartime (Priest 1975, 35, 47). Congress itself took over management of the post because private alternatives were believed to be inadequate.

Overview of the Universal Service Rationale

As early as the 1790s, however, the government's intervention became more oriented toward preserving a politically motivated cross-subsidy from the populous middle states to the relatively sparse west and south. Rural citizens received newspapers and other information at low cost, which furthered federalist aims to preserve and bolster the union. George Washington was one of the first to appreciate the political benefits arising from a monopolized post (Priest 1975, 52). The traditional justification for government control thus developed quite early: subsidizing outlying routes with revenues from relatively densely populated routes.

By the time of the 1845 congressional debates on the postal monopoly, the most extensive ever conducted, private express services were widespread. Members of Congress argued that the private expresses would never provide service to sparsely populated areas and that the government would consequently be left with unprofitable rural routes and massive losses (Priest 1975, 66). Thus, the main justification given in 1845 for legally restricting the carriage of letters by the private expresses was to preserve the rural cross-subsidy.

That argument against competition was used for at least the next 150 years. In 1973 the Board of Governors of the newly reorganized Postal Service stated:

If the Private Express Statutes were repealed, private enterprise, unlike the Postal Service, would be free to move into the most economically attractive markets while avoiding markets that are less attractive from a business standpoint. . . . Without abandoning the policy of self-sufficiency and reintroducing massive subsidies, it is hard to see how the Postal Service could meet rate and service objectives in the face of cream-skimming competition against its major product.[3]

The Postal Service continues to invoke the "cream-skimming" argument today.[4] Ensuring rural service, referred to by the USPS as "universal service," has been the most durable argument for retaining monopoly power. However, the desirability of the uniform rate (which, along with universal service, preserves the rural cross-subsidy) is also used to justify monopoly power. Without monopoly power, the Postal Service argues that it would be forced by competition to abandon uniform rates for particular weight/class categories.

Former Postmaster General Marvin Runyon clearly articulated the link among monopoly power, universal service, and the uniform rate: "The Private Express Statutes provide the financial underpinning that allows the Postal Service to provide universal mail delivery at a uniform postage rate for letter mail" (*Washington Post*, September 23, 1996, A17).

Taking these rationales at face value, one might ask why Congress does not contract out the service to a private, regulated monopoly that is required to maintain universal service and uniform rates. The response seems to be that only by means of government ownership are such terms assured (Tierney 1988, 32). Therefore, maintaining the cross-subsidy of low-density customers today remains the principal traditional justification for all aspects of government intervention: the enforced monopoly, the uniform rate, and government ownership.

Perspectives on the Universal Service Rationale

There are alternative perspectives regarding the universal service rationale. First, elementary economics implies that it is unlikely that rural areas would receive no postal delivery whatsoever if the cross-subsidy were eliminated. Rather, private firms would serve outlying areas but charge them more.[5] Since a substantial number of alternative delivery services, such as United Parcel Service, Federal Express, and newspaper and circular deliveries, frequently cover these same routes, it is likely that they and others would arise to meet the demand.[6] Delivery networks to service these areas already exist and could be coordinated to incorporate letter delivery in their contracts. Rather than becoming isolated, rural customers would simply pay the greater cost of delivery to them.

There is no reason why fairness compels urban residents to subsidize delivery to rural residents. To the extent that people make choices about where they live, they should assume the costs of that decision. If I decide to drive my car longer distances, why should someone else have to subsidize my increased use of gasoline? Similarly, from a distributional perspective, it is possible that the urban-rural cross-subsidy results in wealth redistribution from poor to rich. Currently, for example, inhabitants of the South Bronx are among those who subsidize mail delivery to Aspen, Colorado.

Government could easily contract with private firms to ensure service to rural areas if so desired. The contracts could be competitively awarded, eliminating the need for statutory monopoly. In a study by Harvard economist Andre Shleifer, the Postal Service was singled out as a canonical case of how contracting could be used:

> A common argument for government ownership of the postal service is to enable the government to force the delivery of mail to sparsely populated areas, where it would be unprofitable to deliver it privately. From a contractual perspective, this argument is weak. The government can always bind private companies that compete for a mail delivery concession to go wherever the government wants, or it can alternatively regulate these companies when entry is free. It cannot be so difficult to write the appropriate contract or regulation; after all, the government now tells the U.S. Postal Service where it wants the mail to be delivered. (Shleifer 1998, 136)

Technological Advancement and the Universal Service Rationale

Technological Changes in the Delivery of Printed Matter

Recent technological changes in the process of handling printed matter have been dramatic. Optical character recognition has been central to this process, and the Postal Service has been active in its development. This technology, along with the increased use of computerized bar coding of mail, has led to a highly automated process in which the USPS can process mail with almost no human involvement. Indeed, some mail-sorting centers are known as "lights out" facilities because no human need attend to them.

Many pieces of commercial mail are now bar coded in advance by the sender, which greatly assists in mail sorting and delivery. For pieces without a bar code, the USPS maintains a "remote bar-coding system" that is specifically designed, with the help of optical character readers, to correctly bar code mail. "Multiline optical character readers and facer cancelers" create a video image of the address, which is then processed by a "remote computer reader." This computer attempts to interpret the image electronically in order to affix the proper bar code. If it cannot do so, it automatically transmits the image to a "remote encoding center" where a human enters the address by hand (*1998 Annual Report of the United States Postal Service*).

This technology has been very successful in recognizing printed addresses but, due to the wide divergence of writing styles, much less so in recognizing handwritten addresses. But progress is being made. The remote computer reader could once correctly assess only 2 percent of handwritten mail, but it can now recognize more than 25 percent. The USPS has contracted for software development that will soon result in an estimated 50-percent recognition rate for handwritten addresses, which attests to the pace of technological change (*1998 Annual Report of the United States Postal Service*; also see Crew and Kleindorfer 1992, 8–10, for a more detailed discussion of this technology).

Additional technologies include robots on pedestals that help load and sort the mail trays. The computerized mail-processing system allows the USPS to manage address changes more easily and will support recent efforts to upgrade its mail-tracking capability. Moreover, the USPS recently authorized a private firm, Stamps.com Inc., to sell digital postage online (another, e-Stamp Corporation, got out of the business). This allows computer users to print out an encrypted stamp image if they have established an online account with a postage vendor (Anders 1999, B10). Stamps.com has sold almost 95 million stamps online.

Such developments promise to save on relatively expensive labor costs. However, it is also clear, and the USPS readily admits, that while these technological developments are likely to reduce the cost of mailing personal letters, they particularly favor commercial or "mass" mailings.[7] That is, they facilitate the "targeting" of mail by zip code and other characteristics.

There is much evidence to substantiate the view that the USPS's operations are becoming more commercially oriented. The USPS provides substantial discounts to large mailers that bar code and presort their own material. These discounts are called *work-sharing discounts* (Sidak and Spulber 1996, 20–21). Bar coding and presorting are obviously more easily done by large mailers than by individuals sending personal letters. Such discounts encourage use of the mails by businesses, which frequently issue mass mailings for advertising purposes.

Additional evidence that the mail is increasingly commercial is provided by the changing composition of first-class mail, which can be broken down into "households-to-other-households" mail versus "nonhouseholds-to-households" mail. In 1977, household-to-other-household mail made up 12 percent of the total volume of first-class mail, and nonhousehold-to-household mail was 39 percent. By 1991, household-to-household mail had dropped to 8.4 percent, and nonhousehold-to-household mail had risen to 44.3 percent (Tolley 1994, 28–30). Personal letters between citizens are a relatively small and decreasing component of monopolized first-class mail, whereas the amount of commercial mail is growing. This is consistent with the technological changes lowering the cost of commercial mailing.

First-class mail includes personal correspondence and postcards. The Postal Service describes it as follows: "First-Class Mail, which includes personal correspondence, post cards, and business transactions, affords privacy because it is sealed against inspection (commonly known as the sanctity of the seal)." Standard mail (A) (formerly third-class mail) is mainly business mail. The Postal Service defines it as follows:

> Formerly called third-class mail, Standard Mail (A) generally includes letters, flats and parcels that do not require the security of First-Class Mail nor the speed of Priority Mail. Advertisers or others generally mailing identical pieces of mail in bulk use this class of mail which makes up almost 22 percent of our revenue. (*1996 USPS Annual Report* 39–40)

Figure 11.1 shows the change in this ratio from 1975 to the present. In 1977, first-class revenues were 4.46 times greater than third-class revenues. In recent years, this ratio hit a low of 2.6, descending continuously in intervening years. This suggests that the across-class composition of the Postal Service's revenue stream has also moved away from personal letters and cards and toward more commercial mail.

In other USPS services, such as standard mail (B) (formerly fourth-class, which includes parcel post service) the USPS faces very intense competition. United Parcel Service, Airborne Freight Corporation, and many other companies compete in this market. Given the apparent willingness

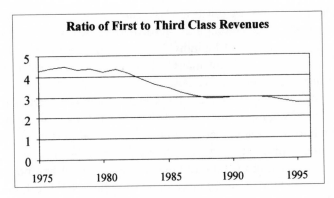

Ratio of First to Third Class Revenues

Figure 11.1

of competitors to provide this service, it would seem that concerns regarding the adequacy of rural service here are specious.

The monopoly is defended as protecting the delivery of printed matter to rural customers. But is the intention to ensure that they are guaranteed delivery of mass-produced advertising matter? The evidence shows that technology is increasingly moving the composition of mail flows in this direction. Defenders of the postal monopoly now must argue that without the cross-subsidy, rural citizens would somehow become isolated from the larger society if they did not receive (or received at higher cost *to the mailer*) mass-produced advertising matter. Given that popular terms for such material include *junk mail*, such arguments seem dubious.

The technological developments described here are moving the Postal Service further from the core activity on which the traditional case for government monopoly is based: the delivery of personal letters. To the extent this is true, the case for a legally enforced monopoly is weakened. Technological progress in substitutes for letter communications, which also reduces the likelihood that rural residents will become isolated, has perhaps been more profound.

Technological Progress in Substitutes for Letter Communications
Letters are only one method of communicating. The number of alternative ways of communicating has burgeoned while the costs have declined. One alternative is the phone. Indeed, many country dwellers may find a phone call more effective in preventing isolation than receiving a letter, since it allows direct interaction. Crandall and Ellig (1997) showed that real long-distance telephone rates fell from 40 to 47 percent between 1984

and 1994. As technological advancement continues to reduce the price of a phone call, rural dwellers will find the phone an increasingly viable alternative to letter communication.

Another alternative is the facsimile, a close substitute for letters in that a written message can be transmitted instantaneously at very low cost. Transmission costs have been falling along with telephone rates. While both sender and receiver must have access to a fax machine to complete the communication, numerous businesses are willing to provide these services, and inexpensive fax machines are widely available. For time-sensitive communications for which a hard copy is preferable, this form outperforms traditional letter mail.

The most formidable technological substitute for letter delivery is electronic mail. This form of communication allows written messages to be transmitted instantaneously, but at much lower cost than that for letters. If both the sender and the receiver have access to a computer, the marginal cost of sending a message is close to zero. The advent of computers designed strictly for Internet access has lowered the cost of using this medium. Given the rapid rate of technological change in the computer industry, the costs of both accessing a computer and sending electronic mail messages will fall still further in the future. Certainly if rural residents fear isolation, they have an incentive to adopt this form of communication, since it provides a fast and convenient method of interacting in which cost is unrelated to distance of residence from urban centers.[8]

The payment of bills by electronic means is also a very close substitute for sending payments through the mail. Bill payment is an important source of USPS revenue, and the Postal Service recognizes that electronic mail places this revenue in jeopardy (*1998 Annual Report of the United States Postal Service*, Management Discussion and Analysis).

The Postal Service also recognizes that alternative technologies represent substantial competition in its two major classes of mail. In discussing first-class mail, the USPS states, "This class of mail faces competition from electronic mail, facsimiles and automatic bill payment systems." And for standard mail (A): "This product faces competition from newspapers, television and mass faxing. The Internet has also emerged as a potentially strong competitor for the revenue generated by Standard Mail (A). The efficiencies of Internet advertising, especially the ability to reach specific groups, will have a significant impact in coming years" (*1996 Annual Report of the United States Postal Service*, 40). The existence and growth of these alternative modes of communicating call into question the traditional justification for government intervention. Given the number and declining price of the options that rural customers now have for keeping in touch, it is unwarranted to claim that if the cross-subsidy were eliminated and rural customers had to pay the full cost of deliveries to them, they would become isolated or otherwise significantly inconvenienced. Not true: they could substitute any one of numerous alternatives.

The Natural-Monopoly Rationale for Government Intervention in Postal Services

Natural-monopoly theory was developed as a rationale for intervening in many network industries. The Postal Service adopted it as a justification in the early 1970s. Next I briefly describe the theory, alternative perspectives on it, and the effects of technological change on its validity.

Overview of the Natural-Monopoly Rationale

Natural monopoly is said to exist when a single firm can supply a good at lower cost than can two or more firms (Sidak and Spulber 1996, 40). This notion is closely related to that of "economies of scale." If a firm's average costs decline as its output increases, it can achieve economies of scale (Carlton and Perloff 1994, 58). If the firm produces a single product, then economies of scale throughout the entire range of output are a sufficient condition for natural monopoly (Carlton and Perloff 1994, 151; Sidak and Spulber 1996, 42).

According to natural-monopoly theory, to achieve least-cost production (i.e., productive efficiency), only one firm is needed in the industry, thus justifying legally protected, territorial monopolies. Because the check of competition has been removed, the monopoly firm must be regulated (or government owned) to prevent price gouging, to ensure that it produces at the correct level of output (i.e., allocative efficiency), and to guarantee that it makes only a "fair" return on its investment (Moorhouse 1986, 423). Government intervention ensures both productive and allocative efficiency and substantially improves on market outcomes.

Natural-monopoly theory provides the main modern defense of government ownership and its monopolization of the postal industry (Sidak and Spulber 1996, 41). In 1970, as part of the Postal Service's reorganization, Congress instructed the USPS to reevaluate the monopoly statutes

(Postal Reorganization Act, sect. 7 [1970]). In their report to Congress, the Board of Governors of the Postal Service argued that the prohibitions on private carriage must be retained and, in addition to relying on the traditional rationale, appealed to the concept of natural monopoly.[9] Commentators continue to assert that at least the local delivery network exhibits natural-monopoly characteristics (Crew and Kleindorfer 1992, 18; Owen and Willig 1983; Panzar 1991).

Perspectives on the Natural-Monopoly Rationale

There are numerous reasons why scholars have become dissatisfied with natural-monopoly theory to justify intervention in industry. First, economists have presented evidence suggesting other motives for intervention besides correcting a natural monopoly (e.g., Hazlett and Spitzer 1997; Jarrell 1978). Second, this approach has been criticized because it lacks a mechanism for translating market failure into regulation. That is, this approach has no framework taking into account the normal behavior of politicians, regulators, or interest groups and translating the demand for corrective intervention into the intended outcomes. Stated somewhat differently, natural-monopoly theory seems to imply that regulators ignore the interests of producers (a powerful pressure group) and concern themselves only with the interests of consumers, a highly unlikely outcome.

Third, a substantial body of research, beginning with Demsetz's seminal 1968 article, "Why Regulate Utilities?" directly confronted the logical consistency of the "natural-monopoly" rationale for regulation. He showed that the existence of a single producer in the market need not lead to monopolistic pricing, that it was possible for competitors to bid for the right to serve the market. Demsetz insisted that the threat of potential entry could discipline those markets that had very few, or indeed only one, producer actually in the market. The notion of potential competition subsequently came to have substantial influence on economics. It was vigorously analyzed in a body of work known as *contestability theory*. Willig (1980) first examined this notion in detail by applying it to postal markets, which are considered highly contestable. It was further developed in a series of papers, including those by Baumol and Willig (1981) and Bailey and Panzar (1981). This inquiry led to a benchmark idealized state termed a *perfectly contestable* market. As Baumol, Panzar, and Willig asserted, "A perfectly contestable market is defined as one in which entry and exit are easy and costless, which may or may not be characterized by economies of scale or scope, but which has no entry barriers" (1988, xiii). This work thus emphasized the ease of entry and exit into a market, rather than cost conditions. It called into question the original notion of natural monopoly and therefore the justification for monopoly rate-of-return regulation.[10] The assets required for letter delivery, such as trucks and buildings for sorting, are easily adaptable to other uses, so the costs of entry and exit are likely to be relatively low. Therefore, contestability is an important consideration in postal markets.

Fourth, many regulated firms produce more than one product. Utilities produce both peak and off-peak power; telephone companies provide both local and long-distance phone service; and the Postal Service delivers several classes of mail. Baumol (1977) showed that economies of scale are neither necessary nor sufficient for an industry to be considered a natural monopoly in a multiproduct case.

Fifth, economists have recognized that even in the presence of economies of scale, private, unregulated ownership nonetheless leads to lower costs than does government ownership. That is, by definition, private ownership creates "residual claimants," or parties with a clear property right to the firm's net cash flows. The existence of residual claims encourages owners to push for efficiency and leads to a number of market-based mechanisms that help control managers (see Geddes 1994 for a detailed discussion of this notion as applied to the postal service). Second, private, deregulated firms have stronger incentives to innovate and to discover new cost-saving technologies (Armstrong, Cowan, and Vickers 1994; Primeaux 1977).

Collectively, these literatures led to a widespread change in perceptions regarding the natural-monopoly rationale for intervention in industries. Whatever the validity of such claims, technological developments have made the natural-monopoly rationale for government intervention in postal services even more dubious (for further criticism of the Postal Service's claims of natural monopoly, see Priest 1975, 71–72; Sidak and Spulber 1996, 43–60).

Technological Advancement and the Natural-Monopoly Rationale

There are several reasons to believe that technology is weakening any aspect of natural monopoly that might have existed in the provision of postal services. First, the USPS's increasing ability to contract out various functions reduces the fixed costs necessary to run its operations. This attenuates any increasing returns to scale that may have existed. There are many examples of contracting. One of the USPS's key functions is the long-distance transportation of mail. Developments in electronic data interchange and computerized reservation systems are lowering the cost of contracting for long-distance transportation with private companies.[11] Selling postage online, as discussed earlier, diminishes the need for a network of window services to sell stamps. It is also easy to contract with private retail stores to sell postage, as is currently done in many European countries. Finally, work sharing discounts shift bar coding and sorting functions onto private companies, effectively contracting out those activities.

Second, demand conditions can change with technology so that natural monopoly is no longer a concern. It is generally conceded that average costs are unlikely to fall forever in most industries, rather that at some level of output, they rise or become constant as output increases. This is particularly true of postal services, since fixed costs are relatively low compared with those of many network industries. For any industry, as technology develops, it becomes more likely that the demand curve will intersect the cost curve in its constant returns-to-scale portion (for an example from the telecommunications industry, see Viscusi, Vernon, and Harrington 1995, 351–53). This occurs for two reasons. First, technological developments spur economic growth, which increases the demand for most goods, including postal services. Second, technology increases the number of available substitutes, which makes the demand curve for postal services flatter, or more price sensitive (i.e., more elastic). This also raises the likelihood that the constant-returns portion of the cost curve is relevant. Both these effects imply that natural monopoly, if it ever existed, is a temporary phenomenon. Just as trucking reduced the natural-monopoly aspects of railroads, the increasing availability of substitutes for letter delivery, such as phone, facsimile machines, and electronic mail, are eliminating any natural-monopoly aspects of postal delivery that may now exist.[12]

Technological developments are also weakening the case for the uniform rate. In addition to ensuring rural service, the USPS has attempted to justify the uniform rate on what are clearly transaction costs grounds. Priest (1975, 72, 70) states,

The Governors further assert that with any varied pricing structure "regulatory red tape" will proliferate and the public will become confused. . . . The Postal Service must charge uniform rates. The Postal Service has found, according to the Governors, that it is only practicable to set rates "according to simple, published formulas of great generality."

In an age of widespread computerization, it is difficult to see how such arguments apply. Providing a computer with weight and destination is sufficient to generate a price, no matter how complex the formula, thus decreasing transaction costs. It is easy to construct a Web site that quickly calculates rates for the consumer. Indeed, United Parcel Service's Web site features a "Quick Cost" rate calculator that rapidly provides prices on the basis of minimal information. Thus, with the help of computers, abandoning the uniform rate and pricing more closely to cost are unlikely to increase confusion, and in any event, competing firms would have an incentive to minimize confusion.

Conclusion

The U.S. Postal Service maintains a legal monopoly over the delivery of any item classified as a "letter," with criminal sanctions imposed for violating this monopoly, as under British rule. The Postal Service remains wholly government owned. But technological developments are calling into question both the traditional and the modern justifications for those arrangements. The increasing availability and the decreasing cost of telephone services, electronic mail, and fax machines provide rural customers with many ways to integrate into society without relying on monopolized mail. The claim that rural Americans would become "cut off" from broader society without subsidies to their postal delivery rings hollow.

These same technological changes undermine the case for viewing postal services as a natural monopoly. Many other delivery firms currently navigate the same routes as does the Postal Service and are willing to enter that market if given the opportunity. Technological change is drastically lowering the cost of contracting. This raises the question of why one extraordinarily large nationwide firm is necessary for mail delivery when smaller regional firms successfully provide many other network services, such as electricity and telephony—not to mention gasoline and candy bars—by relying on contracts. Technological progress is rapidly multiplying the alternatives that consumers and firms face. It is therefore critical to give this market the opportunity to adjust rapidly to these new circumstances and use technology optimally, rather than relying on a fixed institutional structure that predates the founding of our nation.

NOTES

1. 5 Stat. 732 (March 3, 1845). The monopoly is currently established by 18 U.S.C. §§ 1693-99, 1724–25 and 39 U.S.C. §§ 601–6 (1970). See Priest 1975 for a discussion of the other relevant legislation and a legislative history. The monopoly extends to any item considered a "letter." For detailed discussions of the extent of the monopoly, see Miller 1983, 150; and Sidak and Spulber 1996, chap. 2.

2. The USPS instituted a new mail classification system in July 1996. First-class mail includes personal correspondence, postcards, and business transactions. Standard mail (A), formerly called third-class mail, includes letters and flats. Advertisers mailing identical pieces in bulk use this class of mail. For a more complete description of the new mail classes, see the *1996 Annual Report of the United States Postal Service*, 39–40.

3. U.S. Postal Service, Statutes Restricting Private Carriage of Mail and Their Administration 11–13, 68, 186 (House Committee on Post Office & Civil Service, 93d Cong., 1st sess., 1973).

4. Ironically, the USPS blames its current weakening market position on the very universal service mandate that it champions. The *1998 Annual Report of the United States Postal Service* (Management Discussion and Outlook) states: "For the short term, we expect modest growth in our overall markets. However, we also expect that our competitors will further erode our market, especially since they are not bound by the same regulatory restrictions and government mandates that bind us. These competitors are free to target profitable customers and sectors of the market while avoiding others. We, however, are required to serve everyone at the same price."

5. Surprisingly, recent empirical studies indicate that the additional costs of surviving rural routes are small, if they exist at all (see Cohen et al. 1999).

6. See, e.g., Sidak and Spulber 1996, 50: "Even rural areas are served by multiple newspaper delivery routes, which demonstrates that an extremely low-cost service can be maintained simply for the delivery of one item on a daily basis to a substantial proportion of households."

7. For example, the *1998 Annual Report of the United States Postal Service* (Management Discussion and Analysis) states: "Technology has also created opportunities. The increasingly sophisticated use of data allows businesses to go beyond using the mail as a targeted advertising medium to a personalized means of building lasting business relationships. Declining computing costs along with rapid innovation in data base management and demographic analysis contributed to a rapid growth in mail volume in the 1980s. These developments, combined

with the introduction of work-sharing discounts, which helped mailers take advantage of these trends, caused an explosion in mail volume."

8. Forecasts of changes in the technological composition of world communications to 2005 suggest that electronic mail is likely to take a greater share of the market in the future and physical mail a smaller share. A recent Universal Postal Union study found that by 2005, the market share of electronic mail would double over that in 1995 but that the market share of physical communications would decline by 26 percent.

9. U.S. Postal Service, Statutes Restricting Private Carriage of Mail and Their Administration 11–13, 68, 186 (House Committee on Post Office & Civil Service, 93d Cong., 1st sess., 1973). See Priest 1975, 69–71, for a discussion.

10. A number of studies tested contestability theory, including that by Coursey, Isaac, and Smith (1984) who used an experimental approach and concluded that "the most significant result . . . is that the behavioral predictions of the contestable market hypothesis are fundamentally correct. It is simply not true that monopoly pricing is a 'natural' result of a market merely because firms in the market exhibit decreasing costs and demand is sufficient to support no more than a single firm" (1984, 111).

11. The USPS already contracts extensively with private transportation firms in several ways but does maintain its own equipment in this area (see Sidak and Spulber 1996, 44).

12. Viscusi, Vernon, and Harrington (1995, 353) summarize: "This phenomenon is not rare. Railroads possessed significant cost advantages in the late 1800s, and these advantages were eroded considerably with the introduction of trucking in the 1920s. This example introduces a new element, namely, technological change. That is, over long periods of time it is likely that the cost function will shift as new knowledge is incorporated into the production process. Hence, permanent natural monopoly is probably a rare category. Technical change can shift cost functions so as to render competition workable."

REFERENCES

Anders, George. 1999. "Postal Service Soon to Let Two Firms Nationally Sell Computer-Made Stamps." *Wall Street Journal*, July 19, B10.

Armstrong, Mark, Simeon Cowan, and John Vickers. 1994. *Regulatory Reform: Economic Analysis and British Experience.* Cambridge, MA: MIT Press.

Bailey, Elizabeth E., and John C. Panzar. 1981. "The Contestability of Airline Markets during the Transition to Deregulation." *Law and Contemporary Problems* 44, no. 1 (winter): 125–45.

Baumol, William J. 1977. "On the Proper Cost Tests for Natural Monopoly in a

Multiproduct Industry." *American Economic Review* 67, no. 5 (December): 809–22.

Baumol, William J., John C. Panzar, and Robert D. Willig. 1988. *Contestable Markets and the Theory of Industry Structure.* Rev. ed. San Diego: Academic Press.

Baumol, William J., and Robert D. Willig. 1981. "Fixed Costs, Sunk Costs, Entry Barriers, and Sustainability of Monopoly." *Quarterly Journal of Economics* 96, no. 3 (August): 405–31.

Carlton, Dennis W., and Jeffrey M. Perloff. 1994. *Modern Industrial Organization.* New York: HarperCollins.

Cohen, Robert H., William W. Ferguson, John D. Waller, and Spyros S. Xenakis. 1999. "An Analysis of the Potential for Cream Skimming Is the U.S. Residential Delivery Market." In *Emerging Competition in Postal and Delivery Services,* edited by Michael A. Crew and Paul R. Kleindorfer. Boston: Klumer Academic Publishers.

Coursey, Don, R. Mark Isaac, and Vernon L. Smith. 1984. "Natural Monopoly and Contested Markets: Some Experimental Results." *Journal of Law & Economics* 27: 91–113.

Crandall, Robert, and Jerry Ellig. 1997. *Economic Deregulation and Customer Choice: Lessons for the Electric Industry.* Fairfax, VA: Center for Market Processes.

Crew, Michael A., and Paul R. Kleindorfer. 1992. *The Economics of Postal Service: A Research Study Supported by WIK.* Boston: Kluwer Academic Publishers.

Demsetz, Harold. 1968. "Why Regulate Utilities?" *Journal of Law & Economics,* April, 55–65.

Geddes, R. Richard. 1994. "Agency Costs and Governance in the United States Postal Service." In *Governing the Postal Service,* edited by J. Gregory Sidak. Washington, DC: AEI Press.

Hazlett, Thomas W., and Matthew L. Spitzer. 1997. *Public Policy Toward Cable Television: The Economics of Rate Controls.* Cambridge, MA: MIT Press, and Washington, DC: AEI Press.

Jarrell, Greg. 1978. "The Demand for State Regulation of the Electric Utility Industry." *Journal of Law and Economics* 21, no. 2: 269–96.

Miller, James C. III. 1983. "End the Postal Monopoly." *Cato Journal* 5: 149–55.

Moorhouse, John C., ed. 1986. *Electric Power: Deregulation and the Public Interest.* San Francisco: Pacific Research Institute for Public Policy.

Owen, Bruce M., and Robert D. Willig. 1983. "Economics and Postal Pricing." In *The Future of the Postal Service,* edited by Joel Fleishman. Aspen, CO: Aspen Institute.

Panzar, John C. 1991. "Is the Postal Service a Natural Monopoly?" In *Competition and Innovation in Postal Services,* edited by M. A. Crew and P. R. Kleindorfer. Lexington, MA: Lexington Books.

Posner, Richard A. 1974. "Theories of Economic Regulation." *Bell Journal of Economics and Management Science* 5 (autumn): 335–58.

Priest, George L. 1975. "The History of the Postal Monopoly in the United States." *Journal of Law & Economics* 18: 33–80.

Primeaux, Walter J. 1977. "An Assessment of X-Efficiency Gained through Competition." *Review of Economics and Statistics* 59 (February): 105–8.

Shleifer, Andre. 1998. "State versus Private Ownership." *Journal of Economic Perspectives* 12, no. 4 (fall): 133–50.

Sidak, J. Gregory, and Daniel F. Spulber. 1996. *Protecting Competition from the Postal Monopoly.* Washington, DC: AEI Press.

Tierney, John T. 1981. *Postal Reorganization: Managing the Public's Business.* Boston: Auburn House.

———. 1988. *The U.S. Postal Service: Status and Prospects of a Public Enterprise.* Boston: Auburn House.

Tolley, G. S. 1994. "Direct Testimony of George S. Tolley on Behalf of United States Postal Service." *Postal Rate and Fee Changes, 1994* (docket no. R94-1).

U.S. Postal Service. 1973. "Statutes Restricting Private Carriage of Mail and Their Administration." House Committee on Post Office and Civil Service, 93d Cong., 1st sess.

U.S. Postal Service. 1996–1998. *Annual Report of the Postmaster General.* Washington, DC: U.S. Government Printing Service.

Universal Postal Union. 1993. *Survey of Postal Administration* 3. Bern: Universal Postal Union.

Viscusi, W. Kip, John M. Vernon, and Joseph E. Harrington Jr. 1995. *Economics of Regulation and Antitrust.* 2d ed. Cambridge, MA: MIT Press.

Willig, Robert D. 1980. "What Can Markets Control?" In *Perspectives on Postal Services Issues,* edited by Roger Sherman. Washington, DC: AEI Press.

Winston, Clifford. 1993. "Economics Deregulation: Days of Reckoning for Microeconomists." *Journal of Economic Literature* 31, no. 3 (September): 1263–98.

Part IV

Other Areas of Policy

12

The Entrepreneurial Community in Light of Advancing Business Practices and Technologies

Spencer Heath MacCallum

It is generally assumed that local government must be a tax-funded authority. The argument is that so-called market failure necessitates the government's oversight and regulation of community resources. In subdivided areas, which is the traditional settlement pattern in American towns and cities and their suburbs, this may be the case. However, in some areas, land is parceled into its various uses not by selling off lots to form a subdivision but by leasing them.

Such areas, in which the underlying land is owned in one title and the parts are leased, are called, in British terminology, *estates*, and in American, *multiple-tenant income properties* (MTIPs). In these areas, management of the common areas and amenities in the United States is almost invariably private. It may be argued that this is all right as long as the areas are small but that if they were to approach the size and texture of a community, then private management should give way to governmental management. This chapter shows that such areas are indeed approaching the size and texture of communities and that the argument that they ought not be managed privately is being progressively undercut by advancing technology.

The discussion has significant policy implications. Land-lease areas—MTIPs—were once insignificant in the United States, but that is no longer the case. Over the past century, they have grown greatly in number and size. Common examples are hotels, office buildings, apartment complexes, marinas, professional parks, shopping centers, combinations of all these, and more. But as the examples suggest, this explosive growth has taken place almost exclusively in commercial rather than residential real estate. Residential housing is dominated instead by the planned subdivision, which enjoys a virtual monopoly by reason of discriminatory tax policy and federal subsidy. The MTIP has shown great viability in commercial areas, there competing easily with subdivisions. With equal treatment under the law, it might be expected to do the same in the housing field. In doing so, it would offer consumers attractive housing choices beyond the planned subdivision with homeowners' association.

Beyond these policy questions, however, the matter of MTIPs has broader sociological implications that have not been adequately explored. MTIPs are a part of our daily experience, exemplified in familiar forms that resemble local communities in important respects. But because they are relatively prosaic, nonheroic developments of the marketplace, not ideologically inspired as intentional or utopian communities are, they have received little scholarly attention. Nonetheless they have thrived, springing up with the hardiness of weeds. Their success is partly due to their unique organizational strengths. To understand these strengths, we must look at the fundamental difference between subdivision and land lease.

A necessary first step toward forming a community of any kind is to parcel a tract of land into exclusive occupancies while retaining common areas such as parks and access ways. Such parceling can be accomplished in either of two ways. One is to subdivide the landownership into separate fees. The other is to let out the parcels as leaseholds, keeping the land title intact. These two logical possibilities do not have equal merit. The first alternative, subdivision, destroys the locus of authority and certain incentives that are requisite for effective social organization.

Shortcomings of Subdivision

Land subdivision, the familiar pattern of real estate development in the United States, has a robust and profitable business record. When carried out on a large scale, it is frequently called *community development*. But the phrase is misleading. The entrepreneurial interest that gives birth to the subdivision development is not sustained; it dries up as the project progresses and vanishes completely when the last parcel is sold. The "community builders" who practice subdivision are builders, as their name implies, but they are builders of houses—glorified framers, carpenters, bricklayers, plumbers, electricians. To sell their houses, they put in streets and curbing, drainage, utility lines, and the like and landscape the areas. But they do not build communities. They have no commitment to organize, operate, and administer the community assets enjoyed in common. When their inventory of improved lots is sold, these "community builders" move on, leaving the management of the community to the residents, who most likely have no preparation for or expertise in managing and sustaining community resources and have no decisive authority to do so. The residents' continuing community needs, social and physical, are of little concern to the subdivider, to whom it is sufficient that he create a salable product. He may set up a homeowners' association, which is largely boilerplate mandated by the government to qualify the homes for federal mortgage insurance.[1] Thus the entrepreneur who constructs the physical artifacts abandons his customers as they are about to become a community, leaving them to fill the gap as best they can with political devices and institutions.

Because the ownership of the land is fragmented, there can be no concentrated entrepreneurial interest in the management or improvement of "the commons." It follows that as consumers of community services, the residents must provide for themselves the community services they require. The entrepreneurial vacuum leaves just two options. Management must be political or volunteer, and usually it is some combination of the two. Either approach can hire managers, but there is no entrepreneurial interest or effective equity oversight.

Virtually every American city, town, and neighborhood is a subdivision and, as such, exhibits this weakness. The resulting political institutions, whether they are called municipal governments or homeowners' associations, do not differ substantially. Some writers extol homeowners' associations as "privatized" local government.[2] But as David Friedman pointed out, the difference between traditional government and homeowners' associations is largely illusory.[3] Already, as the novelty of homeowners' associations wears off, this is becoming apparent.[4]

Politics and volunteerism, the two options subdivision residents have for obtaining their common services, lack the profit incentive that makes the market an ever evolving process of serving customers competitively in new and different ways. Not only is the vigor of ownership lacking, but the political or bureaucratic administration that attempts to fill the vacuum is irresponsible. Who, for example, in the traditional public-works establishment is liable for injuries caused by water contamination? Democracy affords no answer to this problem; voting, far from being an adequate substitute for responsible proprietary interest, is beset with problems of public ignorance. Moreover, citizens free-ride on the job of holding government accountable—if such a thing as government accountability exists.[5] For all of these reasons, the subdivided community represents, evolutionarily speaking, a dead end.

Multiple-Tenant Income Properties (MTIPs)

The obvious need is for some means of introducing proprietary authority, responsibility, and incentive into community management, including the production and administration of those amenities that traditionally have been provided by politically created monopolies. Such a means is not unknown. It has been discovered, empirically and independently, not once but many times during the past 200 years. It is the application, in an urban setting, of a formula of land tenure that for millennia characterized agrarian societies in many parts of the world. The method, familiar to commercial property managers, is to retain the land title intact, parceling sites among land users by leasing.

Multiple-tenant income properties are relative newcomers in the evolving world of business.[6] From the second quarter of the nineteenth century, and accelerating after World War II in the twentieth, multiple-tenant income properties grew in number, kind, complexity, and size as entrepreneurs in this new kind of business created myriad environments reflecting the specialized needs of a seemingly endless variety of clientele—merchants, travelers, manufacturers, residents, and professionals of every variety. Each specialized type of environment that met with success in the market and so persisted defined an economic niche. In succession, we saw the rise of hotels, apartment buildings, office buildings ("skyscrapers"), luxury liners, commercial airports, shopping centers, RV/camp grounds, mobile home parks, marinas, research parks, professional parks, medical clinics, theme parks, and land-lease manufactured-home communities, as well as, increasingly, integrations and combinations of these and others to form properties more complex and, overall, less specialized. Such an adaptive response to new conditions and opportunities stands out sharply against the stasis of subdivision.

The rapidity of this growth and development of MTIPs is striking. The shopping center at the close of World War II was experimental; fewer than a dozen existed in the United States, and the name had yet to be coined. But by the end of the century, the number of shopping centers in the United States alone exceeded 45,000 and accommodated more than half of the nonautomotive retail activity of the nation.[7]

Each specialized type of MTIP has its characteristic management requirements, differing in emphasis from all others, arising out of and reflecting the needs of the clientele to which it uniquely caters. The shopping center, for example, emphasizes the leadership required to forge a collection of merchant tenants into an effective retailing team. Teams need a coach, which in the shopping mall is the manager. His coaching role includes maintaining peace among highly competitive merchants.[8] The merchants recognize that the manager is uniquely positioned for such a role; he represents the concentrated proprietary interest in the land and consequently has two qualities to be found nowhere else in the center: he is *disinterested* and at the same time vitally *interested* in the success of the center as a whole. Unlike the tenants whom he serves, who inevitably are partisan and to that extent have an incentive to exploit the center as a commons, his direct and personal business interest is the success of the center and every tenant's enterprise in it.

MTIPs resemble a community, and the dividing line is not always clear. Although they have grown larger and more complex over the past century, becoming more like a community as the term is commonly understood, the popular notion of a community implies both a more heterogeneous population and land subdivision. Even so, MTIPs have many of the same features as a community, and when the full range of types is considered, neither the rate of turnover of population nor the degree of social interaction among members sets them apart consistently from what we are accustomed to think of as communities.

Among other notable features of MTIPs is the fact that parceling by leaseholds obviates any need for eminent domain. Whereas subdivision rigidifies the layout of a neighborhood so that it cannot easily be redeveloped short of invoking public powers (or waiting until increasing obsolescence brings down land values to a point that it can be economically reassembled), leasehold permits gradual and continuous change as leases run out and come up for renewal. It preserves for the neighborhood a quality of organic flexibility and growth.

Before discussing their business rationale, I should emphasize that MTIPs are defined by the leasing of sites, without regard for improvements on them. The latter may be constructed and owned independently by either the lessor or the lessee (if the lessee, then the lease generally is for a longer term). This holds true even in the case of an apartment or office building, where the sites are the bare spaces leased or rented: artificially created land stacked up vertically. Furnishing or installing fixtures in such a space, like constructing improvements on a lot, is a separate consideration.

The MTIP's Rationale

However they may be provided, common services and amenities like streets, utilities, parks, and public safety pertain to sites rather than to individuals as such, and individuals enjoy their benefit by occupying those sites. Thus when those who own land sell or lease sites in exchange for price or rent, they are acting as the market purveyor of not only the public services and amenities in that place but of all the locational advantages of that site with respect to things beyond it such as significant natural features and human activities or enterprise.

What landowners actually sell is location with respect to a specific environment. Apart from its context, a site has no ascertainable land value; it comes into demand only if its environs have relevance for the activity that is to take place on the site. A prospective home site for a young family gains in desirability if there is a school nearby; or a mine site if there is a railroad accessible to transport its ores; or a retail site if there are residences nearby, not to mention parking spaces, utility grids, and many other things. A given site is thus valued or disvalued according to its location relative to other things. Although it may have much in common with neighboring sites, each site is the locus of an environment uniquely its own. When a site is sold or leased, what is transferred is exclusive enjoyment of that location and the unique environment defining it. For that reason when we buy or sell land, we are buying or selling what might be called *placement rights*, the rights to place or position ourselves in relation to specific other people and things. It is a cliché among realtors to say that the land's three main factors in land value are location, location, and location. Yet location has no meaning except by reference to environment; the two are correlative terms. Consequently, an aware landowner is closely attuned to and concerned about environment.

An entrepreneurially inclined landowner can create value where before there was little or none, by customizing the environment for its occupants or users, that is, by improving the *location* of a site or sites for specific uses. The majority of landowners have been traditional and conservative, doing little in the way of creating or modifying the environments they lease or sell. But in a growing sector of the economy this is decidedly changing, as private landowners undertake not only the distribution but also the production of common goods and services and into the bargain bring about the spatial integration of complementary land uses. Instead of continuing in the old, atomistic pattern of subdivided lots on Main Street devoid of any unifying proprietary interest, a major portion of retail shops and stores in the United States have moved into arrangements where land is managed under single ownership. Here the landowners (of whom there may be unlimited numbers by virtue of owning stock or other undivided interests) provide many of the services such as streets and parking, sewerage, storm drainage, power distribution, policing, landscaped parks, and public areas that they once would have looked to governments to provide. Nor has retailing been alone in adopting this formula.

The MTIP formula is for the owners of a tract of land intended for multiple tenancy to enhance the value of the sites into which it is parceled by improving the environs of each site from the standpoint of its intended use. The possibilities of upgrading the environment of a site are endless, extending (albeit with diminishing effect) indefinitely beyond the immediate neighborhood of the site itself and even the MTIP of which it is a parcel. That is the overriding reason that entrepreneurial landowners will often cooperate in joint projects.

Having made environmental upgrades, either singly within their own property or jointly over a wider area, a field of competing owners or managers then bid down the rents they ask while a field of prospective tenants, similarly competing among themselves, bid up the rents they are willing to pay. If an owner has succeeded in creating a desirable environment for the sites he offers the public—both social and physical environment which, among other things, will motivate people to be more productive in that place—then the rents will finance the common services and amenities and also return a profit to him.

Thus MTIPs are self-supporting. Because they yield a market revenue, their owners need not resort to taxation, which indeed would destroy the very values they are in business to build. Market revenue not only finances the administration of the MTIP. It also enables the accumulation of reserve funds from which to renovate it as required, even completely rebuilding it to the same or another use, to stay competitive with other locations in the market. This illustrates the immortality of productive capital.

Outgrowing Government As We Know It: Entrepreneurial Communities (Entrecomms)

Sixty-five years ago my grandfather, Spencer Heath, reasoned that if a new town were developed under a unified land title by parceling its land among the occupants by means of long-term ground leasing while maintaining suitable common areas and amenities, it would be a wholly contractual community resembling in principle a hotel carried out of doors on an enlarged plan. Indeed, he perceived hotels as prototypes of the cities of the future.[9] The very scale and complexity of today's larger hotels add plausibility to that novel view. The MGM Grand in Las Vegas is one of many hotels that promote themselves as a "self-contained city." The Grand accommodates not just one or several land uses such as retailing or bedrooms or medical services—following the usual pattern of MTIPs—but also shopping malls, professional offices, convention facilities, restaurants and cafés, chapels, theaters and art galleries, medical services, a security force, a monorail station, and the list goes on. Residents could, if they wished, satisfy nearly all their daily needs without ever leaving the complex. In terms of population size alone, it is interesting to note that the MGM Grand is larger than the city of Boston was at the time the United States became independent of England.

Today it would not seem an altogether radical departure, even though it has never been done, if an enterprising real estate firm developed a stand-alone town on a land-lease basis and operated it as an investment property for income, in other words, developed a wholly nonpolitical, proprietary community, as distinguished from one that was in any way dependent on taxation. The developers of such an enterprise would avail themselves of a new income opportunity, one alien to current "community development" practice: they would offer the residents a full spectrum of on-site utility services. Rather than plugging into political grids for a relatively undifferentiated, generic product, they would instead provide by means of an on-site, integrated, energy management system a selection of highly customized, consumer-driven utilities.

The present reliance on the traditional practice of "plugging into the grid," connecting to whatever utility umbilicals might be extended to their property by local governments, entails a significant loss of flexibility and opportunity for the owners of MTIPs. A substantial part of the cost of land development today is for the escalating list of compliance requirements imposed by municipal authorities. Typically this includes such obstacles as permitting, architectural review, zoning, environmental impact studies, citizens' meetings, and allocation of land to various "public purposes." Most costly of all are the delays and uncertainties at each step of the process. The result of these imposed costs has been to price much land out of the market, resulting in less developable land and inflated land costs for what remains.

The hold of local governments over land developers in this unequal contest, and their main justification for taxing the public, is their monopoly of essential utilities that they have the power to grant or withhold. A generalized MTIP that provided its own utilities on-site with zero discharge into the environment, thereby freeing itself altogether from the grid, might appropriately be called an *entrecomm*—shortened from "entrepreneurial community"—to distinguish it from traditional, tax-dependent communities.

A further defining step, then, in the development of MTIPs in the direction of entrecomms is for their owners to expand the complement of services they now offer their customers by developing an integrated, on-site utility system. Such a step should enable them, with greater dependability and at significant cost savings, to provide utilities tailored to the needs of the users. The requisite technology for the construction and operation of such systems has been progressing steadily for decades in partially self-contained or isolated "community" applications like oil rigs, ships at sea, space vehicles, and arctic workstations, and today no longer presents an insurmountable engineering, economic or financial challenge (see chapters 9 and 10 in this book).

Theoretical Implications

The notion of entrepreneurial communities has relevance for the theoretical discussion of "perfect competition" of "clubs," or private communities, in the technical literature of economics.[10] In the pure competition models, private communities optimally provide local services, thereby achieving efficiency in every sense. However, some of the assumptions of such an arrangement might be challenged. People do not shop for communities in the same way they shop for clothing. A location is not portable. Unlike other goods that can be carried about, a place can be enjoyed only by attaching oneself to it. People make commitments that tie them to a community, and exit is not costless, especially when alternatives are limited or information about how well existing alternatives would satisfy is not readily available.

The concept of entrecomms has relevance in another discussion area. In 1970 Albert Hirschman made the seminal distinction between exit and voice as two kinds of response to unsatisfactory conditions in firms, organizations, and states.[11] While advancing technology clearly strengthens the option of exit, it might also increase the effectiveness of voice and thereby the level of resident participation in a community. An unhappy resident who felt a grievance or, to reverse the coin, a visionary resident who had a constructive suggestion to make about the community, could speedily research, generate, transmit, store, and retrieve information by electronic means. This capability is equally available to residents of subdivisions, including traditional town settings, but residents of an entrecomm would have the advantage of being able to specify a responsible individual, the community entrepreneur, to whom he could direct his voice with the reasonable expectation of a response. Unlike an elected official, who has none of his own property at risk and is in the comfortable position of spending public funds, the landlord of an entrecomm would be a private businessperson dependent on making a profit. He could not let his competitive edge become dull. Finally, it is likely that the entrecomm setting would be conducive to building social capital more effectively than would a subdivision setting. Combined with the benefits of technology, this could also translate into more effective voice and participation.

The Argument against Entrecomms

Because entrecomms are still only a theoretical possibility, no one has either advocated or denigrated them. But we do have something closely resembling them in some respects, namely, company towns. Moreover, company towns have been the target of social criticism in a long spate of popular books, music, and art.[12] They serve very well, therefore, as a straw man for the purpose of argument.

Company towns still exist, but they had their heyday a century ago. These were entire towns often built in remote and unsettled areas by mining, timbering, and other kinds of businesses to provide housing for workers. Frequently they were well built and well managed as an inducement for workers to stay in such areas. As portrayed in the popular literature, however, the interests of the company and its workers were opposed, as the relationship was exploitative. The company store, often lacking competition from independent stores, supposedly gouged the workers by charging high prices while the company charged high rents for substandard housing. But if a company built a model town and manifestly did not exploit the worker/residents, it might be charged with paternalism. The company had to tread a narrow line. Sometimes the charge of paternalism had some basis, as companies have been known to limit drinking or require church attendance with the idea of making the town more attractive to families and the families more stable. Hershey, Pennsylvania, was a model company town attractively laid out with parks, gardens, public library, zoo, amusement park, sports stadium, and well-designed homes. It is said that the elder Milton Hershey could not understand their disloyalty when the workers struck in 1937, seeming to show no appreciation for his efforts on their behalf.[13]

The usual argument against a single ownership town is that the landlord enjoys a monopoly position with a captive clientele and so has an opportunity to be exploitive, patronizing, or neglectful. Having invested in moving to such a town, putting down roots, and making it their home, a family finds it costly to leave. Knowing this, the landlord can exploit them by cutting costs and/or raising the rent at lease-renewal time. Writing long-term contracts to protect against opportunism is costly.[14] In regard to shopping, the family may find it less than satisfactory to buy from an encompassing monopolist. But short of moving elsewhere and establishing roots all over again, they cannot readily know what conditions might be like in another place. Moreover, if the family has built and owns its home, it might be difficult to sell. Hence the argument that community ties, illiquidity of real estate, ignorance of employment and living conditions elsewhere, and difficulties of physically moving conspire to keep a family immobile, making it possible for an opportunistic landlord to raise the rent above what it would be in a more competitive market.

Employee housing is never a company's main product. It is always a sideline activity, a part of its employee benefits package. The fact that the company town, submerged in a larger enterprise, is not an independent profit center constitutes an inherent weakness with two important effects. It makes its manager less sensitive to competition, and it blurs his business role as a community provider. To the extent that this happens, it raises the likelihood that he will indulge any personal idiosyncrasies, ranging from petty tyranny to paternalism.

Changing business practices and advances in technology have all but nullified these traditional arguments against land-lease communities, which today are chiefly found not in company towns but in the myriad varieties of specialized MTIPs in commercial real estate.

Changing Business Practices Favor Entrecomms

MTIPs offer a sharp contrast with company towns. Not only are they operated for profit and stand or fall accordingly, but they compete directly in the market with other MTIPs. Therefore consumer satisfaction becomes a primary rather than a secondary consideration. The desire and need to make a profit allow less room for eccentricity, exploitation, or neglect and create incentives to consistently maintain and upgrade the common services in order to stay competitive.

The contrast with the company towns of a century ago has been further heightened by changing business practices. Corporate organization has widely displaced sole proprietorships throughout the economy, especially in regard to heavily capitalized projects. A corporate firm is more able to pursue a single objective than is a family, which necessarily has a mixed bag of priorities, and it has greater assurance of continuity of policy, being less affected by individual death or inheritance. It is also subject to the discipline of the equities market, where new investors can acquire a controlling interest in a failing or suboptimal venture and restore its profitability. The liquidity of share ownership facilitates this process, since assets can be capitalized in the market. Conversely, certain immaturities in the stock market work against MTIPs, such as the valuation of equities on a quarterly basis, which is too short for most income properties in real estate.

Unlike the company town, the MTIP's dedicated business is building land value as measured by its capitalized revenue stream. Whatever success it has in this direction will of course benefit the owners of improvements as well, since the demand for land readily translates into a demand for improvements on the land. This takes some of the speculation out of home ownership, as the promise of protected value and greater liquidity in one's home makes the prospect of moving less daunting.

The twin goals of profitability and competitiveness have improved the design of MTIPs over that of company towns and have led to better management practices, resulting in a greater liquidity of real estate with respect to both land and improvements. These same goals have also led to better and longer-term leases, offering greater security and satisfactions for both tenants and owners. The writing of leases in itself has opened a whole new area for innovation and competition among MTIPs.[15]

Advancing Technology Favors Entrecomms

Revolutionary advances during the past century in mobility, information, and communications have combined to enhance competition among MTIPs to an altogether unanticipated degree. Improved mobility technology, represented most dramatically by the automobile, has simplified the physical task of moving and dramatically lowered its cost. Nor do families need to live close to work or school if their automobiles can carry them rapidly to and from these destinations. In 1990, vehicle access was nearly universal in the United States, even among the poorest households.[16]

Meanwhile, technological advances in information handling and communication have lessened the psychological costs of moving. It is daily becoming easier to relocate without disrupting established relationships, and soon we all may have the option of virtual travel without leaving home. Some 83 percent of American workers who vacationed for seven or more days during the summer of 2000 remained in contact with their office.[17] The ability to keep in touch while traveling, and the growing option of working at home, which is a second reason why home need no longer be within easy commuting distance of work, have further loosened people's ties to a location. With more freedom and more information about alternatives, a dissatisfied tenant in an MTIP can more readily relocate to a place more to his liking. The costs of moving, both economic and psychic, are incalculably less today than a century ago, and the technological trend shows no signs of abatement.

By lowering the cost of gathering and evaluating information about alternatives and thereby making the market far more transparent than it was a century or even a decade ago, communications technology has increased tenant mobility. Advances in gathering, storing, retrieving, and disseminating information have enormously facilitated comparison shopping. With a minimal investment of time and expense, it is possible from home via the Internet to become informed about not only work opportunities in different places but also lifestyles over a wide range of MTIPs. It is possible to read general posted information, query managers, or interview tenants in cyberspace. An opportunistic landlord creates dissatisfied tenants, and it is they in turn who create his reputation—a reputation ever easier to access and transmit to others. Advances in communications make landlords more accountable than ever before.

The flip side of the technology coin is that the same ease and economy of mobility, information, and communication that enable tenants to comparison shop also enable managers of MTIPs to better customize an inventory of sites for a targeted clientele. Not only can managers, with increasing ease and diminishing cost, discover the needs and preferences of their market, but they can keep apprised of their competition. Furthermore, they can improve their competitive position by a more discriminating selection of tenants. Compatibility and synergy among tenants are significant competitive factors among all classes of MTIPs, from residential apartments to shopping centers. So essential, indeed, is "tenant mix" to the success of shopping centers that it ranks with location. The same technologies of mobility, information, and communication that enable a tenant to comparison shop and then relocate if he chooses also enable a manager to shop the field for tenants who will make compatible, even synergistic, neighbors. This leads to more refined specializations among MTIPs, more options for residents, and hence more competition.

Conclusion

Advancing mobility, information, and communication technology have made MTIPs incomparably more competitive than their country cousin, the company town. This same competitiveness will surely characterize the still hypothetical field of entrepreneurial communities, since these will be but an extension of and a more generalized form of MTIP. Beyond this, technological advancement in a wholly different direction, that of integrated, on-site utilities, promises to make it possible for MTIPs to take the remaining step toward becoming fully self-sustaining local communities administered not politically but voluntarily as other goods and services are, responsive to the pricing system of the marketplace.

Changing business practices and technological advancement have largely dissolved the traditional arguments against single-owner communities. They have done this by lessening the distinction between common goods attaching to sites and other kinds of goods in the market. This trend is significant because it suggests that the way may be opening to an attractive and profitable, exclusively market technique of providing common goods and services. Should this promise materialize, public administration at the local level will be viewed no longer as a paralyzing social problem but as a virgin field of opportunity.

NOTES

1. Evan McKenzie, *Privatopia: Homeowner Associations and the Rise of Residential Private Government* (New Haven, CT: Yale University Press, 1994), 89: "In 1963 FHA released an influential manual entitled Planned-Unit Development with a Homes Association. . . . The manual makes it clear that it will not approve applications for PUD [planned unit development] mortgage insurance unless the developer creates a homeowner association with the power to enforce 'protective covenants.'" See also James L. Winokur, "Choice, Consent, and Citizenship in Common Interest Communities." In *Common Interest Communities: Private Governments and the Public Interest*, edited by Stephen E. Barton and Carol J. Silverman, 98–99 (Berkeley and Los Angeles: University of California Press, 1994).

2. For example, Robert H. Nelson, "Privatizing the Neighborhood," *Liberty* 11, no. 4 (March 1998): 13. Also his "Costly Liberty?" *Liberty* 12, no. 1 (September 1998): 47–50. Nelson so favors the "privatization of government functions" represented by the homeowners' association that he advocates federal enabling legislation that would permit homeowners' associations to be imposed by vote in developed, older neighborhoods nationwide. In his *Edge City: Life on the New Frontier* (New York: Anchor Books, 1988), esp. chap. 6, "Phoenix: Shadow Government," 183–204, Joel Garreau also describes homeowners' associations as "private-enterprise government" but finds the trend deeply disturbing.

3. David Friedman, "Comment: Problems in the Provision of Public Goods," *Harvard Journal of Law and Public Policy* 10 (1987): 505–20, says on p. 506: "Is not the residents' association, with compulsory membership, compulsory dues, and democratic voting rules, simply a local government under a different name? Will it not face exactly the same sorts of problems in running its community—bureaucracy, rational ignorance, corruption, rent-seeking—that make government seem, to many of us, an unattractive and inefficient mechanism for producing goods and services?"

4. For a more thorough discussion of the shortcomings of homeowners' associations as a means of community organization, see Spencer Heath MacCallum, "Entrepreneurship versus Politics in American Life: The Case for Leasing Instead of Subdividing Land." *Critical Review*, forthcoming.

5. Gordon Tullock, "Public Decisions as Public Goods," *Journal of Political Economy* 79 (July/August 1971): 913–18.

6. For a general history of MTIPs before 1970, see Spencer Heath MacCallum, *The Art of Community* (Menlo Park, CA: Institute for Humane Studies, 1970).

7. International Council of Shopping Centers web site 2000 (http://www.icsc .org/srch/ rsrch/scope/current/index.html).

8. Spencer H. MacCallum, "Jural Behavior in American Shopping Centers," *Human Organization: Journal of the Society for Applied Anthropology* 30 (spring 1971): 3–10.

9. Spencer Heath, *Politics versus Proprietorship*, privately published by the author in 1936. See a fuller development of this idea in Heath's major work, *Citadel, Market and Altar* (Baltimore: Science of Society Foundation, 1957). Now distributed by the Heather Foundation, Box 180, Tonopah, NV 89049.

10. James M. Buchanan, "An Economic Theory of Clubs," *Economica* 32 (1965): 1–14; Charles M. Tiebout, "A Pure Theory of Local Expenditures," *Journal of Political Economy* 84 (February 1956): 416–24.

11. Albert O. Hirschman, *Exit, Voice and Loyalty: Responses to Decline in Firms, Organizations, and States* (Cambridge, MA: Harvard University Press, 1970).

12. For a review of company towns, see Price V. Fishback, *Soft Coal, Hard Choices: The Economic Welfare of Bituminous Coal Miners, 1890–1930* (New York: Oxford University Press, 1992), chaps. 8, 9. See also James B. Allen, *The Company Town in the American West* (Norman: University of Oklahoma Press, 1966).

13. Mary Davidoff Houts and Pamela Cassidy Whitenack, *Hershey*, Images of America Series (Charleston, SC: Arcadia, 2000).

14. Victor P. Goldberg, "Regulation and Administered Contracts," *Bell Journal of Economics* 7 (autumn 1976): 426–48; Oliver E. Williamson, "Transaction-Cost Economics: The Governance of Contractual Relations," *Journal of Law and Economics* 22 (October 1979): 233–61.

15. For some of the kinds of possibilities this opens up, see Spencer Heath MacCallum, "Orbis: A Heuristic Exercise in the Private Provision of Public Services," chap. 13 of a book in preparation by the author, *Environment and Community for the 21st Century*, available from the author at <sm@look.net>.

16. Of the 6.4 percent of the population of the United States living in zero-vehicle households in 1990, the majority were retired, older people living in the central part of a large urban area with good transit access who as a rule preferred to walk to errands, social activities, and shopping. See Richard Crepeau and Charles Lave, "Travel by Carless Households," *Access* 9 (fall 1996): 29–31.

17. "Americans Stayed Connected to Their Offices on Summer Vacation," *Business Wire*, September 6, 2000. "According to a survey commissioned by Andersen Consulting . . . some 83 percent of American workers who vacationed for seven or more days since April remained in contact with their office." The article gives the survey results in detail.

13

Technology and the Protection of Endangered Species

Richard L. Stroup and Jane S. Shaw

In the United States, wild animals are unowned and, historically, have represented a commons. The only way to obtain legal ownership of a wild animal is by capturing and (usually) killing it. By the middle of the nineteenth century, the "tragedy of the commons" (Hardin 1968) had led to the decline in numbers of many wild animals, from bison to grizzlies, and resulted in the demise of several well-known species. The passenger pigeon, the heath hen, the Carolina parakeet, the Bachman's warbler, and the ivory-billed woodpecker all disappeared (Mann and Plummer 1995, 75–76).

Late in the nineteenth century, state governments began to take control of access to wildlife, primarily game animals, replacing the commons with some government control (Lueck 2000b). They were assisted by the federal government, beginning with passage of the Lacey Act in 1900, which gave to the secretary of agriculture the authority to preserve and restore "game birds and other wild birds" (Lueck 2000a, 65), and by private individuals, who took steps to rescue particular species such as bison, wood duck, and eastern bluebird.

In 1973, responding to concerns that more species were in danger of extinction, the federal government became more actively involved in protecting wildlife through passage of the Endangered Species Act (ESA). Even though government control has helped reverse the decline of many game animals, the Endangered Species Act has not had such a favorable record. Its passage marked a vast expansion of federal authority, but many animal and plant populations continue to decline nevertheless.

Technology, which has helped improve the survival chances of many species, could do far more to protect species than it does today. One reason it is not used as effectively as it could be is that the government agencies in charge of protection, especially the Fish and Wildlife Service, have little incentive to adopt or develop technologies to increase the carrying capacity of existing habitat or help create new habitat. This chapter shows that as long as the ESA is implemented as it is now, effectively penalizing those who maintain habitat that is attractive to listed species, technological solutions will be underused by both the government and the private sector. This failure to apply new technology will add to the difficulty of protecting endangered species. Only if the penalties are removed from the act will the full potential of wildlife protection technologies be achieved.

The Endangered Species Act

Although several acts preceded the Endangered Species Act of 1973, this act expanded the role of the federal government in protecting threatened and endangered species. The law increased the number of categories that could be endangered to include not just species but subspecies and even "distinct populations." And while previous law had prohibited people from "taking" an endangered animal on public land, this law applied the prohibition to private land and expanded the principle to include "harassing" and "harming"—words that would be further interpreted in the courts.

According to M. Lynne Corn (1992, 1) of the Congressional Research Service, the Endangered Species Act is "widely regarded by its proponents as one of this country's most important and powerful environmental laws." Its particular strength, upheld by court decisions, is that species and populations officially listed as endangered are to be protected, regardless of the cost to individuals, the government, or society generally. This interpretation has been upheld by the courts.[1]

To protect a species or population from risk of extinction, the Endangered Species Act gives federal officials the right to override private property rights, no matter what the cost to the owner of accommodating the species. No goal other than protecting each and every species, and all distinct populations of that species, is supposed to count for anything in bureaucratic determinations.

Although the act was passed by voice votes virtually unopposed, it is not clear that anyone understood its implications. Its passage represented the culmination of efforts by environmental groups, who were beginning to show political muscle, and biologists, especially those in the Fish and Wildlife Service, the organization that would have most of the federal responsibility for enforcing the law (the National Marine Fisheries Service implements the law with respect to marine animals). In the years before passage of the act, Fish and Wildlife biologists had begun creating a list of endangered species, and environmental groups were making the issue of endangered species a high priority. Both groups chose to take a national legislative approach (Lueck 2000a, 65).

There is scant evidence that many extinctions were imminent in the early 1970s. Although a few famous extinctions have occurred in the United States, restorations have also been successful. It is appropriate to distinguish two kinds of problems with wildlife populations—the decline of large mammals and migratory birds such as pronghorn antelope, white-tailed deer, and some migratory waterfowl, and the actual approach of extinction for a few species.

In both cases, the declines were reversed through a combination of government and private actions. For example, in 1924, the number of pronghorn antelope had fallen to 26,600 in the United States. But by 1964, the U.S. population of pronghorn had increased more than thirteen times (Harrington 1981; Lueck 2000b). Many species that had actually been in danger of extinction were saved as well. At the turn of the twentieth century, as the number of bison was dwindling fast, efforts led by naturalist Ernest Harold Baynes formed the American Bison Society, which was instrumental in creating a bison refuge in Montana (Dary 1989, 234–40). Protection of the wood duck and the bluebird was enhanced by the creation, placement, and maintenance of nesting boxes, many on private land. Recently, the wood duck was the second most numerous species of duck on the eastern waterfowl flyway—a sign of complete recovery (Seasholes 1997, 1).

These restorations took place when far less was known than we know today about managing wildlife, tracing animals in the wild, and breeding animals for release or rerelease into the wild. Today, much more could be done, since we now have technologies ranging from biogenetic studies of animal populations to geographical positioning through satellites.

Yet government regulation and management cannot be shown to have been effective. While there is debate over how to measure effectiveness, biologists continue to identify more species in danger, and only a few species have been taken off the endangered or threatened list. Of those that have been removed, only a small number were deleted because they recovered;

others were removed because errors were discovered in the original list or because they became extinct (Stroup 1995, 2–3).

Technology to Enhance Habitat

The technology now exists to increase the productivity of existing habitat, and researchers are continuing to develop new technologies. These could go a long way to recover species that are endangered or threatened. Several are currently available.[2]

- Habitat enrichment or wildlife management is probably the most important area in which more technology could be brought to bear. While such management is an art as well as a science, it draws on a wide (and still developing) variety of techniques, knowledge, and experience. It combines both high-tech and low-tech activities, from conducting DNA analyses to setting controlled fires and planting suitable vegetation. Wildlife management to protect endangered species is used by companies such as International Paper and nonprofit organizations such as the Nature Conservancy.

  Efforts to save the red-cockaded woodpecker illustrate how relatively simple technology can magnify available habitat. Found in the southeastern United States, these endangered birds frequent the longleaf pines and loblolly pines where there is a clear grassy understory and few hardwoods. The birds make nest cavities near the tops of trees, usually very old pines because old trees frequently have heart rot, which softens the wood and makes it easy for woodpeckers to peck out a cavity. But because people have cut down the oldest pines, cultivated the land, and suppressed fire, this woodpecker's preferred habitat has largely disappeared. The remaining pines tend to be younger trees.

  Carole Capeyn and David Allen discovered in the 1980s that it is possible to create an artificial cavity (with a chain saw) near the top of a tree, even a young tree, and place nest boxes inside.[3] The nest boxes are 6 x 9 x 9-inch blocks of rot-resistant wood, typically western cedar, with a 3-inch-diameter chamber bored into them to provide a place to roost, and a 1 7/8-inch entry hole drilled near the top of the block. The boxes cost about $30 each, and some skill with a chain saw is required. The boxes are being used in several places, including the Joseph W. Jones Center, a nonprofit ecological conservation institution at Ichauway, Georgia.

- DNA studies can show whether specific populations are related, helping biologists determine whether a population of, say, grizzly bears, is genetically diverse enough to be viable through natural reproduction (Cronin 1997, 664; Cronin et al. 1999, 622–23). These studies can help biologists foster a specific trait such as disease resistance, growth rate, or antler size.

- In the field, zoos and other private organizations are increasing using captive breeding, followed by release and reintroduction, Captive breeding is a science that depends on integrating a variety of biological techniques from DNA genotyping to determine how to select mates to identification of appropriate release habitat that contains suitable prey for the reintroduced animals.

  One success story was the restoration of the peregrine falcon by the Cornell Laboratory of Ornithology. (Subsequently, the peregrine project, headed by Tom Cade, moved to Boise, Idaho, where it is now known as the World Center for Birds of Prey.) While there is some scientific debate over whether the released birds were "pure" enough to qualify as peregrine falcons, it is apparent that reintroduction would never have occurred without the decades-long study and experimentation at the laboratory (Cade 1988). Cade creatively applied methods of traditional falconry ("hawking") to endangered species, magnifying his success by techniques such as artificial insemination. (This was achieved by using the tendency of newly born falcons to "imprint" on humans and then causing males to copulate on a glove [Urbanski 1992, 105]). Cade succeeded in bringing back falcons to the point that they now are nesting atop skyscrapers in large American cities.

- Reintroduction is an increasingly sophisticated science. The prestigious International Union of Conservation (IUCN) has developed a protocol for introducing animals. Learning from past failures, it emphasizes knowledge of the species' "critical needs," thorough study of the new habitat, and continued monitoring for years or even decades.

- Once introduced, or after being captured, animals can be tracked by collars or implants with transmitters that send signals to satellites. This tracking through the global positioning system (GPS) can be combined with geographic information systems (GIS) to make maps with a continuous record of an animal's location. This is an advance over traditional systems that obtain positions only when the animal is relocated by a person holding a receiver. Radio collars were used to monitor the location of wolves recently brought into Yellowstone National Park.

- FLIR (Forward Looking Infrared Radar) is the use of video cameras on aircraft or on the ground that read infrared signals. It allows biologists to see animals through tree branches and snow (warm looks white; cold looks dark). Remote video and still cameras can also be used to observe animals.

Incentives and the Role of Technology

These technologies are used by the federal government, but the incentive structure created by the Endangered Species Act limits their application. The reason is that biologists at the Fish and Wildlife Service have at their disposal immense power in forbidding owners to modify habitat that may harbor endangered species. Thus they have every incentive simply to maximize the amount of land on which they restrict actions that might harm a listed species. They can order that the land be set aside from uses such as logging, building, and even farming, and the government does not have to compensate landowners. Given this power, the Fish and Wildlife Service has tended to use it rather than apply technology. Indeed, the service's power is limited to forbidding owners from modifying habitat; it cannot require private landowners to apply technology, even as simple as putting up nest boxes.

In economic terms, the effect of the Endangered Species Act has been to cause government biologists to adopt very costly means to produce habitat for listed species. The power they have under the act distorts relative prices.

To view this problem in simplified terms, consider using two inputs, technology and land, in various combinations to produce the habitat needed to support a specific population of a listed species. This habitat can be produced using lots of land and little technology or a smaller amount of land and more technology. The cost or price of each input will help determine the least expensive combination of inputs needed to support the population in question.

Suppose that without the presence of the costly penalties provided in section 9 of the act, the least expensive combination to produce the desired habitat for a specific population of red-cockaded woodpeckers on private land is $20,000 per year to rent the land and $20,000 per year for technology such as nest boxes on trees and the frequent burning of underbrush. The total cost would be $40,000 per year to maintain the habitat.

Now assume the current penalties. The Fish and Wildlife Service can restrict the use of the same land so that nothing done on it would be inconsistent with bird habitat; however, the Fish and Wildlife Service does not have to pay anything. Under these conditions, few landowners would be willing to use technology to support the birds, even for a sum far exceeding the $20,000 that would have been acceptable without the ESA and its rules. Under the ESA, for the owner to enhance the habitat and encourage additional birds to live in the area would risk the loss of freedom to use any or all land owned by that owner and others in the vicinity.

Thus, without the cooperation of the landowner in providing nest boxes, producing habitat for the same number of birds might require twenty times as much land, and the total cost might be ten times as great as using technology, or $400,000. All the money would be spent on land on which economic uses were forbidden or severely limited, and much of it would involve mature timber that had begun to rot, made unharvestable by regulation. However, the Fish and Wildlife Service would pay only the cost of monitoring compliance. (Unfortunately, without the use of technology such as controlled fire and artificial nest cavities, setting aside even this much larger acreage might not guarantee success.)

While this option is far more costly to society, it is far cheaper (and thus more attractive) to the Fish and Wildlife Service.[4] If the Fish and Wildlife Service had to pay the cost of setting aside the land, its budget would be charged $400,000. The agency would be likely to switch to the $40,000 solution instead. Technology would be properly brought to bear.

"Shoot, Shovel, and Shut Up"

The problem is actually even worse than this sketch, however. Private owners are not likely to use these technologies under the present incentive structure. Just the opposite, in fact. To keep federal officials from taking control of their land, property owners may try to keep out endangered species. That is, the penalties of the Endangered Species Act give landowners an incentive to manage their land *against* the listed species. This incentive reportedly leads some landowners, managers, or those who lease government lands to "shoot, shovel, and shut up" (Brown and Stroup 1999, 60).

Thus, technology is a two-edged sword. A Montana biologist reported (in personal conversation with one of the authors) that not only do wildlife biologists rely on radio collars to determine the location of introduced wolves, so do ranchers. While killing a wolf except in unusual circumstances could bring down the arm of the law, killing wolves that don't have radio collars (but that may be in the same pack) is not likely to lead to penalties. As landowners' ability to destroy or block out animals increases, the argument in favor of the Endangered Species Act is further eroded.

Economists Dean Lueck and Jeffrey Michael (1999) looked at what is actually happening to red-cockaded woodpecker habitat in North Carolina. Using data on more than 1,000 forest plots, they found that the closer the plots were to colonies of woodpeckers, the younger the trees were when the plot was logged. In other words, the property owners were keeping out the woodpeckers by cutting down the trees early.

One well-known case illustrates this phenomenon. Ben Cone, a North Carolina landowner who had received commendations for managing his family's land for wildlife, was required to follow Fish and Wildlife restrictions when colonies of woodpeckers were found on his property. According to a consultant he hired, 1,560 out of 7,200 acres were under the control of the Fish and Wildlife Service. Previously, Cone had logged 50 to 60 acres every five to ten years; he began to clear-cut 300 to 500 acres per year on the rest of his land. He told an investigator, "I cannot afford to let those woodpeckers take over the rest of the property. I'm going to start massive clear-cutting. I'm going to a 40-year rotation, instead of a 75- to 80-year rotation" (Sugg 1993, A12). Eventually, however, he worked out a deal with the Fish and Wildlife Service that mitigated this policy.

In a similar vein, an official of the Texas Parks and Wildlife Department commented that the Endangered Species Act had not done anything for two listed birds. "I am convinced that more habitat for the black-capped vireo, and especially the golden-cheeked warbler, has been lost in those areas of Texas since the listing of these birds than would have been lost without the Endangered Species Act at all," wrote Larry McKinney (1993, 74).

Because the cost of providing any given habitat is not paid openly, the total cost of the Endangered Species Act does not appear in any budget. Many environmentalists, most of whom do not realize the unnecessarily high cost of this strategy, applaud the Fish and Wildlife Service for giving an environmental goal (saving each listed species) such high priority without considering costs. They don't recognize that the agency is increasing costs for others while reducing its own and that the law has unintended consequences: counterproductive activities by landowners. Furthermore, individuals who own property with wildlife habitat end up with less respect for government, become more resentful of its power, and are more likely over time to organize politically to oppose the act. The costs do not end there, however. In the long run, attempting to save species with a system that wastes funds and is largely ineffective will lose the support of the general public.

A Budget for the Endangered Species Act

Until the high costs to landowners are removed from the Endangered Species Act, technology will not be used effectively to protect species. It may instead be used by landowners, surreptitiously or otherwise, to reduce or degrade habitat. There is a way to change these incentives: The government should be required to use its funds to compensate owners for taking away ordinary uses of land. The Fish and Wildlife Service should be put "on budget" when it protects habitat.

By compensating landowners and removing the fear of penalties when the land is attractive to listed species, the government will encourage $40,000 solutions that effectively use technologies to enhance habitat, rather than $400,000 solutions that use enormous amounts of land ineffectively. And it will concentrate its funds on those animals that the American public wants to see protected.

Examining Fish and Wildlife Service data, Don Coursey (1994), an economist at the University of Chicago, found that when the agency spent its own funds, it spent much more money on large, dramatic animals, primarily mammals and birds and a few reptiles (sometimes called *charismatic megafauna*), than on small and less attractive animals such as snails and insects. Coursey conducted a survey to determine what the American public thought the endangered species budget should be spent on, and indeed, the public wanted the bigger, well-known animals to be protected.

Thus, when the Fish and Wildlife Service must use its own funds (whether for land acquisition, captive breeding, or other techniques), the money goes toward protecting the animals that the American public wants to protect—grizzly bears, wolves, and crocodiles. Only a small portion of the agency's expenditures go for animals such as the Stephens kangaroo rat, the Karner blue butterfly, or the flower-loving Delhi swamp fly. Yet today the Fish and Wildlife Service makes landowners incur an often high cost to protect these obscure animals on their lands. Putting the Fish and Wildlife Service "on budget" would result in a program for saving species that is far more productive and far more in line with the wishes of the American people than the policies operating today.

Incentives for Land Managers and Owners

With the proper incentives in place, the goal of saving species could be pursued much more effectively. A program in western states commonly known as "ranching for wildlife" illustrates how a different set of incentives could encourage the use and further development of technological innovations (Leal and Grewell 1999).

Ranching-for-wildlife programs, which exist in eight western states, are cooperative arrangements between landowners (often ranchers with large expanses of land) and state wildlife agencies. The programs have their origins in landowners' practice of charging hunters for access to their land ("fee hunting"). To increase their profits, ranchers would like greater freedom from state hunting regulations. Short seasons and tight limits on the number of animals that can be taken can interfere with landowners' management of hunts. Such rules are designed to help the state agency maintain large game populations over broad regions, but such "one-size-fits-all" rules can reduce the ability of landowners to build trophy herds. Under ranching for wildlife, state agencies give landowners incentives to invest in wildlife management that will lead to more wild game in the state and more land with the wild characteristics that make for the best hunting.

In California, for example, in order to join the program, a landowner inventories the wildlife and habitat on his or her property and proposes specific management steps. These activities may include creating fence openings to ease wildlife movement, installing wood duck nest boxes, planting cereal grains and native grasses, and protecting streamside habitat by planting trees. The landowner combines these steps with management of hunting. Without heavy penalties and with the freedom to use more management tools, landowners adopt new techniques. In the state of Utah (which does not even require a specific management plan for participating in the program), landowners have seeded more than 11,500 acres.

Deliberate efforts to manage land this way can succeed spectacularly. For example, in 1976 the Deseret Ranch in northeastern Utah had an elk herd that numbered about 350, and today, through careful management, the herd contains 2,000 animals. The White Mountain Apache Tribe in east-central Arizona has been managing its elk herd since 1977. Today, licenses cost about $12,500 because the chance of taking a trophy elk is so great (Anderson 1999, 19). (Other animals, including black bear, mountain lion, and wild turkey, are sufficiently abundant that they too can be hunted for a price.)

There is no reason why comparable management could not be used to protect endangered species if the penalties for simply having endangered species were removed. In the case of hunting, the market (i.e., hunters who pay) provides the funds to carry out the objective. If preservation of endangered species is a public good, as many argue, then public funds to reward successful management of those species may be appropriate. Alternatively, it is clear that private funds are available to save endangered species, as they were, for example, in restoring the peregrine falcon. Zoos, membership organizations like the Audubon Society, and private foundations all could be a source of funding to develop the management of endangered species.

Conclusion

Technology is increasingly important to the survival of threatened and endangered species. The current Endangered Species Act strongly hinders the application of known technologies to private land and the development of new technologies that could reduce the threat of extinction. It leads some landowners to use technology to reduce habitat rather than increase the value to wildlife. Until the penalties are removed, growing numbers of people will continue to reduce habitat that could, instead, be enriched to enhance the survival of species.

NOTES

1. The *TVA vs. Hill* case required that construction of a nearly completed federal dam be stopped to protect a seemingly endangered fish, the snail darter.

2. For examples of technology used in oceans, see Michael De Alessi's chapter in this volume.

3. Information from Jonathan Stober of the Jones Center in telephone conversation January 26, 2000.

4. The agency would have to monitor land-use restrictions in either case, but that cost should be small either way.

REFERENCES

Anderson, Terry L. 1999. "Truly Sustainable." *PERC Reports*, December.

Brown, Matthew, and Richard L. Stroup. 1999. "The Takings Debate." *Environmental Protection*, June, 59–60.

Cade, Tom J. 1988. "Captive Breeding: Historical Summary." In his *Peregrine Falcon Populations: Their Management and Recovery*. Boise, ID: Peregrine Fund.

Corn, M. Lynne. 1992. *Endangered Species Act Issues*. Washington, DC: Congressional Research Service, May 27.

Coursey, Don. 1994. "The Revealed Demand for a Public Good: Evidence from Endangered and Threatened Species." Report prepared for the national meeting, American Association for the Advancement of Science, January.

Cronin, Matthew A. 1997. "Systematics, Taxonomy, and the Endangered Species Act: The Example of the California Gnatcatcher." *Wildlife Society Bulletin* 25, no. 3: 661–66.

Cronin, M., R. Shideler, J. Hechtel, C. Strobeck, and D. Paetkau. 1999. "Genetic Relationships of Grizzly Bears (*Ursus arctos*) in the Prudhoe Bay Region of Alaska: Inference from Microsatellite DNA, Mitochondrial DNA, and Field Observations." *Journal of Heredity* 90, no. 6: 622–28.

Dary, David A. 1989. *The Buffalo Book: The Full Saga of the American Animal*. Athens: Ohio University Press and Swallow Press.

Hardin, Garrett. 1968. "The Tragedy of the Commons." *Science* 162: 1243–48.

Harrington, Winston. 1981. "Wildlife: Severe Decline and Partial Recovery." In *America's Renewable Resources: Historical Trends and Current Challenges*, edited by Kenneth D. Frederick and Roger A. Sedjo. Washington, DC: Resources for the Future.

Leal, Donald R., and J. Bishop Grewell. 1999. *Hunting for Habitat: A Practical Guide to State-Landowner Partnerships*. Bozeman, MT: Political Economy Research Center.

Lueck, Dean. 2000a. "An Economic Guide to State Wildlife Management." PERC Research Study RS-002. Bozeman, MT: Political Economy Research Center.

————. 2000b. "The Law and Politics of Federal Wildlife Preservation." In *Political Environmentalism*, edited by Terry L. Anderson. Stanford, CA: Hoover Institution Press.

Lueck, Dean, and Jeffrey Michael. 1999. "Preemptive Habitat Destruction under the Endangered Species Act." PERC working paper 99-1. Bozeman, MT: Political Economy Research Center.

Mann, Charles, and Mark Plummer. 1995. *Noah's Choice*. New York: Knopf.

McKinney, Larry. 1993. Reauthorizing the Endangered Species Act—Incentives for Rural Landowners. In *Building Economic Incentives into the Endangered Species Act*, edited by Hank Fischer and Wendy E. Hudson. Washington, DC: Defenders of Wildlife, October.

Seasholes, Brian. 1997. "The Wood Duck." Center for Private Conservation (CPC) Case Study, June 1. Available at www.cei.org/CPCCaseReaderasp?ID=376.

Stroup, Richard. 1995. "The Endangered Species Act: Making Innocent Species the Enemy." PERC Policy Series PS-3. Bozeman, MT: Political Economy Research Center, April.

Sugg, Ike C. 1993. "Ecosystem Babbitt-Babble." *Wall Street Journal*, April 2, A12.

Urbanski, Mark A. 1992. "Birds and Birding: A Case of Private Provision." PERC working paper 92-19. Bozeman, MT: Political Economy Research Center.

About the Contributors

CLYDE WAYNE CREWS JR. is the director of technology studies at the Cato Institute. He is the author of the annual report, *Ten Thousand Commandments: A Policymaker's Annual Snapshot of the Federal Regulatory State.* Crews's writing has been published in the *Wall Street Journal, Forbes, Journal of Commerce, Washington Times, Electricity Journal, Policy Sciences,* and *Journal of Regulation and Social Costs.* Before joining Cato, Crews was director of competition and regulation policy at the Competitive Enterprise Institute. He holds a master's degree in business administration from the College of William and Mary and a bachelor's degree in business administration from Lander College in Greenwood, SC. He is married with three children.

MICHAEL DE ALESSI is the director of natural resource policy at the Reason Public Policy Institute. He received a B.A. in economics and an M.S. in engineering economic systems from Stanford University and an M.A. in marine policy from the Rosenstiel School of Marine and Atmospheric Science at the University of Miami. He is the author of *Fishing for Solutions,* and his articles on private conservation and the oceans have appeared in such publications as *New Scientist, Journal of Commerce, International Herald Tribune, Wall Street Journal Europe* and *Asian Wall Street Journal.* He lives in San Francisco.

FRED E. FOLDVARY received his Ph.D. in economics from George Mason University. He has taught economics at the Latvian University of Agriculture, Virginia Tech, California State University at Hayward, and, currently, Santa Clara University. Foldvary's publications include *The Soul of Liberty, Public Goods and Private Communities, Beyond Neoclassical Economics,* "Municipal Public Finance" in the *Handbook of Public Finance,* "The Completely Decentralized City" in *City and Country,* and *Dictionary of*

Free-Market Economics. His areas of research include the economics of real estate, public finance, public choice, and natural-law philosophy.

DAVID FRIEDMAN is a professor of law at Santa Clara University. He is the author of *The Machinery of Freedom, Price Theory: An Intermediate Text, Hidden Order: The Economics of Everyday Life, Law's Order: What Economics Has to Do with Law and Why It Matters,* and articles in a variety of academic journals. His books have been translated into French, Italian, Spanish, German, and Japanese. He is especially interested in using economics to understand systems of legal rules. His current interest is in the implications, especially the nonobvious implications, of present and near-future technological change.

RICK GEDDES is an assistant professor in the Department of Policy Analysis and Management at Cornell University and a research associate at the Hoover Institution. He holds M.A. and Ph.D. degrees in economics from the University of Chicago. His work has been published by the *American Economic Review, Journal of Regulatory Economics, Encyclopedia of Law and Economics, Journal of Legal Studies,* and *Journal of Law and Economics.* He is currently writing a book on postal reform. His other research interests include the effects of regulation on corporate governance, public utility regulation, and the economics of women's rights. He was a visiting faculty fellow at Yale Law School in 1995 and a national fellow at the Hoover Institution in 1999.

DANIEL B. KLEIN is an associate professor of economics at Santa Clara University. He is the coauthor (with A. T. Moore and B. Reja) of *Curb Rights: A Foundation for Free Enterprise in Urban Transit,* editor of *Reputation: Studies in the Voluntary Elicitation of Good Conduct,* and editor of *What Do Economists Contribute?* In the area of auto-emissions policy, Klein coauthored a report with A. Glazer and C. Lave for the California State Senate Transportation Committee, and together they published related research in *Journal of Transport Economics and Policy.* With P. M. Koskenoja, Klein wrote a lengthy analysis of the remote-sensing approach to controlling auto emissions, published by the Cato Institute.

ALVIN LOWI JR. is a professional engineer in private practice. He received his B.M.E. and M.S. degrees from the Georgia Institute of Technology and served as an engineering officer on various U.S. Navy vessels at sea in the Korean conflict. He taught marine engineering, heat and power laboratory practice, energy management, and power generation courses at the Navy Amphibious Base Coronado Boat Engineers School, Georgia Tech, and the University of Pennsylvania. He has been employed variously as a research specialist, preliminary design engineer, and member of the technical staffs of several prominent aircraft, turbomachinery, and aerospace concerns. During the past thirty-five years, Lowi's engineering practice has led to several product development and entrepreneurial ventures in which he has served as director, officer, or principal. His biography is published in various directories, including *Who's Who in Technology*, *Who's Who in Engineering*, *Who's Who in Science and Engineering*, and the Society of Automotive Engineers' *Directory of Consultants*. He is the author of more than seventy reports, papers, and journal articles and is a patent holder in various fields, including water distillation, solar-thermal energy conversion, internal combustion engines, cogeneration, and emission controls.

SPENCER HEATH MACCALLUM earned his bachelor's degree at Princeton University and his master's degree in social anthropology at the University of Washington and did extensive postgraduate work at the University of New Mexico and the University of Chicago. He is the author of *The Art of Community* and of articles in journals such as *Human Organization*, *The Independent Review*, *Modern Age*, and *Critical Review*. His writings focus on the idea, deriving from his grandfather Spencer Heath's work *Citadel, Market and Altar*, of a community in which an entrepreneurial firm owns and manages the land and leases sites competitively and for profit on a long-term basis. The firm builds land value by optimizing the social and business environment of those leased sites. MacCallum's chapter in this volume explores how modern technologies, particularly electronic communications and automobile transportation, strengthen the case for his grandfather's visionary idea.

KERRY MACINTOSH is a professor at Santa Clara University's School of Law and a member of its high-technology program. She is also a member of the American Law Institute. She has published articles on commercial transactions and electronic commerce in, among other journals, the *Harvard Journal of Law and Technology*, *Berkeley Technology Law Journal*, and *Boston University Journal of Science and Technology Law*. In 1993, the

American College of Commercial Finance Lawyers awarded her the "Best Writing by a Young Lawyer Award." Her current research focuses on electronic payment systems and other law and technology issues.

JOHN C. MOORHOUSE is the Carroll Professor of Economics at Wake Forest University. His articles in applied microeconomics have been published in, among other journals, the *Albany Law Review, Atlantic Economic Journal, Cato Journal, Journal of the History of Economic Thought, Public Choice, Quarterly Review of Economics and Business, Southern Economic Journal, Journal of Technology Transfer,* and *Journal of Urban Economics.* He edited *Electric Power: Deregulation and the Public Interest* and coedited (with Jac C. Heckelman and Robert M. Whaples) *Public Choice: Interpretations of American Economic History.* His current research is on the impact of gun control on crime rates in the United States.

PETER SAMUEL has a B.Comm (Honors) from the University of Melbourne, Australia, and taught economics for two years at Monash University in Australia. He took courses in urban planning. He became economics editor for the *Canberra Times,* the daily newspaper of the Australian capital, and then spent fourteen years reporting and writing commentaries on public policy issues for *The Bulletin,* a weekly newsmagazine. After arriving in the United States in 1980, he wrote for *Reason* magazine on transport topics and won an award for a series on New York's subways. During the 1980s, he wrote mainly on defense and international affairs. In 1995, as a contributor to *Forbes* magazine, he wrote about the plans for the I-91 express lanes and the Dulles Greenway and wrote a paper for the Cato Institute on privatizing highways. The response to those articles persuaded him to specialize in writing on highways, and he founded the *Toll Roads Newsletter* in early 1996. This monthly, thirty-two-page review is regarded in transportation circles as the leading source of news and analysis of developments in road policy. Samuel is also a correspondent for *World Highways* and *ITS International* magazines and has written policy papers for the Cato Institute and the Reason Public Policy Institute.

JANE S. SHAW is a senior associate of PERC, the Center for Free Market Environmentalism, in Bozeman, Montana. PERC is a research and educational organization that explores market solutions to environmental problems. Shaw oversees PERC's outreach program, which extends its research to a broad audience through articles, lectures, and conferences. She coedited with Ronald Utt *A Guide to Smart Growth: Shattering Myths and Exploring Solutions* and wrote with Michael Sanera *Facts, Not Fear: A Guide to Teaching Children about the Environment.* Before joining PERC in 1984, Shaw was an associate economics editor at *Business Week.* Previously, she was a reporter for McGraw-Hill Publications in Chicago and Washington, DC. She is serving on the editorial advisory board of *Regulation* and the academic advisory council of the Institute of Economic Affairs in London. She is a senior editor of *Liberty* and a contributing editor of *Ideas on Liberty.*

DONALD C. SHOUP is a professor and the chair of the Department of Urban Planning at University of California at Los Angeles. He has written many articles on how parking affects transportation and land use. His research on employer-paid parking led to California's legislation requiring employers to offer commuters the option to choose cash in lieu of any parking subsidy offered. He is now writing *The High Cost of Free Parking.* He received his bachelor's degree in electrical engineering and economics at Yale and his Ph.D. in economics, also at Yale.

RICHARD L. STROUP is a professor of economics at Montana State University and a senior associate of PERC, the Center for Free Market Environmentalism, in Bozeman, Montana. His work has been a major force in developing the approach to resource problems known as the *new resource economics* or, more popularly, *free-market environmentalism.* Stroup is the coauthor with James D. Gwartney of a primer on economics, *What Everyone Should Know about Economics and Prosperity;* as well as a coauthor with James D. Gwartney and Russell S. Sobel of a leading college economics textbook, *Economics: Private and Public Choice,* now in its ninth edition. His recent publications have focused on the Superfund program and on alternative institutional arrangements for dealing with endangered species, regulatory takings, and other regulatory issues. His most recent monograph, *What Everyone Should Know about Economics and the Environment,* will be published in 2002. Stroup received his B.A., M.A., and Ph.D. degrees from the University of Washington. From 1982 to 1984, he was director of the Office of Policy Analysis at the U.S. Department of the Interior.

SHIRLEY V. SVORNY is a professor of economics at California State University at Northridge. Her work on occupational licensing has appeared in

Public Choice; Federation Bulletin: Journal of Medical Licensure and Discipline; Contemporary Policy Issues; Applied Economics; Economic Inquiry; Encyclopedia of Law & Economics; and *American Health Care: Government, Market Processes, and the Public Interest.* She earned her Ph.D. in economics at the University of California at Los Angeles.

Index

Absorption distillation, 202–4

Act for the Establishment and Support of Lighthouses, Buoys, and Public Piers, 41

Advanced Very High Resolution Radiometry (AVHRR), 31

Adverse clearings, 10, 117

Aerobic digestion, 194

Ahwah, Ian, and Marty Karpiel: on physician profiling, 150

Akerlof, George A.: on low-quality goods, 128

Allen, David: on red-cockaded woodpecker, 246

Allen, James B.: on company towns, 236, 242n12

American West, branding and barbed wire as private property solutions in, 23–4

Anaerobic digestion, 193–4

Anders, George: on online postage, 212

Andersen Consulting: on staying in contact with the office on vacation, 239, 242n17

Anderson, Terry L.: on elk herds, 253

Anderson, Terry L., and Peter J. Hill: quote on technology and property rights, 15; on enforcing private property rights in the American West, 23

Aquaculture, 27–30; fencing fish, 27–30; genetic manipulation in, 28–9; open-ocean in cages, 29; pollution from, 30; of salmon, advantages, 28; tank advantages, 29–30

Armstrong, Mark, Simeon Cowan, and John Vickers: on incentive to innovate, 218

Arrow, Kenneth J.: quoted on central planning, 6; licensure definition, 145; on markets' failure to give adequate consumer information, 127

Artificial reefs: creating and using, 33

Ashbaugh, Lowell L., et al: on accuracy of remote sensing of tailpipe emissions, 93; on comparison of failing remote sensing and smog check, 94

Aspen CO: parking problems and solutions in, 67–70, 73–4, 84n10

Auto emissions, 9, 86–103; greatest polluting source from few gross polluters, 87. *See also* Emission controls, Remote sensing, Smog-checks

Automatic coin machines on toll motorways, 50–1

Autonomous underwater vehicles (AUVs): robots to map, find, and herd sealife, 32

AUVs. *See* Autonomous underwater vehicles

Avoided-cost contract with the franchised utility, 174

Bailey, Elizabeth E., and John C. Panzar: on contestability theory, 217